중학 내신 완벽 대비 종합서

능률 중학 영어

중1

능률중학영어 중1

지은이 NE능률 영어교육연구소

선임 연구원 김지현

연구원 윤인아 박효빈 남휘영 이희진

영문 교열 August Niederhaus Nathaniel Galletta Patrick Ferraro

디자인 안훈정 김연주

내지 일러스트 박응식 최은미 김동현 정경호

내지 사진 www.shutterstock.com

맥편집 김미진

영업 한기영 이경구 박인규 정철교 김남준 이우현

마케팅 박혜선 남경진 이지원 김여진

Let's grow together

NE능률이 미래를 창조합니다.

건강한 배움의 고객가치를 제공하겠다는 꿈을 실현하기 위해
40년이 넘는 시간 동안 열심히 달려왔습니다.

앞으로도 끊임없는 연구와 노력을 통해
당연한 것을 멈추지 않고

고객, 기업, 직원 모두가 함께 성장하는 NE능률이 되겠습니다.

NE_Books
Grammar Inside Level 1
[2021 개정]
Inside
NELT
1833-8368

"Success is not the key to happiness.
Happiness is the key to success.
If you love what you are doing, you will be successful."

성공은 행복을 얻는 비결이 아닙니다. 행복이 성공을 얻는 비결입니다.
여러분이 하는 일을 사랑한다면, 여러분은 성공할 것입니다.

- Albert Schweitzer -

Structures & Features

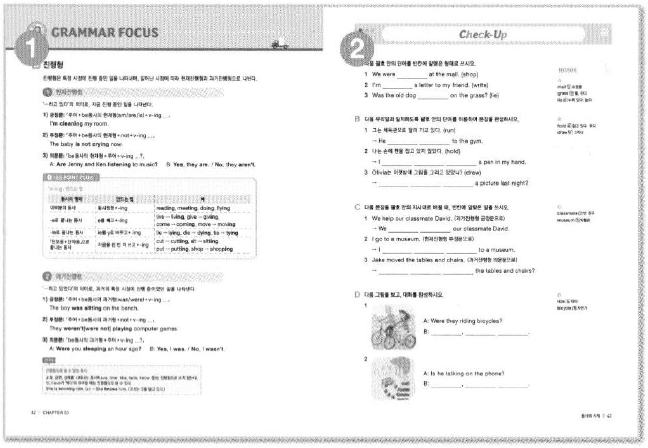

❶ GRAMMAR FOCUS

2015년 개정 교육과정을 분석하여 중학교 1학년에서 알아야 할 필수 문법을 체계적으로 정리했습니다. 시험에 자주 출제되는 내용은 내신 POINT PLUS로, 주의해야 할 문법 사항은 TIPS로 정리하여 쉽게 학습할 수 있습니다.

❷ Check-Up

GRAMMAR FOCUS에서 배운 내용을 간단한 유형의 연습 문제를 통해 확인해 볼 수 있습니다.

❸ Grammar Practice

앞서 배운 문법 사항을 통합하여 Check-Up보다 심화된 문제를 제공하여 이해도를 더 확실하게 점검할 수 있습니다.

❹ 내신 완성 Grammar Practice

학교 시험과 유사한 문제로 구성하여 실전에 대비할 수 있습니다.

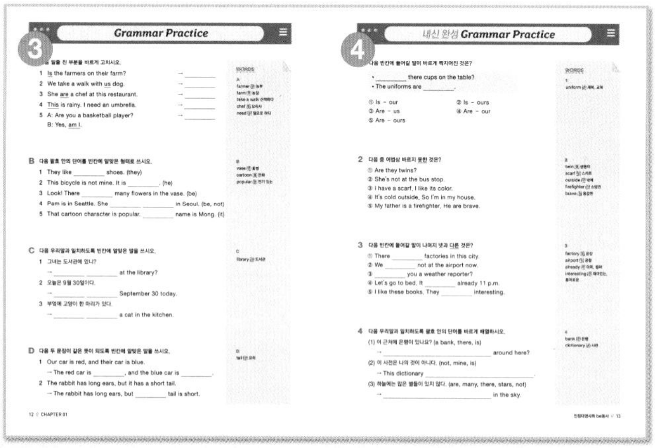

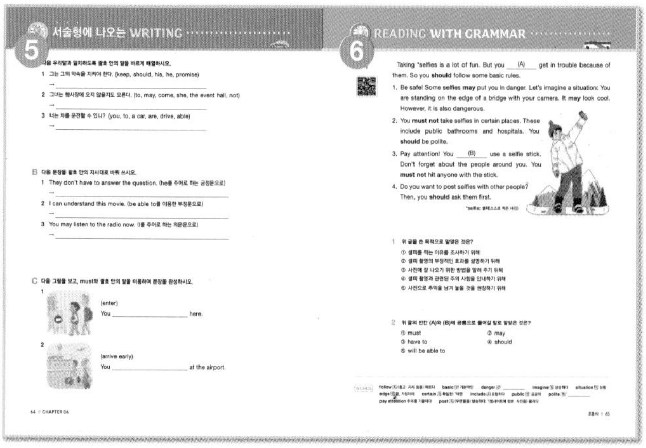

❺ 서술형에 나오는 WRITING

다양한 서술형 문제를 통해 GRAMMAR FOCUS를 반복 학습할 수 있고, 쓰기는 물론 학교 내신 시험의 서술형 주관식 문항 대비도 완벽하게 할 수 있습니다.

❻ READING WITH GRAMMAR

해당 문법 항목이 녹아 있는 흥미로운 내용의 지문을 통해 문법 연습은 물론 독해 실력도 동시에 높일 수 있습니다.

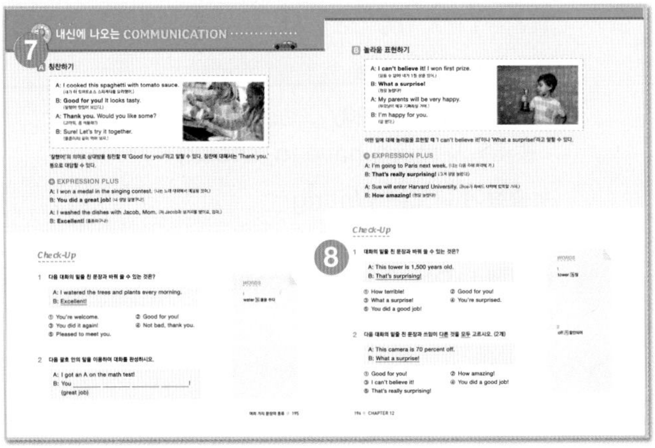

⑦ 내신에 나오는 COMMUNICATION

중학교 1학년 과정의 필수 의사소통 기능을 생생한 대화문을 통해 학습할 수 있습니다. 각 의사소통 기능과 관련된 다른 표현들도 추가로 학습할 수 있습니다.

⑧ Check-Up

학교 시험과 유사한 문제 유형을 통해 학습한 내용을 확인하고 내신에 대비할 수 있습니다.

⑨ FINAL TEST

어휘, 의사소통 기능, 문법 등 앞에서 학습한 내용을 종합적으로 확인해 볼 수 있습니다. 학교 내신 시험과 유사한 난이도의 다양한 문제를 풀어보며 실전에 대비하고 실력도 점검해 볼 수 있습니다.

⑩ 내신 완성 서술형

내신에 자주 출제되는 서술형 주관식 문제를 풀며 서술형 주관식에 대한 자신감을 높일 수 있습니다.

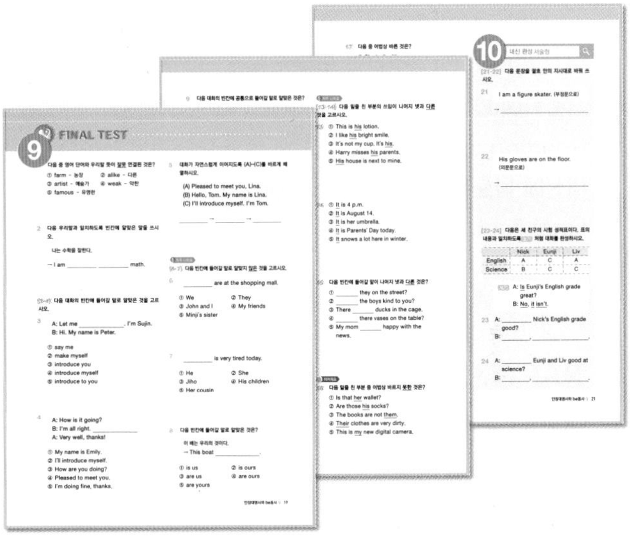

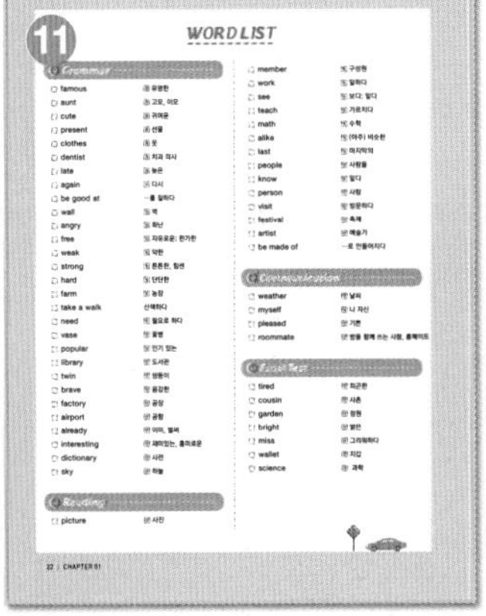

⑪ WORD LIST

해당 과에서 쓰인 어휘 중 핵심 어휘만을 별도로 학습할 수 있습니다. 어휘를 학습하며 한 과를 마무리할 수 있습니다.

Contents

CHAPTER 01

인칭대명사와 be동사

GET READY

I am happy.
(나는 행복하다.)

You are my best friend.
(너는 나의 가장 친한 친구이다.)

He is our teacher.
(그는 우리의 선생님이다.)

'나, 너, 그, 우리의' 등 사람이나 사물을 대신해서 가리키는 말을 인칭대명사라고 해요. 이 인칭대명사는 문장에서 어떤 역할을 하느냐에 따라 다양한 형태로 쓰여요. 그리고 주어 뒤에 오는 be동사는 '…이다, …에 있다'라는 의미를 나타내는데, 주어에 따라 형태가 달라져요.

A 인칭대명사와 be동사

1 인칭대명사의 격

인칭대명사는 사람이나 사물의 이름을 대신해서 가리키는 말로, 인칭, 수, 격에 따라 형태가 달라진다.

수	인칭	주격 (…는/가)	소유격 (…의)	목적격 (…를/에게)	소유대명사 (…의 것)
단수	1인칭	I	my	me	mine
	2인칭	you	your	you	yours
	3인칭	he she it	his her its	him her it	his hers —
복수	1인칭	we	our	us	ours
	2인칭	you	your	you	yours
	3인칭	they	their	them	theirs
역할		문장의 주어	명사 앞에서 소유 관계를 나타냄	동사, 전치사의 목적어	「소유격+명사」를 대신함

Sarah is a swimmer. **She** swims fast. (She = Sarah)
Ben is an artist. **His** paintings are wonderful. (His = Ben's)
I have a pet bird. I love **it**. (it = the pet bird)
My bag is small. **Theirs** are big. (Theirs = Their bags)

2 인칭대명사와 be동사

be동사는 '…이다, …에 있다'라는 뜻을 나타내며, 주어의 인칭과 수에 따라 형태가 달라진다.

1) 주어가 인칭대명사일 때:

수	인칭	주어	be동사의 현재형	줄임말
단수	1인칭	I	am	I'm
	2인칭	You	are	You're
	3인칭	He She It	is	He's She's It's
복수	1인칭	We	are	We're
	2인칭	You	are	You're
	3인칭	They	are	They're

TIPS
비인칭 주어 it
날씨, 시각, 날짜, 요일, 거리, 계절 등을 나타내는 문장의 주어로 it을 쓰는데, 이 it을 비인칭 주어라고 한다. 비인칭 주어 it은 '그것'이라고 해석하지 않는다.
It is sunny. (화창하다.)
It is Friday. (금요일이다.)
It is summer. (여름이다.)

I am[**I'm**] a smart boy.
He is[**He's**] busy now.
It is[**It's**] her cell phone.
They are[**They're**] my classmates.

2) 주어가 일반명사일 때: 단수명사면 be동사 is, 복수명사면 are를 쓴다.

Check-Up

A 다음 괄호 안에서 알맞은 말을 고르시오.

1 (I / You / She) am a student.

2 (You / He / They) is a famous musician.

3 This is your book. That is (she / her / hers).

4 I have a boyfriend. (Our / His / Its) name is Jason.

5 Those are my aunts. I like (they / their / them) very much.

WORDS

A
famous 형 유명한
musician 명 음악가
aunt 명 고모, 이모

B 다음 밑줄 친 부분을 줄여 쓰시오.

1 I am 14 years old. → ________

2 It is a beautiful garden. → ________

3 She is our grandmother. → ________

4 We are in the classroom. → ________

5 You are the best players in your team. → ________

B
grandmother 명 할머니
classroom 명 교실
player 명 선수

C 다음 빈칸에 알맞은 인칭대명사를 쓰시오.

1 This is my camera. ________ is black.

2 Chris is my brother. ________ is cute.

3 Julia is a kind girl. Everybody loves ________.

4 This pen is a present for you. Now it is ________.

5 They are fashion designers. ________ clothes are wonderful.

C
cute 형 귀여운
present 명 선물
fashion 명 패션
designer 명 디자이너
clothes 명 옷

D 다음 밑줄 친 부분을 바르게 고치시오.

1 You is a dentist. → ________

2 They am good students. → ________

3 This is 11:30. I am late again. → ________

4 I play soccer with me friends on Sundays. → ________

5 Joe and I like Beethoven. Us are pianists. → ________

D
dentist 명 치과 의사
late 형 늦은
again 부 다시
pianist 명 피아니스트

B be동사의 부정문과 의문문

1 be동사의 부정문: 「주어+be동사+not ...」

부정문	줄임말	
I am not	I'm not	—
You are not	You're not	You aren't
He/She/It is not	He's/She's/It's not	He/She/It isn't
We/You/They are not	We're/You're/They're not	We/You/They aren't

I **am not** lazy. = I**'m not** lazy.
You **are not** alone. = You**'re not** alone. = You **aren't** alone.
He **is not** at the gym. = He**'s not** at the gym. = He **isn't** at the gym.
They **are not** my parents. = They**'re not** my parents. = They **aren't** my parents.

2 be동사의 의문문: 「be동사+주어 ...?」

의문문	긍정 대답	부정 대답	
Am I ...?	Yes, you are.	No, you aren't.	No, you're not.
Are you(단수) ...?	Yes, I am.	—	No, I'm not.
Is he/she/it ...?	Yes, he/she/it is.	No, he/she/it isn't.	No, he's/she's/it's not.
Are we ...?	Yes, we/you are.	No, we/you aren't.	No, we're/you're not.
Are you(복수) ...?	Yes, we are.	No, we aren't.	No, we're not.
Are they ...?	Yes, they are.	No, they aren't.	No, they're not.

A: **Am I** a good baseball player**?** B: **Yes, you are. / No, you aren't.**
A: **Are you** a teenager**?** B: **Yes, I am. / No, I'm not.**
A: **Are they** popular actors**?** B: **Yes, they are. / No, they aren't.**

내신 POINT PLUS

「There is/are ...」
'…이 있다'라고 해석하며, 뒤에 오는 명사가 단수이면 is, 복수이면 are를 쓴다.
부정문은 「There is/are not ...」으로, 의문문은 「Is/Are there ...?」로 쓴다.

There is *an apple* in the basket. (바구니 안에 사과 한 개가 있다.)
There aren't *enough books* on the desk. (책상 위에 책들이 충분히 있지 않다.)
A: **Are there** *four seasons* here? (이곳에는 사계절이 있니?)
B: **Yes, there are. / No, there aren't.** (응, 있어. / 아니, 없어.)

Check-Up

A 다음 문장을 괄호 안의 지시대로 바꿀 때, 빈칸에 알맞은 말을 쓰시오.

1 You are tall. (부정문으로)

→ ________ ________ ________ tall.

2 They are good at cooking. (의문문으로)

→ ________ ________ good at cooking?

3 She is in the hospital right now. (의문문으로)

→ ________ ________ in the hospital right now?

4 There are three pictures on the wall. (부정문으로)

→ ________ ________ three pictures on the wall.

B 다음 대화의 빈칸에 알맞은 말을 쓰시오.

1 A: Is he angry with me? B: Yes, ________ ________.

2 A: Are you free today, Molly? B: No, ________ ________.

3 A: Are Jane and Laura sisters? B: No, ________ ________.

C 보기 처럼 빈칸에 알맞은 말을 쓰시오.

보기 John is in the bathroom. He isn't in his room.

1 The chair is weak. ________ ________ strong.

2 Rocks are hard. ________ ________ soft.

3 My sister is a dancer. ________ ________ a singer.

4 Steve and I are 13 years old. ________ ________ 14.

D 다음 우리말과 일치하도록 빈칸에 알맞은 말을 쓰시오.

1 바다에 배들이 있다.

→ ________ ________ boats on the sea.

2 침대 위에 곰 인형이 있니?

→ ________ ________ a teddy bear on the bed?

3 냉장고에 우유병이 없다.

→ ________ ________ ________ a milk bottle in the refrigerator.

WORDS

A
be good at …를 잘하다
hospital 명 병원
wall 명 벽

B
angry 형 화난
free 형 자유로운; *한가한

C
weak 형 약한
strong 형 튼튼한, 힘센
rock 명 바위
hard 형 단단한

D
bottle 명 병
refrigerator 명 냉장고

Grammar Practice

A 다음 밑줄 친 부분을 바르게 고치시오.

1 <u>Is</u> the farmers on their farm? → __________

2 We take a walk with <u>us</u> dog. → __________

3 She <u>are</u> a chef at this restaurant. → __________

4 <u>This</u> is rainy. I need an umbrella. → __________

5 A: Are you a basketball player? → __________
B: Yes, <u>am I</u>.

B 다음 괄호 안의 단어를 빈칸에 알맞은 형태로 쓰시오.

1 They like __________ shoes. (they)

2 This bicycle is not mine. It is __________. (he)

3 Look! There __________ many flowers in the vase. (be)

4 Pam is in Seattle. She __________ __________ in Seoul. (be, not)

5 That cartoon character is popular. __________ name is Mong. (it)

C 다음 우리말과 일치하도록 빈칸에 알맞은 말을 쓰시오.

1 그녀는 도서관에 있니?
→ __________ __________ at the library?

2 오늘은 9월 30일이다.
→ __________ __________ September 30 today.

3 부엌에 고양이 한 마리가 있다.
→ __________ __________ a cat in the kitchen.

D 다음 두 문장이 같은 뜻이 되도록 빈칸에 알맞은 말을 쓰시오.

1 Our car is red, and their car is blue.
→ The red car is __________, and the blue car is __________.

2 The rabbit has long ears, but it has a short tail.
→ The rabbit has long ears, but __________ tail is short.

WORDS

A
farmer 명 농부
farm 명 농장
take a walk 산책하다
chef 명 요리사
need 동 필요로 하다

B
vase 명 꽃병
cartoon 명 만화
popular 형 인기 있는

C
library 명 도서관

D
tail 명 꼬리

내신 완성 Grammar Practice

1 다음 빈칸에 들어갈 말이 바르게 짝지어진 것은?

- ________ there cups on the table?
- The uniforms are ________.

① Is - our
② Is - ours
③ Are - us
④ Are - our
⑤ Are - ours

2 다음 중 어법상 바르지 못한 것은?

① Are they twins?
② She's not at the bus stop.
③ I have a scarf. I like its color.
④ It's cold outside. So I'm in my house.
⑤ My father is a firefighter. He are brave.

3 다음 빈칸에 들어갈 말이 나머지 넷과 다른 것은?

① There ________ factories in this city.
② We ________ not at the airport now.
③ ________ you a weather reporter?
④ Let's go to bed. It ________ already 11 p.m.
⑤ I like these books. They ________ interesting.

4 다음 우리말과 일치하도록 괄호 안의 단어를 바르게 배열하시오.

(1) 이 근처에 은행이 있나요? (a bank, there, is)
→ ________________________ around here?

(2) 이 사전은 나의 것이 아니다. (not, mine, is)
→ This dictionary ________________________.

(3) 하늘에는 많은 별들이 있지 않다. (are, many, there, stars, not)
→ ________________________ in the sky.

WORDS

1
uniform 명 제복, 교복

2
twin 명 쌍둥이
scarf 명 스카프
outside 부 밖에
firefighter 명 소방관
brave 형 용감한

3
factory 명 공장
airport 명 공항
already 부 이미, 벌써
interesting 형 재미있는, 흥미로운

4
bank 명 은행
dictionary 명 사전

서술형에 나오는 WRITING

A **다음 우리말과 일치하도록 괄호 안의 말을 바르게 배열하시오.**

1 그는 그들의 영어 선생님이다. (is, English teacher, their, he)

→ ______________________________

2 저 티셔츠는 그녀의 것이 아니다. (is, that, hers, T-shirt, not)

→ ______________________________

3 너는 이탈리아 출신이니? (from, you, are, Italy)

→ ______________________________

B **다음 우리말과 일치하도록 괄호 안의 단어를 이용하여 문장을 완성하시오.**

1 너의 삼촌은 거실에 계시니? (uncle)

→ ____________________ in the living room?

2 내 차는 주차장에 없다. (car)

→ ____________________ in the parking lot.

3 오늘은 토요일이다. (Saturday)

→ ____________________ today.

C **다음 그림을 보고, 괄호 안의 단어를 이용하여 문장을 완성하시오.**

1

(his, cap)

____________________ on the chair.

2

(there, baseball)

____________________ under the desk.

1

Clara: Look! This **is my** family picture.
Jacob: Wow, **your** family **is** big.
Clara: Yes. **There are** six members in **my** family.
Jacob: **Is** this man **your** dad**?**
Clara: **Yes, he is. He's** a *barista. **He** works at a café.
Jacob: **I** see. **Is** this woman **your** mom**?**
Clara: **Yes, she is. She's** a middle school teacher. **She** teaches math.

Jacob: Oh, these boys **are** so alike! **Are they** twins**?**
Clara: **Yes, they are. They're my** little brothers. **Their** names **are** Jay and Sam.
Jacob: And this girl **is you**. Hmm.... <u>그런데, 사진에는 여섯 명이 있지 않네.</u>
Clara: The last member **is** Max. Here **he is**. **He's our** pet cat!

*barista: 바리스타(커피를 전문적으로 만드는 사람)

1 Clara의 가족에 대한 위 대화의 내용과 일치하지 <u>않는</u> 것은?

① Clara의 가족 수는 총 여섯이다.
② Clara의 아버지는 카페에서 일한다.
③ Clara의 어머니는 수학 선생님이다.
④ Clara의 남동생들은 쌍둥이다.
⑤ Clara의 가족은 강아지를 키운다.

서술형

2 위 대화의 밑줄 친 우리말과 일치하도록 괄호 안의 단어를 바르게 배열하시오.

→ But, ______________________ in the picture.
(are, people, not, six, there)

WORDS picture 명 사진 member 명 구성원 work 동 일하다 see 동 보다; *알다 teach 동 [1] __________ math 명 수학 alike 형 (아주) 비슷한 last 형 [2] __________ 문제 people 명 사람들

2

Do you know **me**? **I** live in Sapporo, Japan. **Am I** a person**? No, I'm not**. People from all around the world visit **me** in February. **They** come for the snow festival. **They** look at the ice castles. The castles **are** tall, but I (A) be not tall. Artists make (B) they. But anyone can make **me**!

Just make two big snowballs. One **is** for **my** body, and the other **is** for **my** head. **My** eyes **are** buttons. **My** arms **are** branches. And **my** nose **is** a carrot. Do you know **me** now? Of course **you** do! **I am** a snowman!

1 Which is NOT true about the writer?

① It lives in Japan.
② People can make it.
③ It has buttons for eyes.
④ Branches are its arms.
⑤ Its nose is made of a snowball.

2 Correct the underlined (A) and (B).

(A) __________ (B) __________

WORDS know 동 알다 live 동 살다 person 명 [1] __________ visit 동 방문하다 festival 명 축제 castle 명 성 artist 명 예술가 anyone 대 누구, 누구나 button 명 단추 branch 명 나뭇가지 문제 be made of …로 만들어지다

내신에 나오는 COMMUNICATION

A 안부 묻고 답하기

A: **How is it going**, Emma**?**
(어떻게 지내니, Emma?)

B: **I'm okay, thanks. How is everything?**
(나는 잘 지내, 고마워. 어떻게 지내니?)

A: **Pretty good.**
(아주 잘 지내.)

상대방에게 안부를 물을 때는 'How is it going?'이나 'How is everything?'이라고 말할 수 있다. 친한 사이에서는 'What's up?'이라고 물을 수도 있다. 안부 인사에 답할 때는 'I'm okay, thanks.'나 '(I'm) Pretty good.' 등의 표현을 쓸 수 있다.

EXPRESSION PLUS

1 안부 묻기
- How are you? / How are you doing? (어떻게 지내니?)

2 안부 인사에 답하기
- (I'm) All right. / (I'm) Fine. ((나는) 잘 지내.)
- Very well. / Great. (아주 잘 지내.)
- Not bad. (나쁘지 않아.)
- Not so good. (잘 못 지내.)

Check-Up

1 다음 대화의 빈칸에 들어갈 말로 알맞지 않은 것은?

A: Hello! How is it going?
B: ____________ How are you?

① Pretty. ② Great.
③ All right. ④ I'm fine.
⑤ Not so good.

2 다음 중 쓰임이 나머지 넷과 다른 것은?

① How is it going?
② How is everything?
③ How are you today?
④ How are you doing?
⑤ How is the weather?

WORDS

2
weather 명 날씨

B 소개하고 답하기

A: **Let me introduce myself. My name is** Josh.
(내 소개를 할게. 내 이름은 Josh야.)

B: **Nice to meet you**, Josh. **I'm** Tim.
(만나서 반가워, Josh. 나는 Tim이야.)

A: **Nice to meet you, too.**
(나도 만나서 반가워.)

자신을 소개할 때는 'Let me introduce myself.', 'I'm ...', 'My name is ...'라고 말할 수 있다. 소개에 답할 때는 'Nice to meet you.' 등의 표현을 쓸 수 있다.

⊕ EXPRESSION PLUS

A: **I'll introduce myself**. I'm Bob. (내 소개를 할게. 나는 Bob이야.)
B: **I'm happy to meet you**, Bob! (나는 너를 만나서 기뻐, Bob!)

A: **This is** my friend Jack. (이쪽은 내 친구 Jack이야.)
B: **Glad to meet you**. I'm Cindy. (만나서 반가워. 나는 Cindy야.)
C: **Pleased to meet you**. (만나서 반가워.)

Check-Up

1 다음 대화의 빈칸에 들어갈 말로 알맞은 것은?

A: ______________________
B: Nice to meet you, Kate. I'm Dave.
C: Glad to meet you, Dave.

① I'm fine.
② How are you?
③ This is my new room.
④ Let me introduce myself.
⑤ This is my roommate, Kate.

WORDS

1
roommate 명 방을 함께 쓰는 사람, 룸메이트

2 밑줄 친 ①~⑤ 중 대화의 흐름과 어울리지 않는 것은?

A: I'll introduce myself. ① My name is Jenny.
B: ② What's up? ③ Nice to meet you. ④ I'm Carl.
A: ⑤ Nice to meet you, too.

FINAL TEST

1 다음 중 영어 단어와 우리말 뜻이 잘못 연결된 것은?

① farm - 농장　② alike - 다른
③ artist - 예술가　④ weak - 약한
⑤ famous - 유명한

2 다음 우리말과 일치하도록 빈칸에 알맞은 말을 쓰시오.

나는 수학을 잘한다.

→ I am ________ ________ math.

[3-4] 다음 대화의 빈칸에 들어갈 말로 알맞은 것을 고르시오.

3
A: Let me ____________. I'm Sujin.
B: Hi. My name is Peter.

① say me
② make myself
③ introduce you
④ introduce myself
⑤ introduce to you

4
A: How is it going?
B: I'm all right. ____________
A: Very well, thanks!

① My name is Emily.
② I'll introduce myself.
③ How are you doing?
④ Pleased to meet you.
⑤ I'm doing fine, thanks.

5 대화가 자연스럽게 이어지도록 (A)~(C)를 바르게 배열하시오.

(A) Pleased to meet you, Lina.
(B) Hello, Tom. My name is Lina.
(C) I'll introduce myself. I'm Tom.

________ → ________ → ________

! 자주 나와요

[6-7] 다음 빈칸에 들어갈 말로 알맞지 않은 것을 고르시오.

6
________ are at the shopping mall.

① We　② They
③ John and I　④ My friends
⑤ Minji's sister

7
________ is very tired today.

① He　② She
③ Jiho　④ His children
⑤ Her cousin

8 다음 빈칸에 들어갈 말로 알맞은 것은?

이 배는 우리의 것이다.
→ This boat ____________.

① is us　② is ours
③ are us　④ are ours
⑤ are yours

9 다음 대화의 빈칸에 공통으로 들어갈 말로 알맞은 것은?

A: Claire, ________ that actor from America?
B: Yes, he ________.

① am ② is
③ are ④ isn't
⑤ aren't

[10-11] 다음 대화의 빈칸에 들어갈 말이 바르게 짝지어진 것을 고르시오.

10
A: ________ your parents in the garden?
B: No, ________ aren't.

① Is – you ② Is – they
③ Are – you ④ Are – they
⑤ Am – their

11
• A: Are you and Maria pianists?
B: Yes, ________ are.
• A: Is that your sister's sweater?
B: Yes, it is. It's ________.

① we – her ② we – hers
③ we – theirs ④ you – hers
⑤ you – theirs

12 다음 밑줄 친 부분 중 줄여 쓸 수 없는 것은?

① The stores are not open.
② I am not a fast runner.
③ It is not John's spoon.
④ They are not my friends.
⑤ He is not a famous writer.

! 자주 나와요

[13-14] 다음 밑줄 친 부분의 쓰임이 나머지 넷과 다른 것을 고르시오.

13 ① This is his lotion.
② I like his bright smile.
③ It's not my cup. It's his.
④ Harry misses his parents.
⑤ His house is next to mine.

14 ① It is 4 p.m.
② It is August 14.
③ It is her umbrella.
④ It is Parents' Day today.
⑤ It snows a lot here in winter.

15 다음 빈칸에 들어갈 말이 나머지 넷과 다른 것은?

① ________ they on the street?
② ________ the boys kind to you?
③ There ________ ducks in the cage.
④ ________ there vases on the table?
⑤ My mom ________ happy with the news.

! 어려워요

16 다음 밑줄 친 부분 중 어법상 바르지 못한 것은?

① Is that her wallet?
② Are those his socks?
③ The books are not them.
④ Their clothes are very dirty.
⑤ This is my new digital camera.

17 다음 중 어법상 바른 것은?

① She isn't with me now.
② I like yours white shirt.
③ Is him from Singapore?
④ There are a police car over there.
⑤ The necklace on the desk isn't her.

! 어려워요

18 다음 중 짝지어진 대화가 어색한 것은?

① A: Is he ready now?
B: No, he isn't.
② A: Are you David's friends?
B: Yes, you are.
③ A: Are Bill and Mark 8 years old?
B: No, they aren't.
④ A: Are there flowers in your room?
B: Yes, there are.
⑤ A: Is your bag under mine?
B: Yes, it is.

! 서술형

[19-20] 다음 우리말과 일치하도록 괄호 안의 단어를 바르게 배열하시오.

19 그녀의 이야기는 재미있지 않다.
(story, fun, is, her, not)

→ ______________________

20 이 손목시계는 너의 것이니?
(watch, yours, is, this)

→ ______________________

내신 완성 서술형

[21-22] 다음 문장을 괄호 안의 지시대로 바꿔 쓰시오.

21 I am a figure skater. (부정문으로)

→ ______________________

22 His gloves are on the floor.
(의문문으로)

→ ______________________

[23-24] 다음은 세 친구의 시험 성적표이다. 표의 내용과 일치하도록 보기 처럼 대화를 완성하시오.

	Nick	Eunji	Liv
English	A	C	A
Science	B	C	C

보기 A: Is Eunji's English grade great?
B: No, it isn't.

23 A: ________ Nick's English grade good?
B: ________, ________ ________.

24 A: ________ Eunji and Liv good at science?
B: ________, ________ ________.

WORD LIST

Grammar

□ famous	형 유명한
□ aunt	명 고모, 이모
□ cute	형 귀여운
□ present	명 선물
□ clothes	명 옷
□ dentist	명 치과 의사
□ late	형 늦은
□ again	부 다시
□ be good at	…를 잘하다
□ wall	명 벽
□ angry	형 화난
□ free	형 자유로운; 한가한
□ weak	형 약한
□ strong	형 튼튼한, 힘센
□ hard	형 단단한
□ farm	명 농장
□ take a walk	산책하다
□ need	동 필요로 하다
□ vase	명 꽃병
□ popular	형 인기 있는
□ library	명 도서관
□ twin	명 쌍둥이
□ brave	형 용감한
□ factory	명 공장
□ airport	명 공항
□ already	부 이미, 벌써
□ interesting	형 재미있는, 흥미로운
□ dictionary	명 사전
□ sky	명 하늘

Reading

□ picture	명 사진
□ member	명 구성원
□ work	동 일하다
□ see	동 보다; 알다
□ teach	동 가르치다
□ math	명 수학
□ alike	형 (아주) 비슷한
□ last	형 마지막의
□ people	명 사람들
□ know	동 알다
□ person	명 사람
□ visit	동 방문하다
□ festival	명 축제
□ artist	명 예술가
□ be made of	…로 만들어지다

Communication

□ weather	명 날씨
□ myself	대 나 자신
□ pleased	형 기쁜
□ roommate	명 방을 함께 쓰는 사람, 룸메이트

Final Test

□ tired	형 피곤한
□ cousin	명 사촌
□ garden	명 정원
□ bright	형 밝은
□ miss	동 그리워하다
□ wallet	명 지갑
□ science	명 과학

CHAPTER 02

일반동사

GET READY

Jenny **walks** slowly.
(Jenny는 천천히 걷는다.)

I **don't dance** very well.
(나는 춤을 잘 못 춘다.)

Do you want these movies**?**
(너는 이 영화들을 원하니?)

'걷다', '춤추다', '원하다' 등 동작이나 상태를 나타내는 말을 일반동사라고 해요. 일반동사도 be동사처럼 주어에 따라 형태가 바뀌는데, 바뀌기 전 동사 그대로의 형태를 동사원형이라고 해요.

GRAMMAR FOCUS

A 일반동사의 현재형

1 일반동사

be동사(am, are, is 등)와 조동사(can, may, will, must 등)를 제외한 모든 동사로, 주어의 동작이나 상태를 나타낸다.

예 play(놀다), make(만들다), speak(말하다), like(좋아하다) 등

2 일반동사의 현재형

1) 주어가 1인칭, 2인칭이거나 복수일 때: 동사원형

I **love** you.
You **have** a nice shirt.
We **watch** quiz shows together.
They **plant** trees around the city.
Many people **buy** bread at Holmes Bakery.

2) 주어가 3인칭 단수일 때: 보통 「동사원형+-(e)s」 형태로 쓰지만 예외도 있다.

He **drinks** eight glasses of water every day.
My pet **catches** the ball very well.
She **goes** to church on Sundays.
The baby **cries** very loudly.
Mr. Smith **has** four children.

내신 POINT PLUS

일반동사의 3인칭 단수 현재형

1 규칙 변화

동사의 형태	만드는 법	예
대부분의 동사	동사원형+-s	love**s**, read**s**, buy**s**, come**s**, eat**s**, know**s**, work**s**, play**s**, run**s**, sleep**s**
-ch, -sh, -x, -s, -o로 끝나는 동사	동사원형+-es	watch**es**, catch**es**, wash**es**, finish**es**, mix**es**, cross**es**, go**es**, do**es**
「자음+y」로 끝나는 동사	y를 i로 고치고 +-es	study → stud**ies**, cry → cr**ies**, try → tr**ies**, dry → dr**ies**, fly → fl**ies**

2 불규칙 변화: have → has

Check-Up

A 다음 괄호 안에서 알맞은 말을 고르시오.

1 I (wake / wakes) up late.
2 Emma and I (like / likes) fruit.
3 People (stop / stops) at the red light.
4 The eagle (fly / flies) high in the sky.
5 My sister (wash / washes) the dishes after dinner.

WORDS

A
wake up (잠에서) 깨다
eagle 명 독수리
wash the dishes 설거지를 하다

B 다음 괄호 안의 동사를 알맞은 형태의 현재형으로 쓰시오.

1 They __________ waffles on the street. (sell)
2 Lisa __________ lunch at twelve. (have)
3 Mike __________ soccer with his friends. (play)
4 School __________ at three o'clock. (finish)
5 Some children __________ letters to Santa Claus. (write)

B
sell 동 팔다
finish 동 끝나다

C 다음 밑줄 친 부분을 바르게 고치시오.

1 The sun <u>set</u> in the west. → __________
2 Nora <u>trys</u> her best all the time. → __________
3 Mr. Kim <u>gos</u> to the gym every evening. → __________
4 Bruce and his sister <u>swims</u> very fast. → __________

C
try one's best 최선을 다하다
all the time 내내, 항상
gym 명 체육관

D 다음 빈칸에 들어갈 말을 보기 에서 골라 알맞은 형태의 현재형으로 쓰시오.

보기 worry eat open study

1 They __________ Spanish hard.
2 My mother __________ about my health.
3 The store __________ in the early morning.
4 We __________ pizza for dinner once a week.

D
Spanish 명 스페인어
hard 부 열심히
health 명 건강
once 부 한 번

B 일반동사의 부정문과 의문문

1 일반동사의 부정문: 「주어+do/does not+동사원형 ...」

주어	부정형
1인칭, 2인칭, 복수	do not[don't]+동사원형
3인칭 단수	does not[doesn't]+동사원형

1) 주어가 1인칭, 2인칭, 복수일 때: 동사원형 앞에 do not[don't]을 쓴다.

I **don't**[**do not**] **play** mobile games.
We **don't believe** the news.
They **don't wear** glasses.

2) 주어가 3인칭 단수일 때: 동사원형 앞에 does not[doesn't]을 쓴다.

The market **doesn't**[**does not**] **close** on weekends.
My dog **doesn't bark** loudly.
Seonmi **doesn't check** the weather forecast.

2 일반동사의 의문문: 「Do/Does+주어+동사원형 ...?」

주어	의문문	긍정 대답	부정 대답
1인칭, 2인칭, 복수	Do+주어+동사원형 ...?	Yes, 주어+do.	No, 주어+don't.
3인칭 단수	Does+주어+동사원형 ...?	Yes, 주어+does.	No, 주어+doesn't.

1) 주어가 1인칭, 2인칭, 복수일 때: 「Do+주어+동사원형 ...?」

A: **Do you watch** the drama**?**
B: **Yes, I do.** / **No, I don't.**

A: **Do his children like** cheese**?**
B: **Yes, they do.** / **No, they don't.**

2) 주어가 3인칭 단수일 때: 「Does+주어+동사원형 ...?」

A: **Does your aunt live** in London**?**
B: **Yes, she does.** / **No, she doesn't.**

TIPS

일반동사 do와 조동사 do

1 일반동사 do: '…를 하다'의 의미로, 문장에서 동사로 쓰인다.
I **do** my homework after school. (나는 방과 후에 숙제를 한다.)

2 조동사 do: 일반동사가 있는 문장을 부정문이나 의문문으로 만들 때 쓰인다.
She **doesn't** *have* breakfast. (그녀는 아침을 먹지 않는다.)
Do you *know* Josh? (너는 Josh를 아니?)

Check-Up

A 다음 괄호 안에서 알맞은 말을 고르시오.

1 (Do / Does) you speak German?

2 She (don't / doesn't) like spicy food.

3 (Do / Does) this subway go to Seoul Station?

4 Jane and Chris (don't / doesn't) know each other.

WORDS

A

German 명 독일인; *독일어
spicy 형 (맛이) 매운
subway 명 지하철
each other 서로

B 다음 대화의 빈칸에 알맞은 말을 쓰시오.

1 A: Do you clean your desk? B: Yes, ________ ________.

2 A: Does this machine work well? B: Yes, ________ ________.

3 A: Do Emily and Tom take the school bus? B: No, ________ ________.

B

clean 동 청소하다
work 동 일하다; *작동하다

C 다음 문장을 괄호 안의 지시대로 바꿀 때, 빈칸에 알맞은 말을 쓰시오.

1 I live with my family. (부정문으로)

→ ________ ________ ________ with my family.

2 They prepare for exams. (의문문으로)

→ ________ ________ ________ for exams?

3 She visits her grandmother every Friday. (부정문으로)

→ ________ ________ ________ her grandmother every Friday.

4 Alex grows strawberries in the garden. (의문문으로)

→ ________ ________ ________ strawberries in the garden?

C

prepare 동 준비하다
grow 동 재배하다

D 다음 우리말과 일치하도록 괄호 안의 단어를 이용하여 문장을 완성하시오.

1 그는 휴대 전화가 있니? (have)

→ ________ ________ ________ a cell phone?

2 우리는 이 웹 사이트를 사용하지 않는다. (use)

→ We ________ ________ this website.

3 너는 집에서 에너지를 절약하니? (save)

→ ________ ________ ________ energy at home?

4 코끼리는 고기를 먹지 않는다. (eat)

→ Elephants ________ ________ meat.

D

website 명 웹 사이트
save 동 구하다; *절약하다
meat 명 고기

Grammar Practice

A 다음 밑줄 친 부분을 바르게 고치시오.

1 A balloon flys over the tree. → ________

2 We not sell pasta or steak. → ________

3 Does Nick's friends play basketball? → ________

4 He teach math at a high school. → ________

5 She don't understand their questions. → ________

B 다음 괄호 안의 단어를 이용하여 문장을 완성하시오.

1 Yuri is kind. She ________ the poor. (help)

2 Her grandfather ________ a nice yacht now. (have)

3 Colin wakes up early. He ________ the train. (do, miss)

4 Anna ________ butter cookies for her child. (make)

5 Fish live in water. They ________ on land. (do, live)

C 다음 밑줄 친 부분이 어법상 바르면 O를 쓰고, 틀리면 바르게 고치시오.

1 My sister runes a bookstore. → ________

2 Helen and her brother love their pet. → ________

3 Do Lily and Mason like Mexican food? → ________

4 Does Danny listens to the radio at night? → ________

5 The managers doesn't know my email address. → ________

D 다음 우리말과 일치하도록 괄호 안의 단어를 바르게 배열하시오.

1 우리는 문자 메시지를 보내지 않는다. (do, we, not, send)

→ ________________ text messages.

2 그들은 매 여름 이 호텔에서 지내니? (stay, they, do)

→ ________________ in this hotel every summer?

WORDS

A
balloon 명 풍선
over 전 … 위에[위로]
steak 명 스테이크
understand 동 이해하다

B
yacht 명 요트
train 명 기차
land 명 육지, 땅

C
run 동 달리다; *운영하다
manager 명 운영자, 관리자
email address 이메일 주소

D
send 동 보내다
text message 문자 메시지
stay 동 머무르다; *지내다

내신 완성 Grammar Practice

1 다음 빈칸에 들어갈 말이 바르게 짝지어진 것은?

• Sarah ________ learn Chinese at school.
• He ________ his teeth after meals.

① don't – brushs
② don't – brushes
③ doesn't – brush
④ doesn't – brushs
⑤ doesn't – brushes

WORDS

1
Chinese 명 중국어
meal 명 식사, 끼니
brush 동 솔질[칫솔질]을 하다

2 다음 밑줄 친 부분의 쓰임이 나머지 넷과 다른 것은?

① Do you take a yoga class?
② I do not like horror movies.
③ It does not snow often in Texas.
④ We do exercises after dinner.
⑤ Does Adam have a concert ticket?

2
yoga 명 요가
horror 명 공포
exercise 명 운동

3 다음 중 어법상 바른 문장을 모두 고른 것은?

ⓐ The bus passes City Hall.
ⓑ Do bats come out at night?
ⓒ Carter and I doesn't write Korean.
ⓓ The flower shop closes at 10 o'clock.
ⓔ Does your father watches sports on TV?

① ⓐ, ⓑ, ⓒ
② ⓐ, ⓑ, ⓓ
③ ⓑ, ⓒ, ⓓ
④ ⓑ, ⓓ, ⓔ
⑤ ⓒ, ⓓ, ⓔ

3
city hall 시청
bat 명 박쥐

4 다음 그림을 보고, 괄호 안의 단어를 이용하여 대화를 완성하시오.

A: Does Anna play the flute?
B: No, she ________.
She ________________. (the violin)

4
flute 명 플루트

서술형에 나오는 WRITING

A 다음 우리말과 일치하도록 괄호 안의 말을 바르게 배열하시오.

1 너는 매일 샤워를 하니? (do, take a shower, you)

→ ______________________ every day?

2 James는 식탁을 치우지 않는다. (clear, does, James, not)

→ ______________________ the table.

B 다음 문장을 주어진 주어로 시작하는 문장으로 바꿔 쓰시오.

1 She doesn't skip art class.

→ I ______________________.

2 They go hiking in the spring.

→ He ______________________.

C 다음은 Karl의 토요일 시간표이다. 표를 보고, 보기 처럼 문장을 완성하시오.

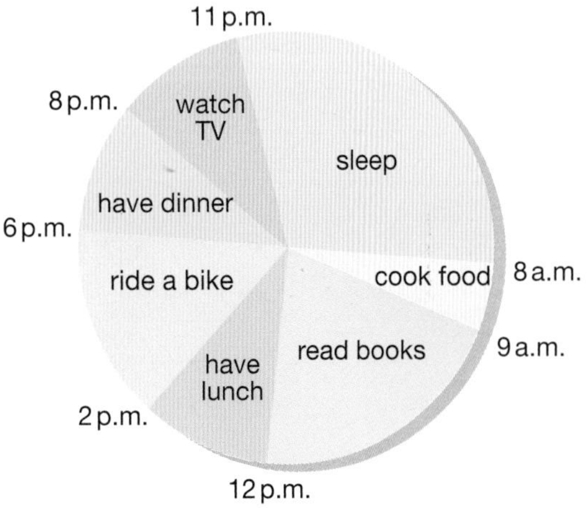

보기 Karl <u>cooks food</u> at 8:30 a.m.

1 Karl ______________ at 10 a.m.

2 Karl ______________ at 4 p.m.

3 Karl ______________ at 9 p.m.

READING WITH GRAMMAR

1

Hi, I **need** some advice! I am too busy. I **have** English class twice a week, piano lessons three times a week, and homework every night. I **don't go** to bed until late at night. And I never **get** to meet my friends. Of course I **want** to skip a lesson. But I'm afraid I'll fall behind. It is too stressful.

Everyone **thinks** I'm a happy, normal student. However, sometimes I **cry** alone in my room. I often **tell** my friends about this. <u>But they doesn't listen carefully.</u> They just **say**, "But you **do** well in school." **Do you understand** my problem**?** What should I do?

1 위 글에서 글쓴이의 고민으로 알맞은 것은?

① 성적이 떨어지는 것
② 학업이 너무 바쁜 것
③ 친구들에게 놀림 받는 것
④ 친구들과의 모임이 너무 많은 것
⑤ 수업에 흥미를 느끼지 못하는 것

2 위 글의 밑줄 친 문장을 바르게 고치시오.

→ But ____.

WORDS
advice 명 조언 **homework** 명 [1]__________ **go to bed** 자다 **get to** …에 도착하다; *(어떤 결과)에 이르다
skip 동 거르다[빼먹다] **afraid** 형 두려워하는 **fall behind** 뒤떨어지다 **stressful** 형 스트레스가 많은 **normal** 형 평범한
alone 부 혼자 **carefully** 부 주의하여 **understand** 동 [2]__________ **problem** 명 문제

2

Amy: What's the matter with you? You **don't look** happy.

Charlie: I'm angry about this bag of potato chips. It **has** too much air in it.

Amy: Air? ① Do you mean the gas inside the bag?

Charlie: **Yes, I do.** The gas almost ② fills up the whole bag. So there aren't many chips. It **doesn't make** sense!

Amy: I ③ understand, Charlie. But it isn't just air. It is *nitrogen gas.

Charlie: Nitrogen gas? **Does the company pack** its snacks with nitrogen gas**?**

Amy: Yes, it ④ does. And the gas **protects** the chips inside.

Charlie: Is the gas safe?

Amy: Yes, it is. It **doesn't have** a smell, taste, or color.

Charlie: Phew.... I **see**. But I ⑤ wants chips, not gas!

*nitrogen gas: 질소 가스

1 Which is NOT true about nitrogen gas?

① It almost fills up the bag.
② It protects the chips.
③ It doesn't smell.
④ It doesn't have a taste.
⑤ It has a white color.

2 Which is NOT grammatically correct?

① ② ③ ④ ⑤

WORDS

matter 명 문제　chip 명 조각; *(얇게 썰어 튀긴) 감자 칩　air 명 1________　mean 동 의미하다　inside 전 … 안에 부 안에
almost 부 거의　fill up …를 가득 채우다　company 명 회사　pack A with B A를 B로 채워 넣다　snack 명 간식
protect 동 2________　smell 명 냄새 동 냄새가 나다　taste 명 맛

내신에 나오는 COMMUNICATION

A 외모 묘사하기

A: **What does** Amanda **look like?**
(Amanda는 어떻게 생겼니?)

B: **She's tall. She has curly hair.**
(그녀는 키가 커. 그녀는 곱슬머리를 가졌어.)

A: Does she wear glasses?
(그녀는 안경을 쓰니?)

B: No, she doesn't.
(아니, 그렇지 않아.)

누군가의 외모를 물을 때는 'What do/does ... look like?'라고 말할 수 있다. 대답할 때는 외모를 나타내는 형용사를 사용하여 '주어+be동사+형용사', '주어+have/has+형용사+명사' 등의 형태로 말할 수 있다.

EXPRESSION PLUS

A: What does he look like? (그는 어떻게 생겼니?)
B: **He is thin. He has blue eyes.** (그는 말랐어. 그는 파란 눈을 가졌어.)

A: What does your cat look like? (네 고양이는 어떻게 생겼니?)
B: **It has a long yellow tail.** (그것은 긴 노란 꼬리를 가졌어.)

TIPS **외모를 나타내는 형용사**
cute(귀여운), short(키가 작은), tall(키가 큰), thin(마른), handsome(잘생긴) 등

Check-Up

1 다음 대화의 빈칸에 들어갈 말로 알맞지 않은 것은?

A: What does his dog look like?
B: ____________

① It is cute. ② It is huge.
③ It is his dog. ④ It has short legs.
⑤ It has brown fur.

2 다음 우리말과 일치하도록 괄호 안의 단어를 이용하여 대화를 완성하시오.

A: Paul은 어떻게 생겼니? (look)
B: 그는 잘생겼어. (be, handsome)

→ A: ________ does Paul ________ ________?
B: He ________ ________.

WORDS
1
huge 형 거대한
fur 명 (동물의) 털

B 음식 권하고 답하기

A: **Would you like some** bread**?**
(빵 좀 먹겠니?)

B: **Yes, please.** They look delicious.
(네, 주세요. 그것들은 맛있어 보이네요.)

A: **Do you want** a glass of orange juice, too**?**
(오렌지 주스도 한 잔 원하니?)

B: **No, thanks.** I'm not thirsty.
(아니요, 괜찮아요. 저는 목이 마르지 않아요.)

음식을 권할 때는 'Would you like (some) ...?'나 'Do you want (some) ...?'라고 말할 수 있다. 수락할 때는 'Yes, please.'로, 거절할 때는 'No, thanks.'로 말할 수 있다.

EXPRESSION PLUS

1 음식 권하기
- **Will you have some** pie**?** (파이를 좀 드시겠어요?)
- **Try this.** (이것 좀 먹어 보세요.) / **Help yourself.** (마음껏 드세요.)

2 대답하기
- **Okay. Thank you.** (네. 감사합니다.)
- **No, I'm full.** (아니요, 저는 배불러요.) / **No, thank you.** (아니요, 괜찮아요.)

Check-Up

1 다음 대화의 빈칸에 들어갈 말로 알맞지 않은 것은?

A: Do you want a cup of milk?
B: ____________________

① Yes, please.
② Okay. Thank you.
③ Help yourself.
④ No, thanks.
⑤ No, I'm full.

2 다음 대화의 밑줄 친 문장과 바꿔 쓸 수 있는 것을 모두 고르시오. (2개)

A: <u>Would you like some vanilla ice cream?</u>
B: Okay. Thank you.

① Is this vanilla ice cream?
② Do you eat vanilla ice cream?
③ Do you make vanilla ice cream?
④ Do you want some vanilla ice cream?
⑤ Will you have some vanilla ice cream?

WORDS

1
a cup of 한 잔의

2
vanilla 명 바닐라

1 다음 중 영어 단어와 우리말 뜻이 잘못 연결된 것은?

① taste - 맛 ② almost - 거의
③ huge - 아주 작은 ④ mean - 의미하다
⑤ carefully - 주의하여

2 다음 우리말과 일치하도록 빈칸에 알맞은 말을 쓰시오.

나는 공부 습관에 관해 네 조언이 필요해.

→ I need your __________ on study habits.

[3-4] 다음 대화의 빈칸에 들어갈 말로 알맞은 것을 고르시오.

3

A: What does Kevin look like?
B: ____________________

① He is kind.
② I know him.
③ He has dark hair.
④ He is my best friend.
⑤ He is nice to everyone.

4

A: Would you like some strawberry cake?
B: ________________ I'm full.

① I like it.
② Yes, please.
③ No, thank you.
④ I'm very hungry.
⑤ That's my favorite.

5 주어진 문장 뒤로 대화가 자연스럽게 이어지도록 (A)~(C)를 바르게 배열하시오.

What does your pet look like?

(A) No, it doesn't.
(B) Does it have curly fur?
(C) My pet is small and white.

__________ → __________ → __________

6 밑줄 친 ①~⑤ 중 대화의 흐름과 어울리지 않는 것은?

A: Mom, that smells good!
B: ① Do you want this spaghetti with cream sauce?
A: ② I don't like spaghetti.
③ Yes, please. I'm hungry.
B: ④ Will you have some iced tea, too?
A: ⑤ Yes. I'm thirsty.

7 다음 중 동사의 3인칭 단수형이 잘못 연결된 것은?

① have - has ② make - makes
③ study - studies ④ enjoy - enjoies
⑤ prepare - prepares

어려워요

8 다음 밑줄 친 부분 중 어법상 바르지 못한 것은?

① Jay talks too much.
② This T-shirt drys quickly.
③ Dan takes a bus to school.
④ Bora puts milk in her coffee.
⑤ Nancy listens to Korean songs.

9 다음 빈칸에 들어갈 말로 알맞지 않은 것은?

_________ goes to the movies once a month.

① He ② She
③ Karen ④ My friends
⑤ Mira's teacher

10 다음 빈칸에 공통으로 들어갈 말로 알맞은 것은?

- Kate _________ not have the key right now.
- A: Liam, _________ Tim live here?
  B: Yes, he _________.

① is ② are
③ do ④ does
⑤ doesn't

! 자주 나와요

[11-13] 다음 질문에 대한 대답을 보기 에서 고르시오.

보기 ⓐ Yes, I do. ⓑ Yes, I am.
ⓒ Yes, we do. ⓓ No, they don't.
ⓔ No, he doesn't.

11 Does your brother study hard?

____

12 Do you live alone, John?

____

13 Do Amy and Jane have bicycles?

____

14 다음 대화의 빈칸에 들어갈 말로 알맞은 것은?

A: Does Jinhee take skiing lessons?
B: _____________ She doesn't like sports.

① Yes, she is. ② Yes, she does.
③ No, she isn't. ④ No, she does.
⑤ No, she doesn't.

15 다음 중 어법상 바른 것은?

① Do Sam play the piano?
② My uncle stays in Seattle.
③ He doesn't cleans his room.
④ The snake move very quietly.
⑤ John and Mary doesn't eat carrots.

! 어려워요

16 다음 밑줄 친 부분의 쓰임이 보기 와 다른 것은?

보기 Walt's children do not take taxis.

① Do oranges grow in Britain?
② I do my homework after school.
③ We usually do not have breakfast.
④ They do not save money.
⑤ Do you know the actor's real name?

[17-18] 다음 문장을 부정문으로 바꿀 때, 빈칸에 알맞은 말을 쓰시오.

17 They bake cookies every Friday.

→ They _________ _________ _________ every Friday.

18 My father comes from New York.

→ My father __________ __________ __________ New York.

자주 나와요

19 다음 중 짝지어진 대화가 어색한 것은?

① A: Does Andy sing well?
B: No, he doesn't.

② A: Does she wear glasses?
B: Yes, she does.

③ A: Do you and Mia often eat fast food?
B: Yes, I do.

④ A: Do your parents listen to rock music?
B: Yes, they do.

⑤ A: Do you make many calls to each other?
B: No, we don't.

서술형

[20-21] 다음 우리말과 일치하도록 괄호 안의 단어를 이용하여 문장을 완성하시오.

20 그들은 토요일에 일을 하나요? (work)

→ ____________________ on Saturday?

21 그녀가 내 전화번호를 아니? (know)

→ ____________________ my phone number?

내신 완성 서술형

[22-23] 다음 대화에서 밑줄 친 부분을 바르게 고치시오.

A: My mom makes dinner every day.
B: Does your dad cooks too?
A: No, he doesn't. But he wash the dishes after dinner.

22 cooks → __________

23 wash → __________

[24-25] 다음은 세 친구가 주말에 주로 하는 활동을 나타낸 표이다. 표의 내용과 일치하도록 대화를 완성하시오.

	Activity
Mason	play tennis
Susan	take pictures
Peter	ride a skateboard

24 A: __________ Mason play tennis on weekends?
B: __________, __________ __________.

25 A: __________ Susan and Peter ride bikes?
B: __________, __________ __________.

WORD LIST

Grammar

□ wake up	(잠에서) 깨다
□ eagle	명 독수리
□ wash the dishes	설거지를 하다
□ sell	동 팔다
□ finish	동 끝나다
□ try one's best	최선을 다하다
□ gym	명 체육관
□ health	명 건강
□ spicy	형 (맛이) 매운
□ subway	명 지하철
□ each other	서로
□ clean	동 청소하다
□ prepare	동 준비하다
□ grow	동 재배하다
□ website	명 웹 사이트
□ save	동 구하다; 절약하다
□ understand	동 이해하다
□ train	명 기차
□ run	동 달리다; 운영하다
□ text message	문자 메시지
□ stay	동 머무르다; 지내다
□ meal	명 식사, 끼니
□ brush	동 솔질[칫솔질]을 하다
□ horror	명 공포
□ city hall	시청

Reading

□ advice	명 조언
□ homework	명 숙제
□ skip	동 거르다[빼먹다]
□ afraid	형 두려워하는
□ stressful	형 스트레스가 많은
□ normal	형 평범한
□ alone	부 혼자
□ carefully	부 주의하여
□ problem	명 문제
□ matter	명 문제
□ air	명 공기
□ mean	동 의미하다
□ inside	전 … 안에 부 안에
□ company	명 회사
□ protect	동 보호하다
□ smell	명 냄새 동 냄새가 나다
□ taste	명 맛

Communication

□ curly	형 곱슬곱슬한
□ huge	형 거대한
□ fur	명 (동물의) 털
□ a cup of	한 잔의

Final Test

□ habit	명 습관
□ enjoy	동 즐기다
□ quietly	부 조용히
□ real	형 진짜의

CHAPTER 03

동사의 시제

GET READY

I **play** soccer. (나는 축구를 한다.)

I **played** soccer. (나는 축구를 했다.)

I **am playing** soccer. (나는 축구를 하고 있다.)

I **was playing** soccer. (나는 축구를 하고 있었다.)

I **will play** soccer. (나는 축구를 할 것이다.)

위 문장들은 모두 축구를 한다는 내용이지만 시제, 즉 동작이 일어나는 시점에 따라서 동사의 형태가 달라져요. 대부분의 동사는 형태가 규칙적으로 변하지만, 몇몇 동사들은 불규칙하게 변해요.

GRAMMAR FOCUS

A 과거시제

과거시제는 과거에 일어난 일이나 상태를 나타낸다.

1 be동사

1) be동사의 과거형: am, is의 과거형은 was이고, are의 과거형은 were이다.
He **was** very sick yesterday.
You **were** an elementary school student in 2016.

2) be동사 과거형의 부정문: 「주어+wasn't/weren't ...」
The house **wasn't**[**was not**] empty that night.
They **weren't**[**were not**] happy with the news.

3) be동사 과거형의 의문문: 「Was/Were+주어 ...?」
A: **Was** she late for school**?** B: **Yes**, she **was**. / **No**, she **wasn't**.
A: **Were** we in Boston at that time**?** B: **Yes**, we **were**. / **No**, we **weren't**.

2 일반동사

1) 일반동사의 과거형: 보통 동사원형 뒤에 -(e)d를 붙이지만, 일부 동사는 불규칙하게 변한다.
I **finished** my science homework.
She **came** to Korea last week.

내신 POINT PLUS

일반동사의 과거형 만드는 법

규칙	대부분의 동사	동사원형+-ed	want**ed**, stay**ed**, open**ed**
	-e로 끝나는 동사	동사원형+-d	like**d**, bake**d**, move**d**, invite**d**
	「자음+y」로 끝나는 동사	y를 i로 바꾸고+-ed	study → stud**ied**, cry → cr**ied**
	「단모음+단자음」으로 끝나는 동사	자음을 한 번 더 쓰고+-ed	stop → stop**ped**, chat → chat**ted**
불규칙	현재형과 과거형이 같은 동사	cut → **cut**, put → **put**, set → **set**, let → **let**, hit → **hit**	
	현재형과 과거형이 다른 동사	do → **did**, go → **went**, come → **came**, have → **had**, say → **said**, take → **took**, leave → **left**, drink → **drank**	

2) 일반동사 과거형의 부정문: 「주어+did not+동사원형 ...」
I **didn't**[**did not**] **read** the newspaper this morning.

3) 일반동사 과거형의 의문문: 「Did+주어+동사원형 ...?」
A: **Did** Bill **go** to the concert**?** B: **Yes**, he **did**. / **No**, he **didn't**.

TIPS
과거시제와 자주 함께 쓰이는 부사(구)
- last night(어젯밤)
- yesterday(어제)
- then/at that time(그때)
- a year ago(일 년 전)

Check-Up

A 다음 괄호 안에서 알맞은 말을 고르시오.

1 We (be / was / were) at the airport.

2 It (is / was / were) very cold yesterday.

3 (Do / Does / Did) you call him last Sunday?

4 She (drink / drinks / drank) tea a minute ago.

5 Jane and I (don't / doesn't / didn't) go out last night.

B 다음 괄호 안의 단어를 빈칸에 알맞은 형태로 쓰시오.

1 We ________ a big party yesterday. (have)

2 Jim ________ to the movies last weekend. (go)

3 The actor ________ in Sydney 10 years ago. (live)

4 She ________ very proud of her victory then. (be)

C 다음 밑줄 친 부분을 바르게 고치시오.

1 He didn't <u>opened</u> the window. → ________

2 <u>Were</u> Sam with you at that time? → ________

3 Kelly <u>moves</u> to L.A. two months ago. → ________

4 <u>Were</u> you see him yesterday morning? → ________

D 다음 문장을 괄호 안의 지시대로 바꿀 때, 빈칸에 알맞은 말을 쓰시오.

1 I worked in a hotel. (부정문으로)

→ ________ ________ ________ in a hotel.

2 He was afraid of ghosts. (부정문으로)

→ ________ ________ ________ of ghosts.

3 They were busy on Monday. (의문문으로)

→ ________ ________ ________ on Monday?

4 The lady visited the bank at 4 o'clock. (의문문으로)

→ ________ ________ ________ ________ the bank at 4 o'clock?

WORDS

A
airport 명 공항
go out 외출하다

B
go to the movies 영화를 보러 가다
be proud of …를 자랑스러워하다
victory 명 승리

C
window 명 창문
move 동 움직이다; *이사하다
month 명 월; *달[개월]

D
be afraid of …를 두려워하다
ghost 명 유령

B 진행형

진행형은 특정 시점에 진행 중인 일을 나타내며, 일어난 시점에 따라 현재진행형과 과거진행형으로 나뉜다.

1 현재진행형

'…하고 있다'의 의미로, 지금 진행 중인 일을 나타낸다.

1) 긍정문: 「주어+be동사의 현재형(am/are/is)+v-ing …」
I**'m cleaning** my room.

2) 부정문: 「주어+be동사의 현재형+not+v-ing …」
The baby **is not crying** now.

3) 의문문: 「be동사의 현재형+주어+v-ing …?」
A: **Are** Jenny and Ken **listening** to music**?** B: **Yes**, they **are**. / **No**, they **aren't**.

내신 POINT PLUS

「v-ing」 만드는 법

동사의 형태	만드는 법	예
대부분의 동사	동사원형+-ing	read**ing**, meet**ing**, do**ing**, fly**ing**
-e로 끝나는 동사	e를 빼고+-ing	live → liv**ing**, give → giv**ing**, come → com**ing**, move → mov**ing**
-ie로 끝나는 동사	ie를 y로 바꾸고+-ing	lie → **lying**, die → d**ying**, tie → **tying**
「단모음+단자음」으로 끝나는 동사	자음을 한 번 더 쓰고+-ing	cut → cut**ting**, sit → sit**ting**, put → put**ting**, shop → shop**ping**

2 과거진행형

'…하고 있었다'의 의미로, 과거의 특정 시점에 진행 중이었던 일을 나타낸다.

1) 긍정문: 「주어+be동사의 과거형(was/were)+v-ing …」
The boy **was sitting** on the bench.

2) 부정문: 「주어+be동사의 과거형+not+v-ing …」
They **weren't[were not] playing** computer games.

3) 의문문: 「be동사의 과거형+주어+v-ing …?」
A: **Were** you **sleeping** an hour ago**?** B: **Yes**, I **was**. / **No**, I **wasn't**.

TIPS

진행형으로 쓸 수 없는 동사
소유, 감정, 상태를 나타내는 동사(have, love, like, hate, know 등)는 진행형으로 쓰지 않는다.
단, have가 '먹다'의 의미일 때는 진행형으로 쓸 수 있다.
She is knowing him. (x) → She **knows** him. (그녀는 그를 알고 있다.)

Check-Up

A 다음 괄호 안의 단어를 빈칸에 알맞은 형태로 쓰시오.

1 We were __________ at the mall. (shop)

2 I'm __________ a letter to my friend. (write)

3 Was the old dog __________ on the grass? (lie)

B 다음 우리말과 일치하도록 괄호 안의 단어를 이용하여 문장을 완성하시오.

1 그는 체육관으로 달려 가고 있다. (run)

→ He __________ __________ to the gym.

2 나는 손에 펜을 잡고 있지 않았다. (hold)

→ I __________ __________ __________ a pen in my hand.

3 Olivia는 어젯밤에 그림을 그리고 있었니? (draw)

→ __________ __________ __________ a picture last night?

C 다음 문장을 괄호 안의 지시대로 바꿀 때, 빈칸에 알맞은 말을 쓰시오.

1 We help our classmate David. (과거진행형 긍정문으로)

→ We __________ __________ our classmate David.

2 I go to a museum. (현재진행형 부정문으로)

→ I __________ __________ __________ to a museum.

3 Jake moved the tables and chairs. (과거진행형 의문문으로)

→ __________ __________ __________ the tables and chairs?

D 다음 그림을 보고, 대화를 완성하시오.

1

A: Were they riding bicycles?

B: __________, __________ __________.

2

A: Is he talking on the phone?

B: __________, __________ __________.

WORDS

A
mall 명 쇼핑몰
grass 명 풀, 잔디
lie 동 누워 있다; 눕다

B
hold 동 잡고 있다, 쥐다
draw 동 그리다

C
classmate 명 반 친구
museum 명 박물관

D
ride 동 타다
bicycle 명 자전거

C 미래시제

미래시제는 앞으로 일어날 일을 나타내며, 주로 조동사 will과 be going to를 써서 나타낸다.

1 조동사 will

'…할 것이다, …하겠다'의 의미로, 미래에 대한 예측이나 의지를 나타낸다.

1) 긍정문: 「주어+will+동사원형 ...」
It **will be** sunny tomorrow. (미래 예측)
I **will**[I'll] **pass** the exam this time. (의지)

2) 부정문: 「주어+will not+동사원형 ...」
They **will not**[**won't**] **arrive** on time.
The child **will not tell** a lie again.

3) 의문문: 「Will+주어+동사원형 ...?」
A: **Will** you **be** at home tonight**?** B: **Yes**, I **will**. / **No**, I **won't**.
A: **Will** Cindy **buy** a new raincoat**?** B: **Yes**, she **will**. / **No**, she **won't**.

2 be going to

'…할 것이다, …할 예정이다'의 의미로, 미래에 대한 예측이나 예정된 계획을 나타낸다.

1) 긍정문: 「주어+be동사+going to+동사원형 ...」
We **are going to go** on a picnic.
He**'s going to play** badminton after school.

2) 부정문: 「주어+be동사+not going to+동사원형 ...」
I'm not going to change my mind.
They **are not going to sell** their car.

3) 의문문: 「be동사+주어+going to+동사원형 ...?」
A: **Are** you **going to wear** that hat**?** B: **Yes**, I **am**. / **No**, **I'm not**.
A: **Is** she **going to join** the drama club**?** B: **Yes**, she **is**. / **No**, she **isn't**.

TIPS

미래시제와 자주 함께 쓰이는 부사(구)
• tomorrow(내일) • soon(곧) • this week(이번 주) • next year(내년)
Is it *going to* snow **this week**? (이번 주에 눈이 올 예정이니?)
She *will* finish her homework **soon**. (그녀는 곧 숙제를 끝낼 것이다.)

Check-Up

A 다음 괄호 안에서 알맞은 말을 고르시오.

1 I (check / will check) the email soon.

2 We are going (plant / to plant) apple trees.

3 They will (contact / to contact) you next week.

4 She (isn't / won't) going to climb the mountain.

WORDS

A
check 동 확인하다
plant 동 심다
contact 동 연락하다
climb 동 오르다, 올라가다

B 다음 밑줄 친 부분을 바르게 고치시오.

1 I not will waste my money. → ________

2 Will the boss taking the train? → ________

3 Are you going to studying late today? → ________

4 Is going Henry to take a yoga class? → ________

B
waste 동 낭비하다
take a class 수업을 받다

C 다음 문장을 괄호 안의 지시대로 바꿀 때, 빈칸에 알맞은 말을 쓰시오.

1 Tommy is a violinist. (will을 이용한 긍정문으로)
→ Tommy ________ ________ a violinist.

2 We're going to meet at 3 o'clock. (will을 이용한 의문문으로)
→ ________ ________ ________ at 3 o'clock?

3 She will go fishing alone. (be going to를 이용한 부정문으로)
→ She ________ ________ ________ ________
________ fishing alone.

C
violinist 명 바이올린 연주자
go fishing 낚시하러 가다
alone 부 혼자서

D 다음 괄호 안의 단어와 will 또는 won't를 이용하여 대화를 완성하시오.

1 A: Your hands are dirty, Andy!
B: I ________ ________ my hands now. (wash)

2 A: This elevator doesn't work.
B: Oh, I ________ ________ the security office. (call)

3 A: Did you bring my umbrella?
B: No, I'm sorry. I ________ ________ next time. (forget)

D
security 명 경비
bring 동 가져오다
forget 동 잊다

Grammar Practice

A 다음 밑줄 친 부분을 바르게 고치시오.

1 We are look for our bikes now. → ________
2 He will visits London next month. → ________
3 They cutted the paper an hour ago. → ________
4 I not am going to exchange the shoe size. → ________

B 다음 우리말과 일치하도록 괄호 안의 단어를 빈칸에 알맞은 형태로 쓰시오.

1 그들은 함께 사진을 찍었다. (take)
→ They ________ a picture together.
2 Harry는 지난 경기에서 홈런을 쳤다. (hit)
→ Harry ________ a home run in the last game.
3 아이들은 점심 식사 후에 디저트를 먹었다. (eat)
→ The children ________ dessert after lunch.

C 다음 괄호 안의 단어를 이용하여 문장을 완성하시오.

1 I ________ ________ the show next week. (not, miss)
2 Sarah ________ Mindy to the party last Friday. (invite)
3 They are ________ ________ ________ a hair shop soon. (open)
4 A: Is he cooking now?
B: Yes. He ________ ________ shrimp. (fry)

D 다음 문장을 괄호 안의 지시대로 바꿀 때, 빈칸에 알맞은 말을 쓰시오.

1 Sally is at the department store. (미래시제 의문문으로)
→ ________ ________ ________ at the department store?
2 David takes a walk with his dog. (과거진행형 부정문으로)
→ ________ ________ ________ a walk with his dog.

WORDS

A
look for …를 찾다
exchange 동 교환하다

B
take a picture 사진을 찍다
dessert 명 디저트, 후식

C
miss 동 놓치다
invite 동 초대하다
shrimp 명 새우
fry 동 (기름에) 튀기다

D
department store 백화점
take a walk 산책하다

내신 완성 Grammar Practice

1 다음 빈칸에 들어갈 말이 바르게 짝지어진 것은?

- Christina ________ up at 7:30 this morning.
- She ________ the alarm clock last night.

① wake - set ② wakes - sets
③ wakes - will set ④ woke - set
⑤ woke - will set

2 다음 밑줄 친 부분 중 어법상 바른 것은?

① Emily isn't jog in the park.
② We are knowing his name.
③ Books will are on the desk.
④ Did people gathered in the stadium?
⑤ It is going to be cloudy all day tomorrow.

3 다음 중 짝지어진 대화가 어색한 것은?

① A: Were you in the theater?
B: Yes, I was.
② A: Are they laughing loudly?
B: Yes, they were.
③ A: Did James play the guitar well?
B: Yes, he did.
④ A: Will our school bus arrive soon?
B: No, it won't.
⑤ A: Is she going to drive the car?
B: No, she isn't.

4 다음 우리말과 일치하도록 괄호 안의 단어를 바르게 배열하시오.

(1) 너는 오늘 저녁 테니스를 칠 거니? (are, going, play, to, you, tennis)
→ ____________________ this evening?

(2) 그들은 무대에서 춤추고 있지 않았다. (were, they, dancing, not)
→ ____________________ on the stage.

WORDS

1
alarm clock 자명종
set 동 놓다; *(시계를) 맞추다 (set - set)

2
jog 동 조깅하다
gather 동 모이다
stadium 명 경기장
cloudy 형 흐린

3
theater 명 극장
laugh 동 웃다
loudly 부 큰 소리로

4
stage 명 무대

서술형에 나오는 WRITING

A 다음 우리말과 일치하도록 괄호 안의 말을 바르게 배열하시오.

1 Nancy는 긴 코트를 입고 있었다. (Nancy, a long coat, wearing, was)

→ ______________________________

2 그들은 그들의 삼촌을 도울 예정이니? (are, to, they, their uncle, help, going)

→ ______________________________

3 나는 그 컵을 버리지 않을 것이다. (not, I, the cup, will, throw away)

→ ______________________________

B 다음 우리말과 일치하도록 괄호 안의 말을 이용하여 문장을 완성하시오.

1 Billy는 며칠 후에 집에 돌아올 것이다. (going, return home)

→ ______________________________ in a few days.

2 너는 가족들과 좋은 시간을 보냈니? (do, have a good time)

→ ______________________________ with your family?

3 그녀는 지난주에 그 그림을 완성하지 않았다. (do, finish the painting)

→ ______________________________ last week.

C 다음은 Fred의 일정표이다. 표를 보고, 보기 처럼 문장을 완성하시오.

Friday		Saturday right now	Sunday
watch a magic show with Emma	buy a pair of jeans	read a novel at home	visit my grandparents

보기 Fred watched a magic show with Emma yesterday.

1 Fred ______________________ yesterday.

2 Fred ______________________ right now.

3 Fred ______________________ tomorrow.

READING WITH GRAMMAR

1

School **ended** at four o'clock. Jenna **put** her notebooks in her bag and **ran** out of the school. She **was** excited. Her uncle from America **was coming**! She **thought**, "My uncle **will bring** me a gift." She **wondered**, "**Will** he **bring** delicious American snacks**? Will** he **bring** a fun American toy**?**"

Jenna **arrived** at her home. Her uncle **was sitting** on the sofa! He **was** happy to see her and **gave** her a big hug. Jenna **jumped** with joy. "____(A)____ you **bring** something from America**?** ____(B)____ you **bring** a special gift**?**" she **asked**. "I'm sorry," her uncle **answered**, "but I only **brought** myself!" Jenna **smiled**. "That's the perfect gift from America," she **said**.

1 위 글의 내용과 일치하지 않는 것은?

① Jenna는 학교에서 달려 나왔다.
② Jenna는 삼촌이 가져올 선물을 궁금해했다.
③ Jenna와 삼촌은 집에서 만났다.
④ 삼촌은 Jenna를 안아주었다.
⑤ 삼촌은 Jenna에게 과자와 장난감을 주었다.

2 위 글의 빈칸 (A)와 (B)에 공통으로 들어갈 알맞은 말을 쓰시오.

____

WORDS
end 동 끝나다 notebook 명 노트, 공책 excited 형 신이 난 uncle 명 삼촌 gift 명 선물 wonder 동 궁금해하다
delicious 형 아주 맛있는 arrive 동 [1] ________ hug 명 포옹 joy 명 기쁨 special 형 특별한 perfect 형 완벽한

2

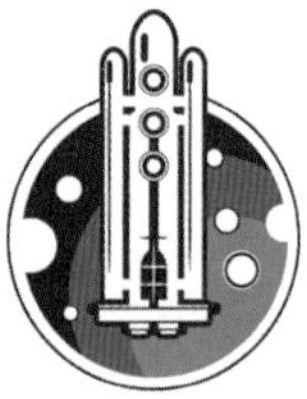

Do you like adventure? Do you dream of a life on a new planet? Then here is your chance. We**'re going to choose** volunteers for Project *Mars. Four of them **will leave** for Mars in 2024.

But the environment there **is going to be** totally different. And your life on Mars **will be** tough. So, we **are going to look** for patient people. Also, you **will go** on some missions on Mars. Therefore, we need brave people. Before the departure, you **will receive** training for several years. You**'ll learn** about survival skills. **Will** you **join** the first human mission to Mars**?** Think carefully. There won't are tickets back to Earth.

*Mars: 화성

1 Which is the best title for the passage?

① Useful Survival Skills
② Mars: The Red Planet
③ Famous Space Scientists
④ The Environment on Mars
⑤ Start a New Life on Mars!

2 Correct the underlined part.

→ ______________

WORDS adventure 명 모험 planet 명 행성 volunteer 명 지원자 environment 명 [1] __________ totally 부 완전히 different 형 다른 tough 형 힘든, 어려운 patient 형 참을성 있는 mission 명 임무; 파견단 brave 형 용감한 departure 명 출발 receive 동 [2] __________ training 명 훈련 several 형 몇몇의 survival 명 생존 skill 명 기술

A 의도 · 계획 묻고 답하기

A: **What are you going to do** after school**?**
(너는 방과 후에 무엇을 할 거니?)

B: **I'm going to** do math homework with Amy. **Will you** join us**?**
(나는 Amy와 수학 숙제를 할 거야. 너도 같이 할래?)

A: Sure. **I will.**
(그래. 그럴게.)

상대방의 의도나 계획을 물을 때는 'What are you going to do?'나 'Will you+동사원형 ...?', 'Are you planning to+동사원형 ...?' 등의 표현을 쓴다. 자신의 계획을 말할 때는 'I'm going to+동사원형 ...' 또는 'I will+동사원형 ...'이라고 말할 수 있다.

⊕ EXPRESSION PLUS

A: **Are you going to** go to the concert**?** (너는 그 콘서트에 갈 거니?)
B: **Yes, I am.** (응, 그럴 거야.) / **No, I'm not.** (아니, 그러지 않을 거야.)

A: **What are you planning to do** this Sunday**?** (너는 이번 일요일에 무엇을 할 계획이니?)
B: **I'm planning to** wash my clothes. (나는 내 옷을 세탁할 계획이야.)

Check-Up

1 다음 질문에 대한 알맞은 응답을 찾아 연결하시오.

(1) What are you going to do? •　　• ⓐ No, I'm not.
(2) Will you play card games with us? •　　• ⓑ Yes, I will.
(3) Are you going to cook curry? •　　• ⓒ I'm going to take a nap.

2 다음 괄호 안의 단어를 이용하여 대화를 완성하시오.

A: ________ ________ ________ ________ ________ a birthday party? (plan, have)
B: Yes, I am.

WORDS

1
curry 명 카레
take a nap 낮잠을 자다

2
have a party 파티를 열다

B 행동 · 동작 묘사하기

A: Jake, **what are** you **doing?**
(Jake, 너 뭐 하고 있니?)

B: **I'm cleaning** my room.
(난 내 방을 청소하고 있어.)

A: **What is** Susan **doing now?**
(Susan은 지금 뭐 하고 있니?)

B: She**'s feeding** her bird.
(그녀는 새에게 모이를 주고 있어.)

현재의 행동이나 동작을 물을 때는 'What+be동사의 현재형+주어+doing?'이라고 말할 수 있다. 질문에 대답할 때는 '주어+be동사의 현재형+v-ing ...'라고 말한다.

EXPRESSION PLUS

A: **What are** the children **doing right now?** (아이들은 지금 무엇을 하고 있나요?)
B: They**'re playing** soccer. (그들은 축구를 하고 있어요.)

A: **Is** the boy **watching** TV? (그 소년은 TV를 보고 있니?)
B: **Yes**, he **is**. (응, 그래.) / **No**, he **isn't**. (아니, 그렇지 않아.)

Check-Up

1 다음 밑줄 친 부분의 쓰임이 나머지 넷과 다른 것은?

① I'm visiting the museum.
② They're singing together.
③ We're taking care of babies.
④ She's going to leave next week.
⑤ Jenny is giving a speech in Korean.

2 다음 대화의 빈칸에 들어갈 말로 알맞은 것은?

A: What is he doing right now?
B: ______________________

① He's putting on jeans.
② He will cook fish soon.
③ He searched the Internet.
④ He drinks soda in the evening.
⑤ He's planning to jump rope tonight.

WORDS

1
take care of …를 돌보다
give a speech 연설하다

2
put on …를 입다
search 동 찾아보다
jump rope 줄넘기를 하다

FINAL TEST

1 다음 중 장소를 나타내는 단어가 아닌 것은?

① mall ② theater
③ museum ④ dessert
⑤ stadium

2 다음 빈칸에 들어갈 단어로 알맞지 않은 것은?

William is a __________ man.

① brave ② special
③ loudly ④ perfect
⑤ patient

[3-4] 다음 대화의 빈칸에 들어갈 말로 알맞은 것을 고르시오.

3
A: ____________________
B: I'm going to rest at home.

① What are you doing?
② When will you go home?
③ What do you do on Sundays?
④ Do you live with your family?
⑤ What are you going to do today?

4
A: What are they doing right now?
B: ____________________

① They were with my aunt.
② They will go out for a walk.
③ They're practicing the violin.
④ They're going to learn Spanish.
⑤ They were reading comic books.

5 대화가 자연스럽게 이어지도록 (A)~(D)를 바르게 배열하시오.

(A) I'm packing my bag.
(B) What are you doing?
(C) Yes. I'm going to go to the beach!
(D) Why? Are you planning to take a trip?

_______ → _______ → _______ → _______

6 다음 중 동사의 과거형이 잘못 연결된 것은?

① hit - hit
② take - took
③ say - sayed
④ study - studied
⑤ stop - stopped

! 자주 나와요

[7-8] 다음 대화의 빈칸에 들어갈 말로 알맞은 것을 고르시오.

7
A: Did Ms. Clark __________ science?
B: Yes, she did.

① teach ② taught
③ teaches ④ teaching
⑤ to teach

8
A: Are they going to visit Sue's home?
B: No, they __________.

① don't ② aren't
③ didn't ④ weren't
⑤ won't

[9-10] 다음 대화의 빈칸에 들어갈 말이 바르게 짝지어진 것을 고르시오.

9 A: ________ you meet her next Friday?
B: Yes, we ________.

① Do - did
② Did - does
③ Did - did
④ Is - is
⑤ Will - will

10 A: Is he ________ in the office now?
B: No, he ________.

① work - is
② works - is
③ work - isn't
④ worked - isn't
⑤ working - isn't

11 다음 빈칸에 들어갈 말로 알맞은 것을 모두 고르시오. (2개)

They went to an amusement park ________.

① soon
② tomorrow
③ yesterday
④ last year
⑤ next Monday

[12-13] 다음 밑줄 친 부분을 바르게 고치시오.

12 The bakery did not has apple jam.

→ ________

13 Is Stacy going rent a car on Sunday?

→ ________

! 어려워요

14 다음 밑줄 친 부분의 의미가 나머지 넷과 다른 것은?

① It will snow a lot tomorrow.
② The movie will begin at 8 p.m.
③ They will arrive at school soon.
④ I will finish this book today.
⑤ She will be home in two hours.

! 자주 나와요

15 다음 중 어법상 바르지 못한 것은?

① He checked the number again.
② I'm going to make cookies.
③ Mason is having a girlfriend.
④ She wasn't listening to her mom.
⑤ Bob didn't brush his teeth this morning.

16 다음 우리말을 영어로 바르게 옮긴 것은?

Nick은 버스를 기다리고 있었다.

① Nick waits for the bus.
② Nick will wait for the bus.
③ Nick is waiting for the bus.
④ Nick was waiting for the bus.
⑤ Nick's going to wait for the bus.

어려워요

17 다음 밑줄 친 부분 중 어법상 바르지 못한 것은?

My family ① went to a lake a week ago. My dad ② putted up a tent. I caught fish. But it rained in the afternoon. And it ③ didn't stop. Dad said, "The sky ④ won't be clear. Let's go home." I ⑤ was really sad!

18 다음 중 짝지어진 대화가 어색한 것은?

① A: Will you walk the dog?
B: Yes, I will.
② A: Was Barbara playing tennis?
B: Yes, she did.
③ A: Did Ted break the window?
B: No, he didn't.
④ A: Are you carrying the bottles now?
B: No, I'm not.
⑤ A: Is she going to clean the floor?
B: No, she isn't.

서술형

[19-20] 다음 우리말과 일치하도록 괄호 안의 단어를 바르게 배열하시오.

19 너희들은 함께 고기를 요리하고 있었니?
(meat, were, cooking, you)

→ ______________________________ together?

20 Jack은 도서관에서 시험공부를 했니?
(study, Jack, for the test, did)

→ ______________________________ in the library?

내신 완성 서술형

21 다음 보기 처럼 문장을 바꿔 쓰시오.

보기 They stayed at home.
→ They were staying at home.

I washed my hair in the bathroom.
→ ______________________________
____

[22-24] 다음은 Brian의 오늘 일정표이다. 표의 내용과 일치하도록 대화를 완성하시오.

Time	Activity
10 a.m.	read a newspaper
5:30 p.m. right now	make spaghetti
8:50 p.m.	write in my diary

22 A: Was Brian reading a letter at 10 a.m.?
B: No, he wasn't. He was ______________________.

23 A: ______________________ right now?
B: Yes, he is.

24 A: ______________________ at 8:50 p.m.?
B: Yes, he will.

WORD LIST

Grammar

☐ be proud of	…를 자랑스러워하다
☐ be afraid of	…를 두려워하다
☐ lie	동 누워 있다; 눕다
☐ hold	동 잡고 있다, 쥐다
☐ museum	명 박물관
☐ ride	동 타다
☐ plant	동 심다
☐ climb	동 오르다, 올라가다
☐ waste	동 낭비하다
☐ bring	동 가져오다
☐ forget	동 잊다
☐ look for	…를 찾다
☐ take a picture	사진을 찍다
☐ invite	동 초대하다
☐ jog	동 조깅하다
☐ gather	동 모이다
☐ cloudy	형 흐린
☐ theater	명 극장
☐ laugh	동 웃다
☐ loudly	부 큰 소리로

Reading

☐ end	동 끝나다
☐ excited	형 신이 난
☐ uncle	명 삼촌
☐ gift	명 선물
☐ wonder	동 궁금해하다
☐ delicious	형 아주 맛있는
☐ arrive	동 도착하다
☐ joy	명 기쁨
☐ special	형 특별한
☐ perfect	형 완벽한
☐ adventure	명 모험
☐ planet	명 행성
☐ volunteer	명 지원자
☐ environment	명 환경
☐ totally	부 완전히
☐ different	형 다른
☐ tough	형 힘든, 어려운
☐ patient	형 참을성 있는
☐ receive	동 받다
☐ survival	명 생존
☐ skill	명 기술

Communication

☐ take care of	…를 돌보다
☐ give a speech	연설하다
☐ put on	…를 입다
☐ search	동 찾아보다

Final Test

☐ beach	명 해변
☐ amusement park	놀이공원
☐ rent	동 빌리다
☐ clear	형 분명한; 맑은
☐ break	동 깨다, 부수다
☐ floor	명 바닥
☐ diary	명 일기

CHAPTER 04

조동사

GET READY

I wear a seat belt.
(나는 안전벨트를 착용한다.)

I **can** wear a seat belt.
(나는 안전벨트를 착용할 수 있다.)

I **must** wear a seat belt.
(나는 안전벨트를 착용해야 한다.)

위 문장들은 모두 동사 wear를 포함하지만 서로 다른 의미를 전달하고 있어요. 문장의 의미를 다르게 만든 것이 바로 can, must와 같은 조동사예요. 조동사는 '동사를 돕는 말'이라는 의미로, 뒤에 오는 동사에 뜻을 더해 주는 역할을 해요.

GRAMMAR FOCUS

A 조동사 can, may

1 조동사

조동사는 동사 앞에 쓰여 뜻을 더해 주는 말이다. 조동사는 주어의 인칭과 수에 따라 형태가 변하지 않으며, 뒤에는 항상 동사원형을 쓴다.

조동사의 종류	기본 형태	부정문	의문문
will, can, may, must, should 등	「조동사+동사원형」	「주어+조동사+not+동사원형 ...」	「조동사+주어+동사원형 ...?」

2 can

1) 능력 · 가능: '…할 수 있다'의 의미이며, be able to로 바꿔 쓸 수 있다. 부정형 cannot 또는 can't는 「be동사+not able to」로 바꿔 쓸 수 있다.

She **can**[**is able to**] cook spaghetti.

I **cannot**[**am not able to**] fly.

A: **Can** you move the boxes? B: **Yes**, I **can**. / **No**, I **can't**.

= A: **Are** you **able to** move the boxes? B: **Yes**, I **am**. / **No**, I**'m not**.

2) 허가: '…해도 된다'

You **can** change the schedule.

You **cannot**[**can't**] run on the stairs.

A: **Can** I borrow this eraser? B: **Yes**, you **can**. / **No**, you **can't**.

TIPS

can의 과거형과 미래형

1 과거형 could: '…할 수 있었다'의 의미로, 과거 시점에서의 능력을 나타낸다. could는 「be동사의 과거형+able to」로 바꿔 쓸 수 있으며, 의문문에 쓰일 경우에는 공손한 부탁을 나타낼 수 있다.
I **could**[**was able to**] read at age 5. (나는 다섯 살 때 읽을 수 있었다.)
Could you wait for me? (저를 기다려 주시겠어요?)

2 미래형 will be able to: '…할 수 있을 것이다'의 의미로, 미래의 능력을 나타낸다.
She **will be able to** fix this car. (그녀는 이 차를 고칠 수 있을 것이다.)

3 may

1) 추측: '…일지도 모른다'의 의미로, 불확실한 추측을 나타낸다.

It **may** rain soon. The rumor **may not** be true.

2) 허가: '…해도 좋다, …해도 된다'의 의미로, can보다 더 정중한 표현으로 쓰인다.

You **may** leave the room now. We **may not** eat anything here.

A: **May** I try on these sneakers? B: **Yes**, you **may**. / Sure. / Of course.
No, you **may not**. / I'm sorry, but you can't.

Check-Up

A **다음 대화의 빈칸에 알맞은 말을 쓰시오.**

1 A: __________ I see your passport?
B: Yes, you may.

2 A: Is he able to solve the problem?
B: Yes, __________ __________.

3 A: Can I have your phone number?
B: No, __________ __________.

4 A: May I use your laptop computer?
B: No, __________ __________ __________.

B **다음 밑줄 친 부분을 바르게 고치시오.**

1 Is she able make music? → __________

2 Can I seeing your textbook? → __________

3 He can't sleeps well these days. → __________

4 May I to borrow your dictionary? → __________

C **다음 우리말과 일치하도록 can 또는 may를 이용하여 빈칸에 알맞은 말을 쓰시오.**

1 Daniel은 간호사가 아닐지도 모른다.
→ Daniel __________ __________ be a nurse.

2 너는 마라톤을 완주할 수 있니?
→ __________ __________ run a full marathon?

D **다음 두 문장이 같은 뜻이 되도록 빈칸에 알맞은 말을 쓰시오.**

1 Can you throw a curve ball?
→ __________ __________ __________ __________ throw a curve ball?

2 Crocodiles cannot live without water.
→ Crocodiles __________ __________ __________ __________ live without water.

3 Ella could participate in the last game.
→ Ella __________ __________ __________ participate in the last game.

WORDS

A
passport 명 여권
solve 동 해결하다
problem 명 문제

B
textbook 명 교과서
borrow 동 빌리다
dictionary 명 사전

C
nurse 명 간호사
marathon 명 마라톤

D
throw 동 던지다
curve ball 명 변화구
crocodile 명 악어
participate in …에 참가하다

B 조동사 must, have to, should

1 must

'…해야 한다'의 의미로, 의무를 나타내며 have to로 바꿔 쓸 수 있다.
Students **must**(= **have to**) follow the school rules.
You **must not** speak loudly in the library.
A: **Must** I go there with you**?** B: **Yes**, you **must**.
No, you **don't have to**. (= **No**, you **need not**.)
No, you must not. (x)

내신 POINT PLUS

must not과 don't have to의 의미
must not는 '…해서는 안 된다'의 의미로 금지를 나타내며, don't have to는 '…할 필요가 없다'의 의미로 불필요를 나타낸다.
You **must not** take pictures here. (너는 여기서 사진을 찍어서는 안 된다.)
You **don't have to** get up early. (너는 일찍 일어날 필요가 없다.)

2 have to

'…해야 한다'의 의미로, 의무를 나타내며 must로 바꿔 쓸 수 있다. have to의 부정문과 의문문은 일반동사의 부정문과 의문문을 만들 때처럼 do를 이용하며, 부정형 don't have to는 need not으로 바꿔 쓸 수 있다.
We **have to**(= **must**) wear school uniforms.
She **has to** take the first train.
I **had to** book the ticket early.
You **don't have to**(= **need not**) hurry.
A: **Does** Minsu **have to** work on Sunday**?** B: **Yes**, he **does**. (= **Yes**, he **has to**.)
No, he **doesn't** (**have to**).

3 should

'…해야 한다, …하는 것이 좋다'의 의미로, must보다 약한 의무, 권유, 충고를 나타낸다.
You **should** see a doctor.
We **should not**[**shouldn't**] waste water.
A: **Should** I eat more vegetables**?** B: **Yes**, you **should**.
No, you **shouldn't**.

Check-Up

A 다음 괄호 안에서 알맞은 말을 고르시오.

1 Should we (picking up / pick up) the trash?
2 They must (learn / to learn) table manners.
3 He (has to / had to) fix his computer last week.
4 Jina (has not to / doesn't have to) return the book.
5 You should (be not / not be) noisy in the museum.

WORDS

A
pick up …를 줍다
trash 명 쓰레기
table manners 식사 예절
return 동 돌아오다; *반납하다
noisy 형 시끄러운

B 다음 대화의 빈칸에 알맞은 말을 쓰시오.

1 A: Must I wear a mask?
B: Yes, ________ ________.
2 A: Must we go to bed now?
B: No, we ________ ________ ________.
3 A: Should they blow up balloons for the party?
B: Yes, ________ ________.
4 A: Do I have to bring my student card to the cafeteria?
B: Yes, you ________ ________.

B
blow up …를 폭파하다; *(공기를) 주입하다
balloon 명 풍선
cafeteria 명 구내식당

C 다음 빈칸에 들어갈 말을 보기 에서 골라 쓰시오. (한 번씩만 쓸 것)

보기 should must not don't have to

1 It's a secret. You ________ tell anyone.
2 I'm doing well. You ________ worry about me.
3 You look nervous. You ________ take a deep breath.

C
secret 명 비밀
nervous 형 불안해하는
take a deep breath 심호흡하다

D 다음 두 문장이 같은 뜻이 되도록 빈칸에 알맞은 말을 쓰시오.

1 We must stand in line at the bus stop.
→ We ________ ________ stand in line at the bus stop.
2 You need not mix the onion and milk.
→ You ________ ________ ________ mix the onion and milk.

D
stand in line 일렬로 나란히 서다
mix 동 섞다

Grammar Practice

A 다음 문장에서 어법상 틀린 곳을 찾아 바르게 고치시오.

1 She mays be a firefighter. ________ → ________
2 Could you showed me the map? ________ → ________
3 We can see a full moon last night. ________ → ________
4 He doesn't has to care for his sister. ________ → ________
5 Is they able to start their work today? ________ → ________

B 다음 빈칸에 들어갈 말을 보기 에서 골라 쓰시오. (한 번씩만 쓸 것)

보기 should must not don't have to

1 It is sunny. I ________ bring an umbrella.
2 The river is very deep. You ________ dive into it.
3 We are too late. We ________ take a taxi to the station.

C 다음 우리말과 일치하도록 괄호 안의 말을 이용하여 문장을 완성하시오.

1 나는 오늘 저녁에 요리를 할 필요가 없다. (have to, cook)
→ I ________ ________ ________ ________ this evening.
2 그는 Taylor에게 소포를 보내지 않을지도 모른다. (may, send)
→ He ________ ________ ________ a package to Taylor.
3 그녀는 아침 식사 후에 샤워를 할 수 있었다. (able, take)
→ She ________ ________ ________ ________ a shower after breakfast.

D 다음 문장을 괄호 안의 지시대로 바꿀 때, 빈칸에 알맞은 말을 쓰시오.

1 She can do ballet. (미래형으로)
→ ________ ________ ________ ________ ________
________ ballet.
2 Jack has to speak in front of many people. (의문문으로)
→ ________ ________ ________ ________ ________ in front of many people?

WORDS

A
full moon 보름달
care for …를 돌보다

B
dive into …로 뛰어들다
station 명 역, 정거장

C
package 명 소포, 꾸러미

D
ballet 명 발레
in front of … 앞에

내신 완성 Grammar Practice

1 다음 빈칸에 들어갈 말이 바르게 짝지어진 것은?

- I'm hungry. ________ I have this apple pie?
- He's very sick. He ________ take this medicine.

① Should - can
② Can - should
③ Must - should
④ Can - may not
⑤ Must - may not

2 다음 중 짝지어진 대화가 어색한 것은?

① A: Can I open the window?
B: Yes, you can.
② A: Do we have to wait long?
B: No, you don't.
③ A: Must Max go to the dentist?
B: No, he must not.
④ A: Will he be able to get a new job?
B: Yes, he will.
⑤ A: May my daughter play with your toys?
B: Yes, she may.

3 다음 우리말을 영어로 바르게 옮긴 것은?

너는 자기 전에 차를 마시는 것이 좋겠어.

① You can drink tea before bed.
② You may drink tea before bed.
③ You must drink tea before bed.
④ You should drink tea before bed.
⑤ You have to drink tea before bed.

4 다음 우리말과 일치하도록 괄호 안의 말을 바르게 배열하시오.

(1) 제가 소스에 설탕을 넣어야 하나요? (do, have to, put, I)
→ ______________________________ sugar in the sauce?

(2) 그들은 시험을 통과할 수 없었다. (able, pass, not, to, were)
→ They ______________________________ the exam.

WORDS

1
medicine 명 약

2
dentist 명 치과 의사

3
tea 명 차

4
sauce 명 소스, 양념
pass 동 지나가다; *(시험에) 통과하다

A 다음 우리말과 일치하도록 괄호 안의 말을 바르게 배열하시오.

1 그는 그의 약속을 지켜야 한다. (keep, should, his, he, promise)

→ ______________________________

2 그녀는 행사장에 오지 않을지도 모른다. (to, may, come, she, the event hall, not)

→ ______________________________

3 너는 차를 운전할 수 있니? (you, to, a car, are, drive, able)

→ ______________________________

B 다음 문장을 괄호 안의 지시대로 바꿔 쓰시오.

1 They don't have to answer the question. (he를 주어로 하는 긍정문으로)

→ ______________________________

2 I can understand this movie. (be able to를 이용한 부정문으로)

→ ______________________________

3 You may listen to the radio now. (I를 주어로 하는 의문문으로)

→ ______________________________

C 다음 그림을 보고, must와 괄호 안의 말을 이용하여 문장을 완성하시오.

1

(enter)

You ______________________ here.

2

(arrive early)

You ______________________ at the airport.

1

Taking *selfies is a lot of fun. But you ___(A)___ get in trouble because of them. So you **should** follow some basic rules.

1. Be safe! Some selfies **may** put you in danger. Let's imagine a situation: You are standing on the edge of a bridge with your camera. It **may** look cool. However, it is also dangerous.
2. You **must not** take selfies in certain places. These include public bathrooms and hospitals. You **should** be polite.
3. Pay attention! You ___(B)___ use a selfie stick. Don't forget about the people around you. You **must not** hit anyone with the stick.
4. Do you want to post selfies with other people? Then, you **should** ask them first.

*selfie: 셀피(스스로 찍은 사진)

1 위 글을 쓴 목적으로 알맞은 것은?

① 셀피를 찍는 이유를 조사하기 위해
② 셀피 촬영의 부정적인 효과를 설명하기 위해
③ 사진에 잘 나오기 위한 방법을 알려 주기 위해
④ 셀피 촬영과 관련된 주의 사항을 안내하기 위해
⑤ 사진으로 추억을 남겨 놓을 것을 권장하기 위해

2 위 글의 빈칸 (A)와 (B)에 공통으로 들어갈 말로 알맞은 것은?

① must ② may
③ have to ④ should
⑤ will be able to

WORDS
follow 동 (충고·지시 등을) 따르다 **basic** 형 기본적인 **danger** 명 [1]__________ **imagine** 동 상상하다 **situation** 명 상황
edge 명 끝, 가장자리 **certain** 형 확실한; *어떤 **include** 동 포함하다 **public** 형 공공의 **polite** 형 [2]__________
pay attention 주의를 기울이다 **post** 동 (우편물을) 발송하다; *(웹사이트에 정보·사진을) 올리다

2

Before landing, pilots ① must report in to *air traffic control at the airport. Pilots are from different countries around the world. So they speak various languages. For communication, they **must** use one language: English.

But there is a problem with letters. The pilot ② may say, "This is flight BE 449." But B **may** sound like P or V. And E **may** sound like I. The similar sounds ③ can confuse the listeners! So pilots use the "spelling alphabet." For example, for BE 449, pilots **have to** say "bravo" (for B), "echo" (for E), "four-four-nine." For IU 108, they ④ have to say "India" (for I), "uniform" (for U), "one-zero-eight." These **may** sound strange. But listeners ⑤ is able to understand each letter!

*air traffic control: 항공 교통 관제 센터

1 Which is the best title for the passage?

① The Life of a Pilot
② Pilot Communication
③ Problems with English Letters
④ The New Language of Airports
⑤ The Favorite Language of Pilots

2 Which is NOT grammatically correct?

① ② ③ ④ ⑤

WORDS
landing 명 착륙 pilot 명 조종사, 비행사 report 동 보고하다 various 형 다양한 language 명 언어
communication 명 의사소통, 연락 letter 명 편지; *글자 flight 명 항공편, 항공기 similar 형 1 ________
confuse 동 혼란시키다 listener 명 듣는 사람 spelling 명 철자법 strange 형 2 ________

A 능력 묻고 답하기

A: **Can you** swim**?**
(너는 수영할 수 있니?)

B: **Yes, I can.** How about you?
(응, 할 수 있어. 너는 어때?)

A: **I can't** swim well. **I can't** float in the water.
(나는 수영을 잘 못해. 나는 물에 뜰 수 없어.)

'…할 수 있니?'의 의미로 능력을 물을 때는 'Can you+동사원형 ...?'으로 표현할 수 있다. 대답할 때는 'Yes, I can.' 또는 'No, I can't.' 등으로 말한다.

EXPRESSION PLUS

A: **Are you able to** carry this box**?** (너는 이 상자를 옮길 수 있니?)
B: **Sure.** (물론이지.) / **No.** It is too heavy for me. (아니. 그건 내게 너무 무거워.)

A: **Are you good at** volleyball**?** (너는 배구를 잘하니?)
B: **Yes, I am.** (응, 잘해.) / **No. I'm not good at** it. (아니. 나는 그걸 잘 못해.)

Check-Up

1 다음 대화의 빈칸에 들어갈 말로 알맞지 <u>않은</u> 것은?

A: Are you good at science?
B: ____________________

① Yes, I am.
② No. It's difficult.
③ Sure. I'm good at it.
④ No. I am a scientist.
⑤ No. I'm not good at science.

WORDS
1
difficult 형 어려운
scientist 명 과학자

2 다음 대화의 빈칸에 들어갈 말로 알맞은 것은?

A: Can you make cheese burger?
B: ____________________

① I need it.
② No, I cannot make it.
③ Yes, I do.
④ Yes, you can make it.
⑤ That's great.

B 조언 · 충고하기

A: I can't wake up early in the morning.
What should I do?
(나는 아침에 일찍 일어날 수가 없어. 내가 무엇을 해야 할까?)

B: **You should** set an alarm.
(너는 알람을 맞춰야 해.)

A: Thanks for your advice.
(조언 고마워.)

상대방에게 조언이나 충고를 구할 때는 'What should I do?'라고 말할 수 있다. 이에 대한 대답으로 상대방에게 조언이나 충고를 할 때는 'You should+동사원형 ...' 등으로 말할 수 있다.

⊕ EXPRESSION PLUS

A: I can't solve this problem. **Can I get some advice?**
(나는 이 문제를 풀 수 없어. 조언을 구할 수 있을까?)

B: **Why don't you** search the Internet**?**
(인터넷을 찾아보는 게 어때?)

Check-Up

1 다음 질문에 대한 알맞은 응답을 찾아 연결하시오.

(1) I'm tired. What should I do? •
(2) I'm not good at dancing. Can I get some advice? •
(3) Alice is angry with me. What should I do? •

• ⓐ You should rest.
• ⓑ You should say sorry to her.
• ⓒ Why don't you practice more?

WORDS

1
rest 동 쉬다

2 다음 우리말과 일치하도록 괄호 안의 말을 이용하여 문장을 완성하시오.

A: I have a stomachache. What should I do?
B: <u>따뜻한 물을 좀 마시는 게 어때?</u> (why, drink)

→ __________ __________ __________ __________ some warm water?

2
stomachache 명 복통
warm 형 따뜻한

FINAL TEST

1 다음 중 영어 단어와 우리말 뜻이 잘못 연결된 것은?

① solve - 해결하다 ② throw - 던지다
③ borrow - 빌리다 ④ include - 제외하다
⑤ confuse - 혼란시키다

2 다음 빈칸에 들어갈 단어로 가장 알맞은 것은?

noisy : quiet = different : ________

① basic ② various
③ strange ④ difficult
⑤ similar

3 다음 대화의 빈칸에 들어갈 말로 알맞은 것은?

A: I have a bad memory. What should I do?
B: ________________

① You should read it.
② I have a good memory.
③ Can I get some advice?
④ Why don't you take notes?
⑤ Do you remember his name?

4 밑줄 친 ①~⑤ 중 대화의 흐름과 어울리지 않는 것은?

A: Can you run the 100 meter race in 20 seconds?
B: ①No, I can't. ②How about you?
A: ③I can run it in 15 seconds.
④I can walk slowly.
B: ⑤You run very fast!

5 대화가 자연스럽게 이어지도록 (A)~(D)를 바르게 배열하시오.

(A) Thank you for your advice.
(B) I lost my camera an hour ago.
(C) You look upset. What happened?
(D) You should go to the lost and found.

________ → ________ → ________ → ________

자주 나와요

6 다음 중 짝지어진 대화가 어색한 것을 모두 고르시오. (2개)

① A: Can you skate?
B: Yes, I can.
② A: Are you good at tennis?
B: No, I am not. I'm good at sports.
③ A: Are you able to bake cookies?
B: No, I'm not.
④ A: I have a headache. What should I do?
B: Why don't you take some medicine?
⑤ A: I can't sleep well. Can I get some advice?
B: I go to bed late, too.

[7-8] 다음 대화의 빈칸에 들어갈 말로 알맞은 것을 고르시오.

7
A: Can you drive well?
B: ____________ I'm a beginner.

① Yes, I can. ② No, I can't.
③ No, I won't. ④ No, you can't.
⑤ Yes, you can.

8

A: May I use your cell phone?
B: ___________ Here it is.

① Yes, I may. ② Yes, you may.
③ Yes, you should. ④ No, you won't.
⑤ No, you may not.

자주 나와요

[9-10] 다음 밑줄 친 부분과 바꿔 쓸 수 있는 것을 고르시오.

9

You must wear a life jacket in the boat.

① will ② can
③ may ④ have to
⑤ are able to

10

A: I didn't have breakfast. I'm hungry.
B: Then you can eat this sandwich.

① will ② may
③ must ④ should
⑤ have to

어려워요

[11-12] 다음 질문에 대한 대답을 보기 에서 고르시오.

보기 ⓐ Yes, you are.
ⓑ Sure, you can.
ⓒ Sorry, I shouldn't.
ⓓ No, you don't have to.

11 Can we see the menu? ___________

12 Must I turn off the gas now? ___________

[13-14] 다음 밑줄 친 부분의 의미가 나머지 넷과 다른 것을 고르시오.

13 ① I can cook *bulgogi*.
② Can you lift this rock?
③ He can sing very well.
④ Can I use your bathroom?
⑤ She can finish her report today.

14 ① He may miss the train.
② We may be late for school.
③ The store may not be open.
④ They may like these presents.
⑤ You may not pick the flowers.

15 다음 밑줄 친 부분의 뜻이 바르지 못한 것은?

① Can I see it one more time?
봐도 될까요?
② You must do your homework.
해야 한다
③ She has to wear a helmet.
착용해야 한다
④ We don't have to go home now.
가면 안 된다
⑤ You may use my computer tonight.
사용해도 된다

[16-18] 다음 우리말과 일치하도록 괄호 안의 단어를 이용하여 문장을 완성하시오.

16

그는 집에 없을지도 모른다. (may, be)

→ He ___________ ___________ ___________ at home.

17 Peter는 영어를 읽을 수 있었다. (able, read)

→ Peter ________ ________ ________ ________ English.

18 내가 운동을 매일 하는 게 좋을까? (should, exercise)

→ ________ ________ ________ every day?

어려워요

19 다음 중 어법상 바르지 못한 것은?

① He didn't have to clean the room.
② I'm able to make a paper airplane.
③ Paul can be able to be a musician.
④ They should be polite to their parents.
⑤ We must not play computer games all day.

자주 나와요

20 다음 중 짝지어진 대화가 어색한 것은?

① A: Can I sit next to you?
B: No, you can't.
② A: Are you able to ride a bike?
B: Of course.
③ A: May I order food now?
B: No, you may not. We're not ready.
④ A: Can we speak loudly?
B: Sure, we can. We should be quiet.
⑤ A: Are you able to swim?
B: No, I'm not. I'm afraid of water.

내신 완성 서술형

[21-22] 다음 문장을 괄호 안의 지시대로 바꿔 쓰시오.

21 David can paint the wall. (미래형으로)

→ ________________

22 Lisa must share a room with her sister. (과거형으로)

→ ________________

____

[23-24] 다음 우리말을 괄호 안의 말을 이용하여 조건에 맞게 영작하시오.

23 그들은 회의에 참석할 필요가 없다. (have to, attend the meeting)

조건: 총 7단어로 작성할 것

→ ________________

24 내가 Joe에게 나중에 전화를 해야 하니? (call Joe later)

조건 1: Do로 시작할 것
조건 2: 총 7단어로 작성할 것

→ ________________

WORD LIST

Grammar

☐ passport	명 여권
☐ solve	동 해결하다
☐ problem	명 문제
☐ textbook	명 교과서
☐ borrow	동 빌리다
☐ dictionary	명 사전
☐ throw	동 던지다
☐ pick up	…를 줍다
☐ trash	명 쓰레기
☐ return	동 돌아오다; 반납하다
☐ noisy	형 시끄러운
☐ balloon	명 풍선
☐ cafeteria	명 구내식당
☐ secret	명 비밀
☐ nervous	형 불안해하는
☐ care for	…를 돌보다
☐ dive into	…로 뛰어들다
☐ station	명 역, 정거장
☐ package	명 소포, 꾸러미
☐ in front of	… 앞에
☐ medicine	명 약

Reading

☐ follow	동 (충고 · 지시 등을) 따르다
☐ danger	명 위험
☐ imagine	동 상상하다
☐ situation	명 상황
☐ include	동 포함하다
☐ public	형 공공의
☐ polite	형 예의 바른
☐ pay attention	주의를 기울이다
☐ landing	명 착륙
☐ pilot	명 조종사, 비행사
☐ report	동 보고하다
☐ various	형 다양한
☐ language	명 언어
☐ communication	명 의사소통, 연락
☐ letter	명 편지; 글자
☐ flight	명 항공편, 항공기
☐ similar	형 비슷한
☐ confuse	동 혼란시키다
☐ strange	형 이상한

Communication

☐ difficult	형 어려운
☐ scientist	명 과학자
☐ rest	동 쉬다
☐ stomachache	명 복통
☐ warm	형 따뜻한

Final Test

☐ memory	명 기억, 기억력
☐ second	명 (시간 단위) 초
☐ happen	동 (일이) 발생하다
☐ headache	명 두통
☐ rock	명 바위
☐ pick	동 고르다; (꽃을) 꺾다
☐ order	동 주문하다
☐ attend	동 참석하다
☐ later	부 나중에

CHAPTER 05

문장의 형식

GET READY

You **look** young.
(너는 어려 보인다.)

He **brought** me a box.
(그는 나에게 상자를 가져다주었다.)

I will **lend** you some money.
(내가 너에게 돈을 조금 빌려줄게.)

동사는 영어 문장의 주요 성분으로, 동사의 종류에 따라 문장의 형태가 달라지기도 해요. look과 같은 감각동사는 뒤에 주어를 설명하는 형용사가 와야 하고, bring, lend와 같은 수여동사는 뒤에 목적어 두 개가 와야 해요.

GRAMMAR FOCUS

A 감각동사가 있는 문장

1 감각동사

'보이다, 들리다, 느끼다' 등 사람의 감각을 표현하는 동사를 감각동사라고 한다.

예 look(…해 보이다), sound(…하게 들리다), smell(…한 냄새가 나다), taste(…한 맛이 나다), feel(…하게 느끼다)

2 「감각동사+형용사」 (2형식)

감각동사만으로는 의미가 충분하지 않으므로, 보충 설명하는 말(보어)이 필요하다. 이때 형용사가 보어로 쓰이며, 형용사 대신 부사를 쓰지 않도록 주의한다.

1) 「look+형용사」: …해 보이다

The boys **look tired**.
The lake **looks calm** and **peaceful**.
The actress looked beautifully. (x)

2) 「sound+형용사」: …하게 들리다

Your voice **sounds great**.
Their plan **sounded perfect**.

3) 「smell+형용사」: …한 냄새가 나다

The flowers **smelled nice**.
These shoes **smell terrible**.

4) 「taste+형용사」: …한 맛이 나다

Chocolate **tastes sweet**.
The sandwiches **tasted delicious**.

5) 「feel+형용사」: …하게 느끼다, (촉감이) …하다

I often **feel happy**.
Nick **felt proud** of the result.
This towel **feels rough**.

+ 내신 POINT PLUS

「감각동사+like+명사(구)」

명사(구)가 감각동사의 보어로 쓰일 때는 명사(구) 앞에 전치사 like를 쓰며, '…처럼 ~하다'라고 해석한다.

That **sounds like** *a good idea*. (그것은 좋은 생각처럼 들린다.)
The robot **looks like** *a human*. (그 로봇은 사람처럼 보인다.)

Check-Up

A 다음 괄호 안에서 알맞은 말을 고르시오.

1 This soup smells (bad / badly).
2 His music sounds (well / good).
3 The powder tasted like (salt / salty).
4 The students look (sad / sadly).

B 다음 빈칸에 들어갈 말을 보기에서 골라 쓰시오.

보기 hungry healthy interesting soft

1 I didn't have breakfast. I feel __________ now.
2 This bed feels __________. I can sleep well on it.
3 The man jogs every morning. He looks __________.
4 The movie sounds __________. I will watch it.

C 다음 우리말과 일치하도록 괄호 안의 단어를 이용하여 문장을 완성하시오.

1 이 커피는 쓴 맛이 난다. (bitter)
→ This coffee __________ __________.
2 Peter는 어제 아파 보였다. (sick)
→ Peter __________ __________ yesterday.
3 나는 인터뷰 전에 초조함을 느꼈다. (nervous)
→ I __________ __________ before the interview.

D 다음 그림을 보고, 괄호 안의 단어를 이용하여 문장을 완성하시오.
(현재시제로 작성할 것)

1

This pizza __________
__________. (delicious)

2

The lemon __________
__________. (sour)

WORDS

A
powder 명 가루
salt 명 소금
salty 형 짠

B
healthy 형 건강한
jog 동 조깅하다

C
bitter 형 (맛이) 쓴
nervous 형 초조해하는
interview 명 면접, 인터뷰

D
sour 형 (맛이) 신

B 수여동사가 있는 문장

1 수여동사

수여동사는 '…에게 ~를 (해)주다'라는 의미를 가진 동사로, '…에게(간접목적어)'와 '~를(직접목적어)'에 해당하는 두 개의 목적어가 필요하다.

예 give(주다), buy(사 주다), bring(가져다주다), send(보내다), teach(가르쳐 주다), cook(요리해 주다) 등

2 「주어 + 수여동사 + 간접목적어 + 직접목적어」 (4형식)

I	gave	her	a birthday present.
주어	수여동사	간접목적어	직접목적어

He **teaches** us English.
Sophia **showed** Logan her photos.
My parents **bought** me a new computer.

TIPS
간접목적어로 대명사가 올 경우, 목적격을 쓴다.
Perry **cooks** *me* pasta.
(Perry는 나에게 파스타를 요리해 준다.)

3 어순 전환: 4형식 ⇨ 3형식

4형식 문장의 간접목적어와 직접목적어의 순서를 바꿔 3형식 문장으로 전환할 수 있다.
이때 간접목적어 앞에 전치사 to, for, of 중 하나를 쓴다.

주어 + 수여동사 + 간접목적어 + 직접목적어 (4형식)

주어 + 수여동사 + 직접목적어 + to/for/of + 간접목적어 (3형식)

1) 전치사 to를 쓰는 동사 예 give, lend, send, show, teach, pass, bring, tell, write 등

The soldier **sent** me a letter.

→ The soldier **sent** a letter **to** me.

2) 전치사 for를 쓰는 동사 예 buy, make, get, cook 등

Erik **made** the customer a cheesecake.

→ Erik **made** a cheesecake **for** the customer.

3) 전치사 of를 쓰는 동사 예 ask

Mr. Park **asked** his students a favor.

→ Mr. Park **asked** a favor **of** his students.

Check-Up

A **다음 문장에서 간접목적어에 밑줄을 긋고, 직접목적어에 동그라미(O) 표시하시오.**

1 My aunt taught me history.

2 I will lend my notebook to you.

3 Jimin made a toy for her brother.

4 Ken brought his friend a recipe book.

B **다음 우리말과 일치하도록 괄호 안의 단어를 이용하여 문장을 완성하시오.**

1 Susan은 그에게 이메일을 쓰고 있다. (an email)

→ Susan is writing _________ _________ _________.

2 나에게 후추를 건네줄래? (the pepper)

→ Can you pass _________ _________ _________?

3 한 남자가 거리에서 그들에게 질문을 했다. (a question)

→ A man asked _________ _________ _________ on the street.

C **다음 빈칸에 전치사 to, for, of 중 알맞은 것을 골라 쓰시오.**

1 He showed his new car _________ us.

2 The reporters asked a favor _________ the singer.

3 The chef is going to make some chicken soup _________ the guests.

D **다음 두 문장이 같은 뜻이 되도록 빈칸에 알맞은 말을 쓰시오.**

1 You told Aiden a lie.

→ You told a lie _________ _________.

2 I will buy him new shoes.

→ I will buy new shoes _________ _________.

3 Julie gave candy bars to her friends.

→ Julie gave _________ _________ _________ _________.

4 Every Sunday, my dad cooks spaghetti for our family.

→ Every Sunday, my dad cooks _________ _________ _________.

WORDS

A
history 명 역사
notebook 명 공책
recipe 명 조리법

B
pepper 명 후추

C
reporter 명 기자
chef 명 요리사
guest 명 손님

D
lie 명 거짓말

Grammar Practice

A 다음 밑줄 친 부분을 바르게 고치시오.

1 I wrote a short note him. → ____________

2 She brought to me a cup. → ____________

3 This hamburger tastes strangely. → ____________

4 The story sounds like scary. → ____________

B 다음 빈칸에 들어갈 말을 보기 에서 골라 쓰시오.

보기 lend smell make feel

1 I sometimes ________ sleepy after lunch.

2 All the dishes on the table ________ spicy.

3 Can you ________ some pancakes for us?

4 Tom doesn't have a bicycle. I will ________ mine to him.

C 다음 두 문장이 같은 뜻이 되도록 빈칸에 알맞은 말을 쓰시오.

1 They bought their children cute dolls.

→ They bought ________ ________ ________ ________ ________.

2 The boy told his classmates a funny joke.

→ The boy told ________ ________ ________ ________ ________ ________.

D 상자 (A)와 (B)에서 알맞은 표현을 하나씩 골라 다음 문장을 완성하시오.
(주어진 표현만 사용할 것)

(A)	(B)
like	red gloves
her son	strawberries
a favor	of the citizens

1 Kate made ____________________.

2 The police officer asked ____________________.

3 The ice cream tasted ____________________.

WORDS

A
note 명 메모, 쪽지
strangely 부 이상하게
scary 형 무서운

B
sometimes 부 때때로
sleepy 형 졸린
dish 명 접시; *요리
spicy 형 (맛이) 매운

C
doll 명 인형
funny 형 웃기는
joke 명 농담

D
glove 명 장갑
citizen 명 시민

내신 완성 Grammar Practice

1 다음 빈칸에 들어갈 말로 알맞은 것을 모두 고르시오. (2개)

Could you get ____________________?

① a cup of coffee me
② me a cup of coffee
③ me for a cup of coffee
④ for a cup of coffee me
⑤ a cup of coffee for me

2 다음 중 어법상 바르지 못한 것은?

① I feel comfortable at home.
② You can ask me questions.
③ The vegetables look fresh.
④ The jazz song sounded sweet.
⑤ She passed the steak sauce me.

3 다음 빈칸에 들어갈 말이 나머지 넷과 다른 것은?

① I showed my report __________ Anne.
② Daniel gave the key __________ me.
③ James made a house __________ his dog.
④ She teaches Korean __________ foreigners.
⑤ Did Henry write a Christmas card __________ you?

4 다음 우리말과 일치하도록 괄호 안의 말을 바르게 배열하시오.

(1) Sam은 나에게 문자 메시지를 보냈다.
(me, a text message, Sam, sent)
→ ____

(2) 나는 나의 부모님께 특별한 저녁 식사를 요리해드릴 것이다.
(a special dinner, cook, my parents, I, will, for)
→ ____

WORDS

2
comfortable 형 편안한
vegetable 명 채소
jazz 명 재즈

3
report 명 보고서
foreigner 명 외국인

4
special 형 특별한

A 다음 우리말과 일치하도록 괄호 안의 단어를 바르게 배열하시오.

1 Linda는 그녀의 친구에게 점심을 사 주었다.
(lunch, Linda, her, bought, friend)
→ ______________________________

2 웨이터가 너에게 계산서를 가져다줄 것이다.
(you, will, the bill, the waiter, bring, to)
→ ______________________________

B 다음 문장을 보기 처럼 바꿔 쓰시오.

보기 Jiho sent the actor a fan letter.
→ Jiho sent a fan letter to the actor.

1 His mother made him fresh orange juice.
→ ______________________________

2 The nurse gave the patients medicine.
→ ______________________________

C 다음 그림을 보고, 보기 와 괄호 안의 단어를 이용하여 문장을 완성하시오. (현재시제로 작성할 것)

보기 thirsty bad delicious bitter

1 Dora's bread ______________________. (taste)
2 Jake's fish ______________________. (smell)
3 William ______________________. (feel)

1

Q I heard about your campaign, Hats for Babies in Africa. But it **sounds strange**. It's very hot in Africa! Do we really have to **send** the babies hats?

A The answer is "Yes." In Africa, millions of babies die on the first night after birth. Surprisingly, they die of cold. Why? In some parts of Africa, it can get very cold at night. And the cold temperatures threaten one-day-old babies. So we started our campaign. We **make** wool hats **for** babies in Zimbabwe and Ethiopia. And we bring our hats to the babies. The hats are saving babies. You can join us, too. You can't *knit at all? Then we'll **give** you *knitting lessons!

*knit: 뜨개질을 하다 *knitting: 뜨개질

1 위 글의 주제로 가장 알맞은 것은?

① 신생아를 돌보는 방법
② 아프리카의 기후 변화
③ 아기 모자 만드는 방법
④ 아프리카의 신생아 수 변화
⑤ 아프리카의 신생아들을 살리는 방법

서술형

2 위 글의 밑줄 친 3형식 문장을 4형식으로 바꿔 쓰시오.

→ And ______________________________.

WORDS
hear 동 듣다 campaign 명 캠페인 birth 명 탄생, 출생 surprisingly 부 놀랍게도 die of …로 죽다 cold 명 추위 형 추운 part 명 일부; *지역 temperature 명 온도 threaten 동 위협하다 wool 명 털실 save 동 [1] __________ join 동 함께 하다, 참여하다

2

A friendly monster met a man. The man **looked** ① cold and hungry. He was blowing air into his hands. The monster **asked** ② him the reason. The man said, "I am making my hands warmer." The monster **felt sorry** for him, so it took ③ him home.

It **brought** the man a blanket and **cooked** a bowl of soup ④ to him. The man **felt grateful**. Then he began blowing air on the soup. The monster **asked** the man another question. It said, "Are you making the soup warmer?" "No. I'm making it cooler," the man replied. The monster **felt** ⑤ confused. It shouted, "You blow hot air and cold air from the same mouth! I can't trust you!" And it chased the man from its house.

1 How did the monster feel at the end?

① bored ② tired
③ angry ④ excited
⑤ thankful

2 Which is NOT grammatically correct?

① ② ③ ④ ⑤

WORDS friendly 형 친절한 monster 명 괴물 blow 동 (입으로) 불다 reason 명 [1] ___________ blanket 명 담요 bowl 명 그릇 grateful 형 고마워하는 reply 동 [2] ___________ confused 형 혼란스러워하는 shout 동 외치다 chase from …에서 쫓아내다

A 전화하기 1

A: Hello, **can I talk to** Sujin**?**
(여보세요, 수진이랑 통화할 수 있을까요?)

B: **Speaking. Who's calling, please?**
(전데요. 누구시죠?)

A: **This is** John.
(나 John이야.)

전화를 걸어 통화할 사람을 찾을 때는 'Can I talk to ...?'라고 말할 수 있다. 이에 대한 대답으로 본인이 당사자라고 밝힐 때는 'Speaking.'이라고 말하며, 전화를 건 사람이 누구인지 물을 때는 'Who's calling, please?'라고 말할 수 있다.

EXPRESSION PLUS

A: **May I speak to** Sean**?** (Sean과 통화할 수 있을까요?)
B: **This is he. Who's this?** (전데요. 누구시죠?)

A: This is Jennifer. **Is** Sori **there?** (저 Jennifer예요. 소리 있나요?)
B: Yes. **Who am I speaking to?** (네. 누구시죠?)

Check-Up

1 다음 대화의 빈칸에 들어갈 말로 알맞은 것은?

A: Hello, is Christine there?
B: ____________________

① Yes, I can. ② What about you?
③ That's great. ④ Yes. Who's this?
⑤ Can I talk to Christine?

2 다음 대화의 밑줄 친 문장과 바꿔 쓸 수 있는 것은?

A: May I talk to Professor Choi?
B: This is she. <u>Who's calling, please?</u>

① How are you? ② Are you there?
③ Can I talk to you? ④ Who am I speaking to?
⑤ Is Professor Choi there?

WORDS

2
professor 명 교수

B 전화하기 2

A: Can I speak to Mr. Brown?
(Brown 씨와 통화할 수 있을까요?)

B: **I'm sorry. He's out. Can I take a message?**
(죄송합니다. 그는 외출했어요. 제가 메모를 남겨 드릴까요?)

A: No, thanks. **I'll call again** later.
(아니요, 괜찮아요. 제가 나중에 다시 전화할게요.)

상대방이 찾는 사람이 부재중일 경우에는 'I'm sorry. He's / She's out.'이라고 말할 수 있다. 메모를 남길 것인지 물어볼 때는 'Can I take a message?'라고 표현할 수 있다. 다시 전화하겠다고 말할 때는 'I'll call again (later).'이라고 말한다.

EXPRESSION PLUS

1 찾는 사람이 없을 때
- Sorry, he just went out. (죄송한데, 그는 방금 나갔어요.)
- She's not here at the moment. (그녀는 지금 여기에 없어요.)

2 메모 남기기
- May I leave a message? (제가 메모를 남겨도 될까요?)
- Do you want to leave a message? (당신은 메모를 남기길 원하세요?)

Check-Up

1 다음 대화의 빈칸에 들어갈 말로 알맞지 않은 것은?

A: Can I speak to the manager?
B: ____________________

① Speaking. ② This is she.
③ She's not here. ④ Can I take a message?
⑤ Sorry, she just went out.

2 대화가 자연스럽게 이어지도록 (A)~(D)를 바르게 배열하시오.

(A) Sorry, he is out.
(B) Of course, you can.
(C) Hello, is Sean there?
(D) Can I leave a message?

__________ → __________ → __________ → __________

WORDS

1
manager 명 경영자, 관리자
go out 외출하다

FINAL TEST

1 다음 중 영어 단어와 우리말 뜻이 잘못 연결된 것은?

① lie - 거짓말 ② blow - 불다
③ shout - 외치다 ④ grateful - 화난
⑤ friendly - 친절한

2 다음 보기 의 단어를 대표할 수 있는 것으로 가장 알맞은 것은?

보기 salty bitter sour spicy

① taste ② smell
③ sound ④ feeling
⑤ touch

3 다음 대화의 빈칸에 들어갈 말로 알맞은 것은?

A: Hello. May I speak to Wendy?
B: Sorry, she's out. Who's calling, please?
A: ______________

① This is Ian.
② She's not here.
③ May I take a message?
④ No, thanks. I'll call again.
⑤ Do you want to leave a message?

4 다음 중 짝지어진 대화가 어색한 것은?

① A: Who's this, please?
B: This is your dad.
② A: May I leave a message?
B: No, thank you.
③ A: May I speak to Ms. Johnson?
B: Speaking.
④ A: Hello, is Philip there?
B: Yes, this is he.
⑤ A: Hello, can I talk to Sue?
B: She's not here at the moment.

5 밑줄 친 ①~⑤ 중 대화의 흐름과 어울리지 않는 것은?

A: Hello. ① May I talk to Peter?
B: ② This is he. ③ Who is he?
A: Hi, Peter. ④ This is Julia. What are you doing?
B: ⑤ I'm listening to music.

[6-7] 다음 빈칸에 들어갈 말로 알맞은 것을 고르시오.

6 My best friend bought a beautiful rose ________ me.

① of ② to
③ at ④ for
⑤ on

7 The man showed his old paintings ________ the guests.

① in ② to
③ at ④ on
⑤ by

(!) 자주 나와요

[8-9] 다음 빈칸에 들어갈 말로 알맞지 않은 것을 고르시오.

8 My mom's cookies look ________.

① well ② delicious
③ good ④ great
⑤ like apples

9 I will ________ a thank-you letter to Jane.

① make ② send
③ give ④ bring
⑤ write

13 다음 빈칸에 들어갈 말이 나머지 넷과 다른 것은?

① He cooked beef ________ her.
② Can you get milk ________ me?
③ I didn't buy the book ________ you.
④ John gave 20 dollars ________ his sister.
⑤ Irene made a sweater ________ her daughter.

[10-11] 다음 대화의 빈칸에 들어갈 말이 바르게 짝지어진 것을 고르시오.

10 A: The wind sounds ________ a ghost.
B: Stop! I ________ scared.

① in – look ② for – feel
③ for – look ④ like – feel
⑤ like – sound

11 A: This soup ________ very salty!
B: Really? Should I get some water ________ you?

① feels – for ② feels – to
③ tastes – for ④ tastes – of
⑤ smells – of

12 다음 밑줄 친 부분 중 어법상 바르지 못한 것은?

① Monica looks fine now.
② This tea smells like vanilla.
③ The radio sounded very quiet.
④ Jack may lend you his camera.
⑤ She told the teacher to my secret.

! 어려워요

14 다음 중 어법상 바르지 못한 것은?

① This red pepper tastes really hot.
② My brother made me a sandwich.
③ The teacher asked him a question.
④ His parents looked kind and friendly.
⑤ The seafood salad smells very freshly.

! 서술형

[15-16] 다음 우리말과 일치하도록 괄호 안의 단어를 바르게 배열하시오.

15 저 구름은 토끼처럼 보인다.
(looks, cloud, like, that, a rabbit)

→ ______________________________

16 나는 그녀에게 시를 써 줄 것이다.
(her, a poem, will, write, I)

→ ______________________________

[17-18] 다음 우리말을 영어로 바르게 옮긴 것을 고르시오.

17 그는 온종일 차분해 보였다.

① He felt calmly all day.
② He was calm all day.
③ He looked calm all day.
④ He sounded calm all day.
⑤ He looked like calm all day.

18 그 점원은 나에게 표 두 장을 건네주었다.

① The clerk passed two tickets me.
② The clerk passed me two tickets.
③ The clerk passed me to two tickets.
④ The clerk passed two tickets of me.
⑤ The clerk passed to two tickets me.

서술형

[19-20] 다음 문장을 바르게 고쳐 쓰시오.

19 The music sounds strangely.

→ ____________________

20 My uncle taught us to science.

→ ____________________

내신 완성 서술형

21 다음 밑줄 친 부분 중 어법상 틀린 것을 찾아 바르게 고치시오.

A: You ① look busy.
B: It's my mom's birthday soon.
So I'm making ② a cushion her.
A: That ③ sounds nice.

__________ → __________

[22-23] 다음 문장을 보기 처럼 바꿔 쓰시오.

보기 He sent me a card.
→ He sent a card to me.

22 Diego is cooking me tacos.

→ ____________________

23 The man asked his neighbor a favor.

→ ____________________

24 다음 글을 읽고, 밑줄 친 우리말을 조건에 맞게 영작하시오.

You are at a store. You are trying on a pair of shoes. They are comfortable. So, you say to the clerk, "이 신발들은 편하게 느껴져요."

조건 1: 위에 쓰인 형용사를 이용할 것
조건 2: 감각동사를 포함하여 4단어로 작성할 것

→ ____________________

WORD LIST

Grammar

□ salt	명 소금
□ salty	형 짠
□ healthy	형 건강한
□ bitter	형 (맛이) 쓴
□ interview	명 면접, 인터뷰
□ sour	형 (맛이) 신
□ history	명 역사
□ recipe	명 조리법
□ pepper	명 후추
□ reporter	명 기자
□ chef	명 요리사
□ guest	명 손님
□ lie	명 거짓말
□ scary	형 무서운
□ sleepy	형 졸린
□ funny	형 웃기는
□ comfortable	형 편안한
□ vegetable	명 채소
□ jazz	명 재즈
□ report	명 보고서
□ foreigner	명 외국인
□ special	형 특별한

Reading

□ hear	동 듣다
□ campaign	명 캠페인
□ birth	명 탄생, 출생
□ surprisingly	부 놀랍게도
□ die of	…로 죽다
□ cold	명 추위 형 추운
□ part	명 일부; 지역
□ temperature	명 온도
□ threaten	동 위협하다
□ wool	명 털실
□ save	동 구하다
□ friendly	형 친절한
□ monster	명 괴물
□ blow	동 (입으로) 불다
□ reason	명 이유
□ bowl	명 그릇
□ grateful	형 고마워하는
□ reply	동 대답하다
□ confused	형 혼란스러워하는
□ shout	동 외치다
□ chase from	…에서 쫓아내다

Communication

□ professor	명 교수
□ manager	명 경영자, 관리자
□ go out	외출하다

Final Test

□ painting	명 그림
□ wind	명 바람
□ ghost	명 유령
□ daughter	명 딸
□ cloud	명 구름
□ poem	명 시
□ clerk	명 점원
□ store	명 가게
□ try on	입어(신어) 보다
□ a pair of	한 쌍의

CHAPTER 06

의문사가 있는 의문문

GET READY

A: **Who** is the girl?
(그 소녀는 누구니?)

B: She is my sister.
(그녀는 나의 여동생이야.)

A: **Where** were you yesterday afternoon?
(너는 어제 오후에 어디에 있었니?)

B: I was at a café.
(나는 카페에 있었어.)

위 질문들처럼 사람, 장소 등의 구체적인 내용을 물을 때 사용하는 말을 의문사라고 해요. 의문사가 쓰인 의문문에는 Yes나 No가 아닌 구체적인 대답을 해야 해요.

A 의문사 who, what, which

1 의문사가 있는 의문문

1) 의문사: '누가, 무엇을, 언제, 어디서, 어떻게, 왜' 등 구체적인 정보를 물을 때 사용하는 말이다. 의문사가 있는 의문문에는 Yes나 No로 대답하지 않는다.

2) 의문사가 있는 의문문의 어순

문장의 종류	의문문의 어순	예
동사가 be동사인 문장	「의문사+be동사+주어 ...?」	**Where** *is* my card?
동사가 일반동사인 문장	「의문사+조동사(do/will/can 등)+주어+동사원형 ...?」	**When** *do* you *go* to school? **What** *will* you *buy*?
의문사가 주어인 문장	「의문사+동사 ...?」 (※ 의문사 주어는 3인칭 단수로 취급)	**Who** *plays* the drums?

2 who: '누구'

A: **Who** is that pretty girl? B: She is *my new classmate*.
A: **Who** ate this hamburger? B: *I* did.

3 what: '무엇'

A: **What** is this animal? B: It is *a polar bear*.
A: **What** did you do at the park? B: I *walked my puppy*.
A: **What** does your mother do? B: She *treats patients*.

4 which: '어느[어떤] 것'

여러 가지 정해진 대상 중에서의 선택을 물을 때 사용한다. 참고로, 정해지지 않은 대상 중에서의 선택을 물을 때는 what을 쓴다.

A: **Which** is her bike? B: *The yellow one* is hers.
A: **Which** do you prefer, ice hockey or skiing? B: I prefer *ice hockey*.

TIPS

「what/which+명사」의 쓰임

의문사 what과 which는 형용사처럼 뒤에 오는 명사를 수식하기도 한다. 이때, what과 which는 '무슨, 어떤 …'으로 해석한다.

What color do you like best? (너는 무슨 색을 가장 좋아하니?)

Which subject does he teach? (그는 어떤 과목을 가르치니?)

Check-Up

A 다음 우리말과 일치하도록 빈칸에 알맞은 의문사를 쓰시오.

1 누가 기사를 불렀나요?
→ ________ called the engineer?

2 2호선과 6호선 중 어떤 지하철이 시청으로 가나요?
→ ________ subway goes to City Hall, line 2 or 6?

3 저 낡은 기계는 무엇입니까?
→ ________ is that old machine?

WORDS

A
engineer 명 기사[엔지니어]
machine 명 기계

B 다음 대화의 빈칸에 들어갈 말을 보기에서 골라 쓰시오.

보기 Who What Which

1 A: ________ cake do you like, cheese or strawberry?
B: I like cheese cake.

2 A: ________ is this guy in the picture?
B: That is my boyfriend, Joe.

3 A: ________ will you have for dessert?
B: I'll have the ice cream.

B
guy 명 남자

C 다음 질문에 대한 알맞은 대답을 찾아 연결하시오.

1 What did you buy? •
2 Who are you waiting for? •
3 Which do you want, a hot dog or a sandwich? •

• ⓐ My friend, Joshua.
• ⓑ I want a hot dog.
• ⓒ I bought a new jacket.

C
jacket 명 재킷

D 다음 문장의 밑줄 친 부분을 묻는 의문문을 만들 때, 빈칸에 알맞은 의문사를 쓰시오.

1 It is <u>July 15</u>.
→ ________ is the date today?

2 <u>Lucas</u> visited Italy during the holiday.
→ ________ visited Italy during the holiday?

3 My favorite season is <u>winter, not summer</u>.
→ ________ is your favorite season, summer or winter?

D
date 명 날짜
holiday 명 휴가[방학]
favorite 형 매우 좋아하는
season 명 계절

B 의문사 when, where, why, how

1 when: '언제'

A: **When** is Christmas Eve? B: It's *December 24*.
A: **When** do you have breakfast? B: I have breakfast *at 8:30*.

2 where: '어디에(서)'

A: **Where** are my new shoes? B: They are *on the shelf*.
A: **Where** does your grandmother live? B: She lives *in Boston*.

3 why: '왜'

의문사 why로 묻는 질문에 대답할 때는 보통 because(왜냐하면, … 때문에)를 사용한다.

A: **Why** do you like pancakes? B: **Because** *they are delicious*.
A: **Why** are you so angry at Mark? B: **Because** *he told me a lie*.

4 how: '어떻게, 어떤'

방법이나 수단 또는 상태를 물어볼 때 사용한다.

A: **How** can I get to Busan Station? B: You can *take bus number 26*. (수단)
A: **How** is the weather today? B: It's *snowy and cold*. (상태)

5 「how+형용사/부사」: '얼마나 …한/하게'

How many+셀 수 있는 명사의 복수형	수	A: **How many** hats do you have? B: I have *seven hats*.
How much+셀 수 없는 명사	양	A: **How much** money does he need? B: He needs *five dollars*.
How much	가격	A: **How much** is this ring? B: It is *40 dollars*.
How old	나이	A: **How old** is she? B: She is *14 years old*.
How often	빈도	A: **How often** do you go camping? B: I go camping *twice a year*.
How far	거리	A: **How far** is it to the museum? B: It's *about 10 kilometers*.
How long	길이	A: **How long** is the Golden Gate Bridge? B: It's *2,737 meters long*.
	기간	A: **How long** does it take? B: It takes *two hours*.
How tall	키·높이	A: **How tall** is the tree? B: It is *three meters*.

Check-Up

A 다음 괄호 안에서 알맞은 말을 고르시오.

1 (How / How tall) did you solve the puzzle?
2 (When / Where) is the animal hospital?
3 (How old / How far) is the beach from here?
4 (How much / How many) tickets does he have?

B 다음 질문에 대한 알맞은 대답을 찾아 연결하시오.

1 Why should we hurry? •	• ⓐ For a week.
2 When did the leaves fall off? •	• ⓑ At the gift shop.
3 Where did you get this postcard? •	• ⓒ This morning.
4 How long are you going to stay here? •	• ⓓ Because we don't have much time.

C 다음 대화의 빈칸에 알맞은 말을 쓰시오.

1 A: __________ __________ is this ship?
B: It is about 500 meters long.

2 A: __________ will Kate go to the market?
B: She will go to the market on Sunday.

3 A: __________ are you so worried?
B: Because I didn't study for the math test.

D 다음 대화의 밑줄 친 부분을 바르게 고치시오.

1 A: How far does he exercise? → __________
B: He exercises three times a week.

2 A: How many water did you bring? → __________
B: About 8 liters.

3 A: Where will the tourists ride horses? → __________
B: Tomorrow afternoon.

WORDS

A
solve 동 (문제를) 해결하다
beach 명 해변

B
hurry 동 서두르다
fall off 떨어지다
postcard 명 엽서

C
ship 명 배
worried 형 걱정하는

D
exercise 동 운동하다
liter 명 리터
tourist 명 관광객

Grammar Practice

A 다음 빈칸에 들어갈 말을 보기 에서 골라 쓰시오.

보기 Why How What Who

1 A: ________ was the concert yesterday?
B: It was really fun.

2 A: ________ is Oliver holding?
B: He is holding his toy car.

3 A: ________ did he buy broccoli?
B: Because he will make broccoli soup for his family.

B 다음 대화의 밑줄 친 부분을 바르게 고치시오.

1 A: <u>Why</u> does she practice dancing? → ________
B: She practices at the stadium.

2 A: <u>How much</u> times did you call me? → ________
B: I called you three times.

3 A: <u>What</u> painting is yours, the left one or the right one? → ________
B: The left one.

C 다음 우리말과 일치하도록 괄호 안의 단어를 이용하여 문장을 완성하시오.

1 누가 은메달을 획득했니? (win)
→ ________ ________ the silver medal?

2 너는 어디에서 그 쇼를 보았니? (see)
→ ________ ________ ________ ________ the show?

D 다음 문장의 밑줄 친 부분을 묻는 의문문을 만들 때, 빈칸에 알맞은 말을 쓰시오.

1 The accident happened <u>at nine</u>.
→ ________ ________ ________ the accident happen?

2 She wants <u>a new piano</u> for her birthday.
→ ________ ________ ________ want for her birthday?

WORDS

A
hold 동 잡다, 들고 있다
broccoli 명 브로콜리

B
painting 명 그림

C
win a medal 메달을 획득하다
(win - won - won)

D
accident 명 사고
happen 동 발생하다

내신 완성 Grammar Practice

1 다음 대화의 빈칸에 들어갈 말이 바르게 짝지어진 것은?

- A: ________ did you finish your work?
  B: An hour ago.
- A: ________ invented *Hangeul*?
  B: King Sejong did.

① What - Who ② When - What
③ When - Who ④ How long - Who
⑤ How long - What

2 다음 중 짝지어진 대화가 <u>어색한</u> 것은?

① A: Where is the bus stop?
B: It is next to the bakery.
② A: How do you know her?
B: We went to the same school.
③ A: Why was she absent from school?
B: Because she had a cold.
④ A: What is in your wallet?
B: I bought it online.
⑤ A: How far is it to the gym?
B: It is about 1 kilometer from here.

3 다음 빈칸에 들어갈 말이 나머지 넷과 <u>다른</u> 것은?

① ________ old is your cat?
② ________ long did he live in Rome?
③ ________ type of person is your boss?
④ ________ many books do you read in a year?
⑤ ________ often does Hannah go to the theater?

4 다음 우리말과 일치하도록 괄호 안의 단어를 바르게 배열하시오.

(1) 누가 그 주제에 대해 나에게 동의하니? (agrees, me, who, with)
→ ____________________ about the issue?
(2) 너는 어젯밤에 무슨 영화를 봤니? (see, you, movie, did, what)
→ ____________________ last night?

WORDS

1
invent 동 발명하다

2
next to 전 … 바로 옆에
be absent from …에 결석하다
have a cold 감기에 걸리다
wallet 명 지갑

3
type 명 유형, 타입

서술형에 나오는 WRITING

A 다음 우리말과 일치하도록 괄호 안의 단어를 바르게 배열하시오.

1 제가 어디에서 정보를 얻을 수 있나요? (I, get, where, information, can)

→ ______________________________

2 네 형은 얼마나 크니? (is, your, tall, brother, how)

→ ______________________________

3 그녀는 얼마나 자주 파스타를 요리하니? (often, she, cook, how, pasta, does)

→ ______________________________

B 다음 우리말과 일치하도록 괄호 안의 단어를 이용하여 영작하시오.

1 너는 왜 잡지를 읽니? (read, magazines)

→ ______________________________

2 누가 그의 장갑을 만들었니? (make, gloves)

→ ______________________________

C 다음은 비행기 시간표이다. 괄호 안의 단어를 이용하여 보기 처럼 대답에 대한 질문을 완성하시오.

Flight No.	From / Time	To / Time	Gate
OJ8931	Gimpo / 08:00	Jeju / 09:05	8
OJ8945	Gimpo / 10:00	Ulsan / 10:55	9

보기 A: Which gate does OJ8931 leave from? (which)
B: It leaves from Gate 8.

1 A: ______________________ from Gimpo to Jeju? (how)
B: It takes one hour and five minutes.

2 A: ______________________ in Ulsan? (when)
B: It arrives in Ulsan at 10:55.

1

Agency:	This is Dubai Travel. **How** can I help you?
Customer:	I'm going to travel to Dubai next month. **What kind** of tours do you have?
Agency:	We have a Camel Tour and a Dubai City Tour.
Customer:	The Camel Tour sounds interesting. **What** is it?
Agency:	It's a short trip to a camel farm. You can ride a camel there. And you can also enjoy *sandboarding.
Customer:	That sounds fun! <u>그 관광은 얼마인가요?</u>
Agency:	It's 200 dollars per person.
Customer:	**What time** does the tour begin? And **how long** does it last?
Agency:	We leave for the camel farm at 8 a.m. And it takes all day.
Customer:	Okay. **How** can I book the tour?
Agency:	Please give me your name.

*sandboarding: 모래 썰매

1 다음 여행 예약 내역 중 위 대화의 내용과 일치하지 <u>않는</u> 것은?

✈ 관광 상품 예약

① 여행사	⊙ Dubai Travel		
② 관광 상품	⊙ 낙타 관광	○ 두바이 시내 관광	
③ 관광 활동	⊙ 낙타 타기	○ 모래 썰매 체험	○ 시내 방문
④ 가격	○ $100	⊙ $200	
⑤ 소요 시간	⊙ 하루	○ 2박 3일	

(!) 서술형

2 위 글의 밑줄 친 우리말을 괄호 안의 단어를 이용하여 영작하시오.

→ ______________________________ (how, the tour)

WORDS agency 명 대리점, 대행사 customer 명 고객, 손님 kind 명 종류, 유형 tour 명 [1]__________ camel 명 낙타 interesting 형 흥미로운 farm 명 농장 enjoy 동 [2]__________ per 전 …당[마다] last 동 계속되다 book 동 예약하다

2

Which country has the most languages in the world? The answer is Papua New Guinea. It's a small country near Australia. About 7 million people live in the country. ___(A)___ languages are spoken there? Surprisingly, there are more than 820!

___(B)___ are there so many languages in Papua New Guinea? Because of high mountains, thick forests, and wide rivers, the native people from different places could not meet easily. Over many years, each native group developed its own language. So **how** can visitors communicate with people in Papua New Guinea? They can speak English, because it's one of the country's official languages!

1 **Which is the best title for the passage?**

① How Languages Develop
② A Country with Many Languages
③ The History of Papua New Guinea
④ Papua New Guinea's Native People
⑤ The Natural Environment of Papua New Guinea

2 **Which is the best pair for blanks (A) and (B)?**

	(A)		(B)		(A)		(B)
①	How	–	When	②	How many	–	Why
③	How many	–	Where	④	How much	–	Why
⑤	How much	–	Where				

WORDS
country 명 국가, 나라 **language** 명 언어 **million** 형 100만의 **thick** 형 두꺼운; *(나무 등이) 빽빽한[울창한]
wide 형 ________ **native** 형 원주민의 **easily** 부 쉽게 **develop** 동 발달시키다, 발달하다 **official language** 공용어

A 슬픔 · 실망의 원인 묻기

A: You look worried. **What's the matter?**
(너 걱정스러워 보여. 무슨 일이니?)

B: I lost my puppy.
(나는 내 강아지를 잃어버렸어.)

A: Really? Let's look for him together!
(정말이니? 같이 찾아보자!)

상대방이 슬퍼 보이거나 실망한 것처럼 보일 때 'What's the matter?' 또는 'What's bothering you?' 등으로 말하여 그 원인을 물을 수 있다.

EXPRESSION PLUS

A: **What's wrong?** (무슨 일이니?)
B: I didn't bring my homework. (나는 내 숙제를 가져오지 않았어.)

A: **What's the problem**, Tiffany**?** (뭐가 문제니, Tiffany?)
B: I have too much work. (나는 일이 너무 많아.)

A: You look sad. **Is there something wrong with you?** (너 슬퍼 보여. 네게 무슨 안 좋은 일이 있니?)
B: I failed my audition again. (나는 오디션에 또 떨어졌어.)

Check-Up

1 다음 대화의 빈칸에 들어갈 말로 알맞지 <u>않은</u> 것을 <u>모두</u> 고르시오. (2개)

A: You look sad. ____________
B: My favorite teacher moved to another school.

① What's wrong?
② What's the matter?
③ What are you doing?
④ Is there something wrong?
⑤ Which one do you prefer?

2 다음 괄호 안의 단어를 바르게 배열하여 대화를 완성하시오.

A: You look unhappy. ____________?
(you, bothering, what's)
B: I missed the school bus.

WORDS

1
move 동 움직이다; *옮기다

2
unhappy 형 불행한, 슬픈

B 동정 · 유감 표현하기

A: I cut my finger with a knife in a cooking class.
(나는 요리 수업에서 칼에 손가락을 베었어.)

B: **What a pity!** Are you okay now?
(정말 안됐구나! 지금은 괜찮니?)

A: Yes, I am.
(응, 괜찮아.)

'정말 안됐구나!'의 의미로 상대방에게 동정이나 유감을 표현할 때는 'What a pity!'라고 말할 수 있다.

EXPRESSION PLUS

A: My soccer team lost the game today. (오늘 우리 축구 팀이 경기에서 졌어.)
B: **I'm sorry to hear that.** (그것 참 유감이다.)

A: Julie is very sick. She's in the hospital. (Julie가 매우 아파. 그녀는 입원 중이야.)
B: **That's too bad.** (참 안됐구나.)

A: I couldn't get a ticket for my favorite band's concert. (나는 내가 정말 좋아하는 밴드의 콘서트 티켓을 못 구했어.)
B: **That's a pity!** (그것 안됐구나!)

Check-Up

1 다음 대화의 빈칸에 들어갈 말로 알맞지 않은 것은?

A: Garam broke his leg yesterday.
B: ____________________

① What a pity!
② That's a pity!
③ That's too bad.
④ That's very nice!
⑤ I'm sorry to hear that.

2 대화가 자연스럽게 이어지도록 (A)~(C)를 바르게 배열하시오.

(A) What a pity!
(B) What's the matter, Tom?
(C) I left my laptop computer on the bus.

__________ → __________ → __________

WORDS

1
break 동 부러지다
(broke - broken)

2
laptop computer 노트북

FINAL TEST

1 다음 중 영어 단어와 우리말 뜻이 잘못 연결된 것은?

① hurry - 서두르다 ② invent - 발명하다
③ wallet - 지갑 ④ develop - 줄어들다
⑤ favorite - 매우 좋아하는

2 다음 우리말과 일치하도록 빈칸에 알맞은 말을 쓰시오.

Wilson은 그 회의에 결석했다.

→ Wilson was ________ ________ the meeting.

3 다음 대화의 빈칸에 들어갈 말로 알맞은 것은?

A: You look sad. ____________
B: My new shoes got dirty in the mud.

① That's great. ② What a pity!
③ How are you? ④ What's wrong?
⑤ That's too bad.

4 다음 대화의 밑줄 친 문장과 바꿔 쓸 수 있는 것은?

A: I got a bad grade on the science test.
B: Again? What a pity!

① You look sad.
② That's too bad.
③ I'm sorry again.
④ You will do better!
⑤ I understand your problem.

5 대화가 자연스럽게 이어지도록 (A)~(C)를 바르게 배열하시오.

(A) I feel better now.
(B) I caught a cold last week.
(C) I'm sorry to hear that. How do you feel now?

________ → ________ → ________

6 밑줄 친 ①~⑤ 중 대화의 흐름과 어울리지 않는 것은?

A: Is there something wrong?
B: ①I lost my English textbook!
A: ②Do you like English? ③That's a pity!
B: ④Can I borrow yours?
A: ⑤Sure.

자주 나와요

7 다음 대화의 빈칸에 들어갈 말이 바르게 짝지어진 것은?

A: ________ is his name?
B: His name is Simon.
A: ________ tall is he?
B: He's 165 centimeters tall.

① Who - Why ② Who - What
③ What - How ④ What - Who
⑤ When - How

8 다음 빈칸에 들어갈 말로 알맞지 않은 것은?

How many ________ are there?

① fish ② salt
③ pants ④ dishes
⑤ children

[9-10] 다음 대화의 빈칸에 들어갈 말로 알맞은 것을 고르시오.

9
A: How often do you exercise?
B: ________________

① At a gym.
② Tomorrow.
③ I like running.
④ Twice a week.
⑤ About two hours.

10
A: I'm looking for a new dress.
B: ________________
A: Pink or sky blue.

① How much is it?
② Where did you get it?
③ What size do you want?
④ What color do you want?
⑤ Why don't you buy this one?

자주 나와요

[11-13] 다음 대화의 빈칸에 알맞은 의문사를 쓰시오.

11
A: ________ do you look so happy?
B: Because I passed the exam.

12
A: ________ is the man with curly hair?
B: He's my little brother.

13
A: ________ was the weather in San Diego?
B: It was cloudy.

14 다음 질문에 대한 대답을 보기 에서 고르시오.

보기
ⓐ It's 800 won.
ⓑ There are five.
ⓒ He comes by subway.
ⓓ Around six in the morning.

(1) How does Sam get here? ________

(2) How much is this yogurt? ________

(3) What time do you get up? ________

[15-16] 다음 우리말과 일치하도록 괄호 안의 단어를 이용하여 문장을 완성하시오.

15
너는 사과와 배 중에 어떤 과일을 먹었니?

→ ________ ________ did you eat, apples or pears? (fruit)

16
얼마나 많은 물이 병에 있나요?

→ ________ ________ ________ is in the bottle? (water)

[17-18] 다음 문장에서 틀린 부분을 찾아 바르게 고치시오.

17
What did happen to your sister?

________ → ________

18
Who you are going to meet after school?

________ → ________

! 자주 나와요

19 다음 밑줄 친 부분의 뜻이 바르지 못한 것은?

① How old is Karen?
얼마나 나이 든

② How tall is the giraffe?
얼마나 키가 큰

③ How far is it to the East Sea?
얼마나 먼

④ How long does it take from here?
얼마나 긴

⑤ How many people are there in the hall?
얼마나 많은

20 다음 중 짝지어진 대화가 어색한 것은?

① A: Who knows the secret?
B: Nobody knows.

② A: When is Minho's birthday?
B: It's March 16.

③ A: What kind of food do you like?
B: I like Mexican food.

④ A: Where does your dad work?
B: He works at the post office.

⑤ A: Why do you go to the market?
B: I go to the market on foot.

! 어려워요

21 다음 중 어법상 바르지 못한 것은?

① Why is he so tired?
② When will they come back?
③ What time she closes her shop?
④ When can we visit the top floor?
⑤ How much money did you spend?

내신 완성 서술형

[22-23] 다음은 Paul과 Alice의 주말 공부 계획이다. 표의 내용과 일치하도록 대화를 완성하시오.

	Saturday	Sunday
Paul	math	x
Alice	English	science

22 A: __________ will study science on Sunday?
B: Alice will.

23 A: __________ subject will Paul study on Saturday, math or English?
B: He will study __________.

24 다음 대화의 빈칸에 알맞은 말을 쓰시오.

A: ______________ for lunch?
B: I want Chinese food.

조건: 총 4단어로 작성할 것

→ ______________________

25 다음 대화의 빈칸에 들어갈 말을 조건에 맞게 영작하시오.

A: Oh, no! I dropped my cell phone! It doesn't work.
B: ______________

조건 1: sorry와 hear를 이용할 것
조건 2: 총 5단어로 작성할 것

→ ______________________

WORD LIST

Grammar

□ engineer	명 기사[엔지니어]
□ machine	명 기계
□ guy	명 남자
□ jacket	명 재킷
□ date	명 날짜
□ holiday	명 휴가[방학]
□ favorite	형 매우 좋아하는
□ season	명 계절
□ beach	명 해변
□ hurry	동 서두르다
□ fall off	떨어지다
□ postcard	명 엽서
□ ship	명 배
□ worried	형 걱정하는
□ tourist	명 관광객
□ accident	명 사고
□ happen	동 발생하다
□ invent	동 발명하다
□ next to	전 … 바로 옆에
□ be absent from	…에 결석하다

Reading

□ agency	명 대리점, 대행사
□ customer	명 고객, 손님
□ kind	명 종류, 유형
□ tour	명 여행, 관광
□ camel	명 낙타
□ interesting	형 흥미로운
□ farm	명 농장
□ enjoy	동 즐기다
□ per	전 …당[마다]
□ last	동 계속되다
□ book	동 예약하다
□ country	명 국가, 나라
□ language	명 언어
□ million	형 100만의
□ thick	형 두꺼운; (나무 등이) 빽빽한[울창한]
□ wide	형 넓은
□ native	형 원주민의
□ easily	부 쉽게
□ develop	동 발달시키다, 발달하다
□ official language	공용어

Communication

□ move	동 움직이다; 옮기다
□ unhappy	형 불행한, 슬픈
□ break	동 부러지다
□ laptop computer	노트북

Final Test

□ dirty	형 더러운
□ mud	명 진흙
□ grade	명 성적
□ catch a cold	감기에 걸리다
□ dish	명 접시
□ twice	부 두 번
□ pear	명 배
□ bottle	명 병
□ giraffe	명 기린
□ on foot	걸어서, 도보로
□ drop	동 떨어뜨리다

CHAPTER 07

명사와 관사

GET READY

Hyobin is wearing **a baseball uniform**.
(효빈이는 야구복을 입고 있다.)

I felt **the love** of my **parents**.
(나는 나의 부모님의 사랑을 느꼈다.)

'효빈, 야구복, 부모님'과 같이 모든 사람과 사물에는 이름이 있어요. 또 '사랑'과 같이 추상적인 개념을 나타내는 이름도 있어요. 이런 이름들을 바로 명사라고 해요. 그리고 명사 앞에는 a, an, the와 같은 관사가 올 수 있답니다.

GRAMMAR FOCUS

A 명사의 종류

1 셀 수 있는 명사

셀 수 있는 명사는 개수를 헤아릴 수 있는 명사이다. 단수형은 명사 앞에 부정관사 a/an을 붙이고, 복수형은 일반적으로 명사 뒤에 -s/-es를 붙인다.

There are some **apples** and **peaches** on **a plate**.

Two **men** are working in **an office**.

내신 POINT PLUS

명사의 복수형

1 규칙 복수형

명사의 형태	복수형 만드는 법	예
대부분의 명사	단수형+-s	bag**s**, train**s**, spider**s**, umbrella**s**
-s, -ss, -sh, -ch, -x로 끝나는 명사	단수형+-es	bus**es**, class**es**, dish**es**, watch**es**, box**es**
-o로 끝나는 명사	단수형+-s/-es	piano**s**, photo**s**, potato**es**, hero**es**
「자음+y」로 끝나는 명사	y를 i로 고치고+-es	lady → lad**ies**, city → cit**ies**
-f, -fe로 끝나는 명사	f, fe를 v로 고치고+-es	leaf → lea**ves**, knife → kni**ves** (※ roof → roof**s**)

2 불규칙 복수형: man → **men**, woman → **women**, child → **children**, tooth → **teeth**, foot → **feet**, mouse → **mice**, goose → **geese**, person → **people**

3 단수형과 복수형이 같은 명사: sheep → **sheep**, fish → **fish**

2 셀 수 없는 명사

셀 수 없는 명사는 개수를 헤아릴 수 없는 명사이다. 단수형으로만 쓰며 앞에 부정관사 a/an을 쓰지 않는다.

1) 고유명사: 사람, 사물, 장소 등의 고유한 이름

Alice traveled around **Europe**.

2) 추상명사: 추상적인 개념을 나타내는 명사 예 love, hope, peace, luck, death 등

There is good **news**.

3) 물질명사: 정해진 형태가 없는 물질이나 재료를 나타내는 명사 예 water, gold, paper, bread, salt 등

We can't live without **water**.

TIPS

물질명사의 수량표현

1 cup(컵), glass(잔), piece(조각, 장), bottle(병), slice(얇게 썬 조각) 등의 단위로 수량을 나타낸다.

a **cup** of milk(우유 한 컵) two **glasses** of juice(주스 두 잔) three **pieces** of paper(종이 세 장)

four **bottles** of water(물 네 병) five **slices** of cheese(치즈 다섯 조각)

2 a lot of[lots of](많은), much(많은), some(약간), a little(약간) 등으로 양을 나타낸다.

many는 셀 수 없는 명사 앞에 쓰일 수 없다.

a lot of trash(많은 쓰레기) **some** salt(약간의 소금)

Check-Up

A 다음 명사의 복수형을 쓰시오.

1 table	– ________	2 fish	– ________
3 tomato	– ________	4 hobby	– ________
5 fly	– ________	6 dress	– ________
7 wolf	– ________	8 mouse	– ________
9 woman	– ________	10 box	– ________

WORDS

A
fly 명 파리
wolf 명 늑대

B 다음 괄호 안에서 알맞은 말을 고르시오.

1 Andy has a (sister / sisters).
2 The cook added (salt / a salt) to the food.
3 I didn't have much (luck / lucks) yesterday.
4 Korea has four (season / seasons) in a year.

B
luck 명 운, 행운
season 명 계절

C 다음 빈칸에 들어갈 말을 보기 에서 골라 쓰시오.

보기 slice pieces cup bottles

1 I drank a ________ of coffee this morning.
2 My father put five ________ of bread on the plate.
3 We bought two ________ of wine for the party.
4 Helen gave me a ________ of mushroom pizza at lunch.

C
plate 명 접시
mushroom 명 버섯

D 다음 밑줄 친 부분을 바르게 고치시오.

1 Thiefs are climbing the wall. → ________
2 Billy bought two glass of milk. → ________
3 Those man are basketball players. → ________
4 The waters in the river didn't look clean. → ________

D
thief 명 도둑
climb 동 오르다, 올라가다
wall 명 벽, 담

B 관사

1 부정관사 a/an

부정관사 a/an은 셀 수 있는 명사의 단수형 앞에 쓰며 자음 소리 앞에는 a, 모음 소리 앞에는 an을 쓴다.

1) 특정하지 않은 하나를 나타낼 때

Do you have **a** spoon?

2) 하나를 나타낼 때 (one의 의미)

She went to Japan **a** month ago.

3) '…마다, …당' (per의 의미)

I wash my face three times **a** day.

The bus goes 70 km **an** hour.

2 정관사 the

정관사 the는 명사의 단수형과 복수형 앞에 모두 쓰이며 자음 소리 앞에서는 [ðə], 모음 소리 앞에서는 [ði]로 발음된다.

1) 앞에 언급된 명사를 다시 언급할 때

Jessie bought *a watch* last week. She wears **the** watch every day.

2) 말하는 사람과 듣는 사람이 모두 아는 것을 가리킬 때

Can you bring me **the** newspaper?

3) 수식어구의 수식을 받는 명사 앞

The man in that picture is my teacher.

4) 관용적으로 사용하는 경우 예 유일한 자연물(**the** sun, **the** earth, **the** sky, **the** sea, **the** world 등), 악기 이름(**the** piano, **the** violin 등), 인터넷(**the** Internet) 등

We saw many stars in **the** sky.

She is playing **the** violin.

TIPS

관사를 생략하는 경우

1 식사 이름 앞: breakfast, lunch, dinner 등
They had **dinner** together. (그들은 함께 저녁을 먹었다.)

2 운동 경기 이름 앞: basketball, soccer 등
We played **soccer** after school. (우리는 방과 후에 축구를 했다.)

3 「by+교통수단」
I came here **by subway**. (나는 지하철을 타고 여기에 왔다.)

4 공항·역 이름 앞
She is at **Incheon Airport**. (그녀는 인천공항에 있다.)

5 본래의 용도로 쓰인 장소 앞: go to school / bed / church 등
George **goes to school** on foot. (George는 걸어서 학교에 간다.)

Check-Up

A 다음 괄호 안에서 알맞은 말을 고르시오.

1 (A / The) sun rises in the east.
2 I go to a hair shop once (a / the) month.
3 Yuri had (a / an) egg sandwich this morning.
4 He has a cat. (A / The) cat is 3 years old.

B 다음 빈칸에 들어갈 말을 보기 에서 골라 쓰시오. (필요 없는 경우에는 X표 할 것)

보기 a   an   the

1 This hammer is ________ useful tool.
2 Two boys are playing ________ tennis.
3 Do you go to school by ________ bus?
4 Jefferson is ________ amazing singer.
5 ________ flowers in my garden are really beautiful.

C 다음 밑줄 친 부분을 바르게 고치시오.

1 The baby looks like <u>a angel</u>. → ________
2 We go hiking twice <u>the week</u>. → ________
3 My family has <u>the breakfast</u> every day. → ________
4 He did not <u>go to the bed</u> late at night. → ________

D 다음 우리말과 일치하도록 괄호 안의 단어를 이용하여 문장을 완성하시오.

1 인터넷에는 많은 정보가 있다. (Internet)
→ There is lots of information on ________ ________.
2 누가 그 아이스크림을 먹었니? (ice cream)
→ Who ate ________ ________ ________?
3 너는 한 시간 동안 기다려야 한다. (hour)
→ You have to wait for ________ ________.

WORDS

A
rise 동 오르다; *(해·달이) 뜨다
east 명 동쪽
hair shop 미용실

B
hammer 명 망치
useful 형 유용한
tool 명 도구, 연장
amazing 형 놀라운

C
angel 명 천사
hiking 명 하이킹, 도보 여행

D
information 명 정보

Grammar Practice

A 다음 괄호 안에서 알맞은 말을 고르시오.

1 It is the oldest palace in (a / the) world.

2 They saw a (bear / bears) in the forest.

3 Jackson takes a walk after (lunch / the lunch).

B 다음 문장에서 어법상 틀린 곳을 찾아 바르게 고치시오.

1 He is not a honest person. ________ → ________

2 Matt drinks a lot of milks every day. ________ → ________

3 They will order two or three cup of tea. ________ → ________

4 She told us some storys about the past. ________ → ________

C 다음 우리말과 일치하도록 괄호 안의 단어를 이용하여 문장을 완성하시오.

1 이 강에는 물고기가 많다. (fish)

→ There are many ________ in this river.

2 Harold는 한 달에 한 번씩 자원봉사를 한다. (month)

→ Harold does volunteer work once ________ ________.

3 물 한 병을 어디서 살 수 있나요? (bottle, water)

→ Where can I buy ________ ________ ________ ________?

D 다음 그림을 보고, 괄호 안의 단어를 이용하여 빈칸에 알맞은 말을 쓰시오.

1

(potato)

There are ________ ________ in the basket.

2

(piece)

There is ________ ________ ________ bread on the plate.

WORDS

A
palace 명 궁전
forest 명 숲

B
honest 형 정직한
order 동 주문하다
tea 명 차
past 명 과거

C
volunteer work 자원봉사

내신 완성 Grammar Practice

1 다음 밑줄 친 부분 중 바르지 못한 것은?

① Leaves are falling from the tree.
② Can you bring me five knives?
③ They fixed the roofs of the houses.
④ He is raising six sheeps on his farm.
⑤ You should wash your hands and feet first.

2 다음 밑줄 친 부분의 쓰임이 보기 와 같은 것은?

보기 He can run 400 meters a minute.

① Did you prepare a gift for him?
② Her daughter is a famous writer.
③ I have four math classes a week.
④ We moved to this city a year ago.
⑤ We saw four zebras and an elephant.

3 다음 중 빈칸에 the[The]를 쓸 수 없는 것은?

① I practice ________ guitar after school.
② May I turn off ________ air conditioner?
③ Olivia built a nice house by ________ sea.
④ ________ umbrellas in Norah's car are ours.
⑤ We will meet our cousin at ________ Busan Station.

4 다음 우리말과 일치하도록 괄호 안의 단어를 바르게 배열하시오.

(1) 그들은 일 년에 세 번 놀이공원에 간다. (a, times, three, year)
→ They go to the amusement park ________________.

(2) 그는 그의 샌드위치에 치즈 두 장을 얹었다. (slices, cheese, of, two)
→ He put ________________ on his sandwich.

WORDS

1
fall 동 떨어지다
raise 동 들어 올리다; *키우다

2
prepare 동 준비하다
city 명 도시

3
turn off …를 끄다
air conditioner 에어컨

4
amusement park 놀이공원

서술형에 나오는 WRITING

A **다음 우리말과 일치하도록 괄호 안의 말을 바르게 배열하시오.**

1 나는 인터넷에서 그녀의 사진을 보았다.
(saw, the, Internet, her, on, photo)
→ I ______________________________.

2 그 남자들은 목요일에 저녁을 먹으러 나갔다.
(dinner, the, went out, men, for)
→ ______________________________ on Thursday.

B **다음 우리말과 일치하도록 괄호 안의 말을 이용하여 문장을 완성하시오.**

1 그녀의 아이들은 그 영화에 나오는 영웅들을 좋아한다. (child, like, hero)
→ ______________________________ in the movie.

2 나는 지난 여름에 자전거를 타고 런던에 여행을 갔다. (travel to London, by, bicycle)
→ ______________________________ last summer.

C **다음은 David 가족의 식사 영수증이다. 목록을 보고, 보기 처럼 질문에 대한 대답을 완성하시오.**

Restaurant Bill

- pizza ...... 2 pieces
- sandwich 4
- coffee ...... 3 cups
- water ...... 2 bottles

보기 A: How much pizza did they have?
B: They had two pieces of pizza.

1 A: How many sandwiches did they order?
B: They ______________________________.

2 A: How much coffee did they drink?
B: They ______________________________.

3 A: How much water did they buy?
B: They ______________________________.

1

Welcome to Joe's cooking class! It's cold today, so we'll make something hot and nutritious—meatballs! We have 500 grams of ground beef, 100 grams of *bread crumbs, **a** small onion, ①an egg, some olive oil, and ②a jar of tomato sauce. Let's get started!

First, mix **the** beef, **the** onion, **the** bread crumbs, and **the** egg in **a** large bowl. Shape ③the mixture into small balls. Now put **the** olive oil in **a** pan. Heat it for a few minutes. Then fry ④the meatballs in **the** pan. Add **the** tomato sauce to **the** meatballs. Roll **the** meatballs until they're covered in **the** sauce. Then put **a** lid on ⑤a pan. Finally, heat **the** meatballs for 20 minutes. Now, enjoy your delicious food!

*bread crumb: 빵가루

1 위 글의 제목으로 가장 알맞은 것은?

① The Meatball Recipe
② The New Meatball Machine
③ The Meatball Cooking Contest
④ Foods That Go Well with Meatballs
⑤ The Meatball: A Healthy Food

2 위 글의 밑줄 친 부분 중 어법상 틀린 것은?

① ② ③ ④ ⑤

WORDS nutritious 형 영양분이 많은 ground 형 간; 가루로 만든 beef 명 소고기 mix 동 [1] __________ bowl 명 그릇 shape A into B A를 B 모양으로 만들다 heat 동 뜨겁게 만들다 a few 어느 정도, 약간 fry 동 부치다, 튀기다 roll 동 굴리다 until 접 …까지 be covered in …로 덮이다 lid 명 뚜껑 문제 go well with …와 잘 어울리다

2

An old man was walking down **a** street. He saw ___(A)___ boy in front of **a** house. **The** boy was trying to ring **the** doorbell. However, he was very short and **the** doorbell was too high. So he couldn't reach it. **The** man watched him for some time. Then **the** man walked up to **the** boy. ___(B)___ man asked, "Do you need any help, little boy?" "Yes, please," **the** boy answered. **The** gentleman stood behind **the** boy and rang **the** bell for him. "Now, you can go in," he said with **a** smile. Then ___(C)___ boy replied, "Sir, we should run!"

1 **Which best describes the atmosphere of the story?**

① boring ② festive
③ touching ④ romantic
⑤ humorous

2 **Which is the best choice for blanks (A)~(C)?**

	(A)		(B)		(C)
①	a	–	A	–	a
②	a	–	The	–	a
③	a	–	The	–	the
④	the	–	A	–	the
⑤	the	–	The	–	the

WORDS
in front of ··· 앞에 **ring** 동 전화하다; *(초인종을) 누르다 (rang – rung) **doorbell** 명 초인종 **reach** 동 1 ___________
behind 전 2 ___________ **smile** 명 미소 **reply** 동 대답하다 **sir** 명 (이름 모르는 남성에 대한 존칭) 선생님
문제 **atmosphere** 명 공기; *분위기 **festive** 형 축제의, 흥겨운 **touching** 형 감동적인

내신에 나오는 COMMUNICATION

A 의견 묻고 답하기

A: **What do you think of** our science teacher**?**
(너는 우리 과학 선생님에 대해 어떻게 생각해?)

B: **I think that** she's professional. How about you?
(나는 선생님이 전문적이라고 생각해. 너는 어때?)

A: **In my opinion**, she's not kind.
(내 의견으로는, 선생님은 친절하지 않아.)

'…에 대해 어떻게 생각하니?'의 의미로 상대방의 의견을 물을 때는 'What do you think of ...?'라고 말할 수 있다. 자신의 의견은 'I think (that) ...'나 'In my opinion, ...'으로 표현할 수 있다.

EXPRESSION PLUS

A: **How do you feel about** the story**?** (너는 그 이야기에 대해 어떻게 생각해?)
B: **I feel that** it's terrible. (나는 그것이 끔찍하다고 생각해.)
(※ 'How do you feel about ...?' 대신 'How do you think about ...?'이라고 말하지 않도록 주의한다.)

A: **How do you like** Seoul**?** (너는 서울을 어떻게 생각해?)
B: I think that it's a lot of fun. (나는 그 도시가 매우 재미있다고 생각해.)

Check-Up

1 다음 질문에 대한 알맞은 응답을 찾아 연결하시오.

(1) How do you like the food? •
(2) What do you think of him? •
(3) How do you feel about the dress? •

• ⓐ I feel that it's pretty.
• ⓑ I think that he's nice.
• ⓒ I don't think it's delicious.

2 다음 대화의 빈칸에 들어갈 말로 알맞은 것은?

A: I feel that the song is good. How about you?
B: ____________________

① I feel cold.
② I don't think of it.
③ I'm fine. Thank you.
④ That's a good idea.
⑤ In my opinion, it's fantastic.

WORDS

2
fantastic 형 환상적인

B 동의하기

A: I think that Andrew should be class president.
(나는 Andrew가 반장이 되어야 한다고 생각해.)

B: **I agree with you.**
(난 네 말에 동의해.)

A: **I don't agree with you.** He isn't a good student.
(나는 네 말에 동의하지 않아. 그는 좋은 학생이 아니야.)

상대방의 의견에 동의할 때는 'I agree with you.', 동의하지 않을 때는 'I don't agree with you.'라고 말할 수 있다.

⊕ EXPRESSION PLUS

A: **Do you agree with me?** (너는 내 말에 동의하니?)
B: **Yes, I agree.** (응, 동의해.) / **No, I don't agree.** (아니, 동의하지 않아.)

A: I think that it will rain soon. (나는 곧 비가 올 거라고 생각해.)
B: **I think so, too.** (나도 그렇게 생각해.) / **I don't think so.** (나는 그렇게 생각하지 않아.)

A: Let's go to the beach for summer vacation. (여름휴가로 해변에 가자.)
B: **That's a good idea.** (그거 좋은 생각이야.)

Check-Up

1 다음 대화의 밑줄 친 문장과 바꿔 쓸 수 있는 것은?

A: The math test was very difficult.
B: I agree with you.

① Not really.
② I don't agree.
③ I think so, too.
④ I don't like math.
⑤ I think that it was easy.

2 다음 대화의 빈칸에 들어갈 말로 알맞은 것을 모두 고르시오. (2개)

A: I think our school uniform is cool.
B: ________________ It's not stylish.

① Yes, I agree.
② I don't think so.
③ I agree with you.
④ That's a good idea.
⑤ I don't agree with you.

WORDS

1
difficult 형 어려운

2
school uniform 교복
cool 형 시원한; *멋진
stylish 형 유행을 따르는, 멋진

FINAL TEST

1 다음 중 영어 단어와 우리말 뜻이 잘못 연결된 것은?

① past - 과거 ② east - 서쪽
③ thief - 도둑 ④ roll - 굴리다
⑤ useful - 유용한

2 다음 우리말과 일치하도록 빈칸에 알맞은 말을 쓰시오.

내가 TV를 꺼도 되니?

→ Can I ________ ________ the TV?

3 다음 대화의 빈칸에 들어갈 말로 알맞은 것은?

A: How do you like the painting?
B: ____________________

① That's too bad.
② I don't think so.
③ I agree with you.
④ I like the painter so much.
⑤ I think that it's wonderful.

4 다음 대화의 밑줄 친 문장과 바꿔 쓸 수 있는 것은?

A: What do you think of my plan?
B: In my opinion, it's a bad idea.

① What are you planning to do?
② How do you feel about my plan?
③ Why do you think about my plan?
④ How do you know about my plan?
⑤ How do you think about my plan?

5 다음 문장이 들어갈 위치로 가장 알맞은 곳은?

But I think that it's a nice car.

A: How do you feel about this car? (①)
B: (②) I feel that it's too expensive. Do you agree?
A: (③) Yes, I agree. (④)
B: I think so, too. (⑤)

자주 나와요

6 다음 중 짝지어진 대화가 어색한 것은?

① A: This T-shirt is pretty.
B: I think so, too.
② A: Science is too difficult.
B: I don't agree. It's easy.
③ A: How do you like the show?
B: I agree with you.
④ A: Let's go on a picnic this weekend.
B: That's a good idea.
⑤ A: What do you think of the new worker?
B: I think that he's friendly.

7 다음 중 명사의 복수형이 잘못 연결된 것은?

① foot - feet ② key - keys
③ baby - babies ④ piano - pianos
⑤ church - churchs

[8-9] 다음 빈칸에 들어갈 말로 알맞은 것을 고르시오.

8 Hans drank a ________ of soda.

① lots ② much
③ slice ④ piece
⑤ bottle

9 The geese ________ swimming across the river.

① is ② are
③ do ④ does
⑤ will

[10-11] 다음 빈칸에 들어갈 말이 바르게 짝지어진 것을 고르시오.

10 Rob bought ________ new computer. ________ computer was not cheap.

① a - A ② a - The
③ an - The ④ an - The
⑤ the - A

11 A: Can I have a ________ of coffee with sugar?
B: Sure. Anything else?
A: I want a ________ of cake, too.

① cup - pair ② cup - piece
③ cups - slice ④ slice - little
⑤ slice - piece

[12-14] 다음 우리말과 일치하도록 괄호 안의 단어를 이용하여 문장을 완성하시오.

12 우리는 일본에 있는 도시 세 개를 방문할 것이다. (city)

→ We will visit ________ ________ in Japan.

13 Tommy는 오늘 아침 주스 두 잔을 마셨다. (glass)

→ Tommy drank ________ ________ ________ juice this morning.

14 독서 모임 회원들은 일 년에 책 열 권을 읽는다. (year)

→ The book club members read ten books ________ ________.

자주 나와요

15 **다음 밑줄 친 부분의 쓰임이 나머지 넷과 다른 것은?**

① I saw a letter in her bag.
② Sue has a beautiful nose.
③ She bought a yellow raincoat.
④ He found an album in the drawer.
⑤ The bus stops here twice an hour.

어려워요

16 다음 중 빈칸에 the[The]가 들어갈 수 없는 것을 모두 고르시오. (2개)

① People are surfing in ________ sea.
② Kate doesn't play ________ flute well.
③ He opened ________ notebook on the desk.
④ ________ baseball is a popular sport in Korea.
⑤ Potatoes are two dollars ________ kilogram.

[17-18] 다음 밑줄 친 부분 중 어법상 틀린 것을 고르시오.

17 ① Who are those ladies?
② He put four dishes in the box.
③ Many kinds of fish live in the pond.
④ The firefighters saved people's lifes.
⑤ We will eat hamburgers for lunch.

18 ① A sun is very bright.
② They live in an apartment.
③ This is an interesting book.
④ I go to the dentist once a month.
⑤ The birds on the roof are singing.

[19-20] 다음 밑줄 친 부분을 바르게 고치시오.

19 Many people really want a peace.

→ ________________

20 Will you go to Rome by the train?

→ ________________

내신 완성 서술형

[21-23] 다음 우리말과 일치하도록 괄호 안의 말을 이용하여 문장을 완성하시오.

21 우리는 평일에 학교에 간다.
(go to, school)

→ ________________ on weekdays.

22 그녀는 빵 네 조각을 먹었다.
(have, piece)

→ ________________ bread.

23 그들은 일주일에 아홉 시간 운동을 한다.
(exercise, hour, week)

→ They ________________.

24 다음 대화의 빈칸에 들어갈 말을 조건에 맞게 영작하시오.

A: How do you like the movie *White Shark*?
B: I think it's scary. ________
A: Yes, I agree!

조건 1: 의문문으로 작성할 것
조건 2: agree를 포함하여 총 5단어로 쓸 것

→ ________________

WORD LIST

Grammar

□ fly	명 파리
□ wolf	명 늑대
□ luck	명 운, 행운
□ season	명 계절
□ thief	명 도둑
□ rise	동 오르다; (해 · 달이) 뜨다
□ east	명 동쪽
□ useful	형 유용한
□ tool	명 도구, 연장
□ amazing	형 놀라운
□ angel	명 천사
□ information	명 정보
□ forest	명 숲
□ honest	형 정직한
□ tea	명 차
□ past	명 과거
□ volunteer work	자원봉사
□ fall	동 떨어지다
□ raise	동 들어 올리다; 키우다
□ prepare	동 준비하다
□ city	명 도시
□ turn off	…를 끄다
□ air conditioner	에어컨
□ amusement park	놀이공원

Reading

□ nutritious	형 영양분이 많은
□ beef	명 소고기
□ mix	동 섞다
□ bowl	명 그릇
□ shape A into B	A를 B 모양으로 만들다
□ heat	동 뜨겁게 만들다
□ a few	어느 정도, 약간
□ fry	동 부치다, 튀기다
□ roll	동 굴리다
□ until	접 …까지
□ in front of	… 앞에
□ ring	동 전화하다; (초인종을) 누르다
□ doorbell	명 초인종
□ reach	동 …에 닿다
□ behind	전 … 뒤에
□ smile	명 미소
□ reply	동 대답하다
□ sir	명 (이름 모르는 남성에 대한 존칭) 선생님
□ atmosphere	명 공기; 분위기

Communication

□ fantastic	형 환상적인
□ school uniform	교복
□ stylish	형 유행을 따른, 멋진

Final Test

□ soda	명 소다, 탄산음료
□ cheap	형 (값이) 싼
□ raincoat	명 비옷
□ drawer	명 서랍
□ surf	동 파도타기를 하다
□ apartment	명 아파트
□ roof	명 지붕
□ peace	명 평화
□ weekday	명 평일

CHAPTER 08

형용사와 부사

GET READY

I picked **red** tulips.
(나는 빨간 튤립을 꺾었다.)

Do you **usually** wash your hair in the morning?
(너는 보통 아침에 머리를 감니?)

This cap is **bigger than** that one.
(이 모자는 저것보다 더 크다.)

형용사와 부사는 다른 말을 수식하여 의미를 더해 주거나 여러 대상들을 비교하는 데 쓰여요. 부사 중에서 어떤 일이 얼마나 자주 일어나는지를 나타낼 때 사용하는 부사를 빈도부사라고 해요.

GRAMMAR FOCUS

A 형용사와 부사

1 형용사

1) 역할: 명사나 대명사를 수식하거나, 주어나 목적어를 보충 설명한다.

He sold the **old** car. (명사 수식)   The car is **old**. (주어를 보충 설명)

2) 수와 양을 나타내는 형용사

의미	셀 수 있는 명사의 복수형 앞	셀 수 없는 명사 앞
조금 있는, 약간의 (긍정적)	a few	a little
거의 없는 (부정적)	few	little
많은	many	much
	a lot of, lots of	

There are **a few** dishes on the table.   This fan uses **little** energy.

2 부사

1) 역할: 동사, 형용사, 다른 부사, 문장 전체를 수식한다.

She walks **slowly**. (동사 수식)   This game is **really** interesting. (형용사 수식)

I studied **very** hard. (다른 부사 수식)   **Luckily**, they won the match. (문장 전체 수식)

2) 부사의 형태

대부분의 형용사	형용사+-ly	slow → slow**ly**, kind → kind**ly**
-y로 끝나는 형용사	y를 i로 고치고+-ly	happy → happ**ily**, easy → eas**ily**
형용사와 형태가 같은 부사		fast(빠른 / 빨리), early(이른 / 일찍), late(늦은 / 늦게), hard(열심히 하는 / 열심히), high(높은 / 높이)

TIPS

-ly로 끝나지만 부사가 아닌 형용사(friendly, daily, lovely 등)에 유의한다.

내신 POINT PLUS

빈도부사

빈도부사는 어떤 일이 얼마나 자주 발생하는지를 나타내는 부사로, 조동사나 be동사의 뒤, 일반동사의 앞에 위치한다.

0% → 100%

never	sometimes	often	usually	always
결코 … 않다	때때로	자주	보통, 대개	항상

I *will* **never** be late again. (나는 결코 다시 늦지 않을 것이다.)

Sue *is* **usually** nice to everybody. (Sue는 대개 모두에게 친절하다.)

He **often** *goes* to Chinese restaurants. (그는 자주 중국 식당에 간다.)

Check-Up

A 다음 밑줄 친 부분이 수식하는 말에 동그라미(O) 표시하시오.

1 Tom is too lazy.

2 Kangaroos have short fur.

3 Junhee ran very slowly in the race.

4 Listen carefully to your English teacher.

WORDS

A
lazy 형 게으른
fur 명 (동물의) 털
race 명 경주
carefully 부 주의하여

B 다음 괄호 안에서 알맞은 말을 고르시오.

1 I don't have (much / many) time.

2 My classmates are very (friend / friendly).

3 She found a (few / little) coins under the sofa.

4 Lucas prayed (silent / silently) for a few minutes.

5 (Sad / Sadly), my grandfather passed away last month.

B
coin 명 동전
pray 동 기도하다
silent 형 조용한
pass away 돌아가시다

C 다음 괄호 안의 빈도부사가 들어갈 위치로 알맞은 곳을 고르시오.

1 I (①) drink (②) green tea (③) after lunch (④). (always)

2 He (①) is (②) busy (③) with his work (④). (usually)

3 You (①) can (②) see (③) dolphins (④) here. (sometimes)

C
be busy with …로 바쁘다

D 다음 빈칸에 들어갈 수 있는 것을 보기 에서 모두 고르시오.

보기 ⓐ few ⓑ a little ⓒ many ⓓ a lot of

1 There is __________ air on this planet.

2 They met __________ models in the show.

3 We bought __________ cheese at the market.

4 Last month, __________ kids visited the amusement park.

D
planet 명 행성

GRAMMAR FOCUS

B 비교 구문

1 형용사와 부사의 비교급과 최상급

둘 이상의 대상을 비교할 때 형용사와 부사의 비교급과 최상급을 쓰며, 형용사와 부사의 기본 형태를 원급이라고 한다.

1) 비교급과 최상급 만드는 법

	형용사 · 부사의 형태	비교급 / 최상급 만드는 법	원급	비교급	최상급
규칙 변화	대부분의 단어	원급+-er/-est	thick	thick**er**	thick**est**
	-e로 끝나는 단어	원급+-r/-st	nice	nice**r**	nice**st**
	「자음+y」로 끝나는 단어	y를 i로 고치고+-er/-est	pretty	pretti**er**	pretti**est**
	「단모음+단자음」으로 끝나는 단어	자음을 한 번 더 쓰고 +-er/-est	hot	hot**ter**	hot**test**
	일부 2음절 단어, 3음절 이상의 단어	more/most+원급	amazing	**more** amazing	**most** amazing
불규칙 변화			good/well	better	best
			bad/ill	worse	worst
			many/much	more	most
			little	less	least

2 비교 구문

1) 원급 비교 「as+원급+as」: '…만큼 ~한[하게]'

Sarah is **as kind as** her sister.

He sings **as well as** Justin.

2) 비교급 비교 「비교급+than」: '…보다 더 ~한[하게]'

Her eyes are **darker than** yours.

Beef is **more expensive than** pork.

3) 최상급 비교 「the+최상급」: '가장 …한[하게]'

This is **the tallest** tower in the world.

The most exciting part was the parade.

TIPS

「the+최상급+in/of+명사」

1 **「the+최상급+in+장소나 범위를 나타내는 단수명사」**: '~에서 가장 …한[하게]'
He is **the smartest** boy **in his class**. (그는 그의 반에서 가장 똑똑한 소년이다.)

2 **「the+최상급+of+비교 대상이 되는 복수명사」**: '~ 중에서 가장 …한[하게]'
English is **the easiest of all subjects**. (영어는 모든 과목들 중에서 가장 쉽다.)

Check-Up

A 다음 괄호 안에서 알맞은 말을 고르시오.

1 My cat jumps higher (as / than) your dog.
2 This is the (longer / longest) river in Asia.
3 Volleyball is as interesting (as / than) basketball.
4 Health is the (more / most) important thing in our life.

B 다음 괄호 안의 단어를 이용하여 빈칸에 알맞은 말을 쓰시오.

1 This ball is ________ than that ball. (light)
2 He is as ________ ________ his neighbors. (wise)
3 My dress is ________ ________ than hers. (beautiful)
4 Your house is ________ ________ building in our town. (old)

C 다음 밑줄 친 부분을 바르게 고치시오.

1 Karl swims well than Paul. → ________
2 This book is as thinner as a notebook. → ________
3 Tomorrow will be more warm than today. → ________
4 Colin is the most tall student in his school. → ________

D 다음 우리말과 일치하도록 괄호 안의 단어를 이용하여 문장을 완성하시오.

1 나는 Dan보다 더 일찍 일어났다. (early)
→ I got up ________ ________ Dan.
2 네 손은 내 것만큼 크다. (big)
→ Your hands are ________ ________ ________ mine.
3 바이칼호는 지구에서 가장 깊다. (deep)
→ Lake Baikal is ________ ________ on Earth.

WORDS

A
river 명 강
volleyball 명 배구

B
light 형 가벼운
neighbor 명 이웃
wise 형 지혜로운

C
thin 형 얇은

D
lake 명 호수

Grammar Practice

A 다음 괄호 안에서 알맞은 말을 고르시오.

1 I had (a few / a little) money at that time.
2 You should walk (careful / carefully) on the ice.
3 Tim is the (younger / youngest) boy in the group.
4 This movie is (as gloomy / more gloomy) as the novel.

WORDS

A
careful 형 조심하는
gloomy 형 우울한, 침울한
novel 명 소설

B 다음 밑줄 친 부분을 바르게 고치시오.

1 I solved the math problem easy. → ________
2 He works hard than anyone else. → ________
3 She fried a little potatoes in a pan. → ________
4 The playground is largest place in this school. → ________
5 Alexander writes often letters to his parents. → ________

B
playground 명 운동장

C 다음 괄호 안의 단어를 빈칸에 알맞은 형태로 쓰시오.

1 Maria comes home very ________. (late)
2 This candy is ________ than ice cream. (sweet)
3 Wednesday is the ________ day of the week. (busy)
4 Madison Avenue is the ________ street from here. (close)

C
sweet 형 달콤한
avenue 명 거리

D 다음 두 문장과 같은 뜻이 되도록 괄호 안의 단어를 이용하여 문장을 완성하시오.

1 Carrie weighs 50 kg. Joanna weighs 53 kg, and Anna weighs 49 kg.
→ Joanna is ________ ________ of the three girls. (heavy)
2 Andrew runs 100 meters in 12 seconds. Billy runs 100 meters in 14 seconds.
→ Andrew runs ________ ________ Billy. (fast)

D
weigh 동 무게가 …이다
heavy 형 무거운
second 명 (시간 단위의) 초

내신 완성 Grammar Practice

1 다음 빈칸에 들어갈 말이 바르게 짝지어진 것은?

• We have too __________ homework today.
• New York is the most crowded city __________ all the cities.

① many - of
② many - in
③ much - at
④ much - in
⑤ much - of

2 다음 표의 내용과 일치하지 않는 것은?

Item	Coat	Scarf	Gloves	Boots
Price	$70	$40	$40	$60

① The scarf is as cheap as the gloves.
② The gloves are cheaper than the boots.
③ The coat is the most expensive item of all.
④ The boots are cheaper than the scarf.
⑤ The cheapest items are the scarf and the gloves.

3 다음 밑줄 친 부분 중 어법상 바르지 못한 것은?

① John practiced jump rope hard.
② Who is the tallest man over there?
③ I will never forget our promise again.
④ You should wear a warmly sweater in winter.
⑤ The white vest is better than the brown one.

4 다음 우리말과 일치하도록 괄호 안의 말을 바르게 배열하시오.

(1) 나는 보통 자기 전에 양치한다. (my teeth, usually, brush)
→ I ______________________ before bed.

(2) 우리는 스마트폰으로 항상 날씨를 확인할 수 있다.
(always, the weather, check, can)
→ We ______________________ with a smartphone.

WORDS

1
crowded 형 붐비는, 혼잡한

2
scarf 명 스카프
cheap 형 (값이) 싼

3
jump rope 줄넘기
promise 명 약속
vest 명 조끼

서술형에 나오는 WRITING

A 다음 우리말과 일치하도록 괄호 안의 단어를 바르게 배열하시오.

1 나는 자주 내 여동생에게 화가 난다. (angry, I, often, am)

→ ______________________ with my sister.

2 그는 이전에 수많은 실수를 저질렀다. (made, lots, he, mistakes, of)

→ ______________________ before.

B 다음 Lena의 일상을 나타낸 표를 보고, 보기 처럼 괄호 안의 단어를 이용하여 문장을 완성하시오.

Activity	Mon.	Tue.	Wed.	Thu.	Fri.	Sat.	Sun.
eat breakfast							
draw pictures	○	○	○		○		
do her homework		○		○			
walk her dog	○	○	○	○	○	○	○

보기 Lena sometimes does her homework. (sometimes)

1 Lena ______________________. (never)

2 Lena ______________________. (always)

3 Lena ______________________. (usually)

C 다음 가수들의 인기투표 결과를 보고, popular를 이용하여 비교하는 문장을 완성하시오.

1 Sam is ______________ Emma.

2 Emma is ______________ Scarlet.

3 Sam is ______________ singer of the three.

READING WITH GRAMMAR

1

Do you want to see **the longest** staircase in the world? Then visit Mt. Niesen in Switzerland. The staircase goes up to the top of the mountain. It is 3.4 kilometers long, with 11,674 steps. That's **a lot of** steps! Climbing to the top is **hard**. It is the same as climbing the *Empire State Building **more than** seven times.

Most of the year, the staircase is **closed** to visitors. However, it is **open** for one day in June every year. On that day, the Niesenlauf, a **special** staircase race, is held. Hundreds of participants try to climb the staircase <u>다른 주자들보다 더 빠르게</u>. **The fastest** time on record was one hour and two minutes!

*Empire State Building: 엠파이어 스테이트 빌딩
(뉴욕시 소재 102층 고층 건물)

1 Niesen산의 계단에 대한 위 글의 내용과 일치하지 <u>않는</u> 것은?

① 세계에서 가장 긴 계단이다.
② 10,000개 이상의 단으로 이루어졌다.
③ 6월 한 달 동안 방문객에게 개방된다.
④ 이 계단을 오르는 대회에 수백 명이 참가한다.
⑤ 이 계단을 오르는 대회의 최단 기록은 1시간 2분이다.

서술형

2 위 글의 밑줄 친 우리말을 괄호 안의 말을 이용하여 영작하시오.

→ ________ ________ ________ ________ ________
(quickly, other runners)

WORDS staircase 명 계단 top 명 맨 위 (부분), 꼭대기 climb 동 [1] ________ hard 형 어려운, 힘든 closed 형 문을 닫은, 폐쇄된 visitor 명 방문객 hundreds of 수백의 participant 명 참가자 on record 기록되어 있는, 기록상의
문제 quickly 부 빨리[빠르게]

2

Q Yesterday, I was watching an Olympic medal ceremony on TV. The gold medalist looked like **the happiest** person in the world. The bronze medalist seemed **very happy**, too. However, the silver medalist looked (A) sad than the others. Why didn't she feel **happier than** the bronze medalist?

A The medalists feel **happy** or **unhappy** because of ________. Silver medalists may think, "I **almost** won. I could be (B) good than the gold medalist." And bronze medalists may think, "At least I got a medal! I **almost** missed it." In other words, silver medalists compare themselves with the winners. However, bronze medalists compare themselves with the non-medalists. That's why bronze medalists feel **happier than** silver medalists.

1 **Which is the best choice for the blank?**

① the winner
② their scores
③ their attitude
④ the Olympic Games
⑤ their coaches' support

2 **Write the correct forms of (A) and (B).**

(A) ________ (B) ________

WORDS medal ceremony 시상식 medalist 명 메달리스트 bronze 명 동, 구리 seem 동 [1] ________ other 대 다른 사람[것] almost 부 거의 at least 적어도, 최소한 miss 동 [2] ________ compare A with B A와 B를 비교하다
문제 score 명 득점, 점수 attitude 명 태도[자세], 사고방식 coach 명 코치 support 명 지지, 지원

A 습관 묻고 답하기

A: **What do you usually do** after school**?**
(넌 방과 후에 주로 무엇을 하니?)

B: I **usually** play baseball with my friends.
(난 주로 친구들과 야구를 해.)

A: Sounds fun! **How often do you** play**?**
(재미있겠다! 얼마나 자주 해?)

B: **Three times a week.**
(일주일에 세 번.)

'너는 주로 무엇을 하니?'의 의미로 상대방의 습관을 물을 때는 'What do you usually do ...?'라고 말할 수 있으며, 이에 대해 'I usually ...'로 대답할 수 있다. 어떤 행동을 얼마나 자주 하는지 물을 때는 'How often do you ...?'라고 말할 수 있으며, 이에 대한 대답은 once(한 번), twice(두 번), 숫자+times 등으로 말할 수 있다.

EXPRESSION PLUS

A: **Do you often** eat out**?** (너는 자주 외식을 하니?)
B: Yes, I do. **I usually** eat out at lunch. (응, 그래. 나는 주로 점심에 외식을 해.)

A: **Do you** take a shower **every day?** (너는 매일 샤워를 하니?)
B: Yes. I take a shower **once a day**. (응. 나는 하루에 한 번 샤워를 해.)

Check-Up

1 다음 대화의 빈칸에 들어갈 말로 알맞은 것은?

A: How often do you check your email?
B: ______________________

① Five times a day.
② I got some emails.
③ I'm sorry, but I can't.
④ I'm writing an email to you.
⑤ What is your email address?

WORDS
1
check 동 확인하다
address 명 주소

2 다음 우리말과 일치하도록 빈칸에 알맞은 말을 쓰시오.

너는 일요일 아침에 주로 무엇을 하니?

→ ________ ________ ________ ________ ________ on Sunday mornings?

B 요청하고 답하기

A: **Can you do me a favor?**
(부탁 좀 들어주겠니?)

B: **Sure.** What is it, Mom?
(물론이죠. 뭔데요, 엄마?)

A: **Can you** clear the table**?**
(식탁 좀 치워 줄래?)

B: **Okay.**
(알겠어요.)

상대방에게 부탁을 할 때는 'Can you do me a favor?'나 'Can you ...?'라고 말할 수 있다. 요청을 받아들일 때는 'Sure.', 거절할 때는 'I'm sorry, but I can't.' 등으로 대답한다.

EXPRESSION PLUS

A: Can you return my book to the library? (내 책을 도서관에 반납해 줄래?)
B: **Sure. No problem.** (그래. 문제없어.) / **I'm afraid I can't.** (미안하지만 못해.)

A: **Wash** the dog, **please**. (개를 좀 목욕시켜줘.)
B: **Sorry, but I'm busy.** (미안하지만, 난 바빠.)

Check-Up

1 다음 대화의 빈칸에 들어갈 말로 알맞은 것은?

A: Can you do me a favor?
B: ______________________

① I'm afraid I can.
② Okay. What is it?
③ What do you do?
④ Can you tell me why?
⑤ You can say that again.

2 다음 우리말과 일치하도록 괄호 안의 단어를 이용하여 문장을 완성하시오.

나에게 다시 알려 주겠니? (can, remind)

→ ________ ________ ________ ________ again?

WORDS

2
remind 동 상기시키다, 다시 한 번 알려 주다

FINAL TEST

1 다음 빈칸에 들어갈 단어로 가장 알맞은 것은?

open : closed = light : ________

① lazy ② wise
③ heavy ④ careful
⑤ crowded

2 다음 밑줄 친 부분의 뜻이 바르지 못한 것은?

① It was the hottest year on record.
기록상의
② You should try at least once.
최대한
③ Hundreds of people gathered at the zoo.
수백의
④ She is busy with her homework.
…로 바쁘다
⑤ He compared himself with me.
…와 ~를 비교하다

[3-4] 다음 대화의 빈칸에 들어갈 말로 알맞은 것을 고르시오.

3
A: ____________________
B: Twice a year.

① How's it going?
② When do you eat lunch?
③ How long is your vacation?
④ How often do you cut your hair?
⑤ What do you usually do on Saturdays?

4
A: ____________________
B: I'm sorry, but I can't.

① How can I help you?
② Do you need the key?
③ What can I do for you?
④ Can you wash the dishes?
⑤ May I open the door, please?

5 대화가 자연스럽게 이어지도록 (A)~(D)를 바르게 배열하시오.

(A) Okay, I will.
(B) Sure. What is it, Steven?
(C) Please turn down the music.
(D) Can you do me a favor?

______ → ______ → ______ → ______

자주 나와요

6 다음 중 짝지어진 대화가 어색한 것은?

① A: Please plant the trees.
B: Okay, I will.
② A: Can you do me a favor?
B: Sure. No problem.
③ A: Can you pick up some trash?
B: I'm afraid I can't.
④ A: What do you usually do at 7 p.m.?
B: I usually have dinner.
⑤ A: How often do you eat vegetables?
B: Sorry, but I'm busy.

7 다음 중 형용사와 부사가 잘못 연결된 것은?

① fast - fastly ② free - freely
③ good - well ④ quiet - quietly
⑤ happy - happily

8 다음 중 원급-비교급-최상급이 잘못 연결된 것은?

① little - less - least
② fat - fatter - fattest
③ bad - worse - worst
④ ugly - uglyer - uglyest
⑤ easily - more easily - most easily

9 다음 빈칸에 들어갈 말로 알맞은 것은?

Bill is as ________ as you.

① strong ② stronger
③ strongest ④ more strong
⑤ most strong

자주 나와요

[10-11] 다음 대화의 빈칸에 들어갈 말이 바르게 짝지어진 것을 고르시오.

10
A: Add ________ milk to the bowl.
B: Sorry, but I don't have milk.
A: Do you have ________ eggs, then?
B: Yes, I do.

① a few - few ② a few - a few
③ much - a little ④ a little - a few
⑤ a little - a little

11
A: The ending of this novel is ________.
B: But, ________, the main character doesn't die.

① sad - lucky ② sad - luckier
③ sad - luckily ④ sadly - lucky
⑤ sadly - luckily

12 다음 빈칸에 들어갈 말이 나머지 넷과 다른 것은?

① Tony is as rich ________ Chris.
② My hair is longer ________ Joe's.
③ Jack's room is bigger ________ this one.
④ The sun is brighter ________ the moon.
⑤ My bag is more useful ________ yours.

[13-14] 다음 우리말과 일치하도록 괄호 안의 단어를 이용하여 문장을 완성하시오.

13 너는 네 형보다 더 날씬해 보인다. (thin)

→ You look ________ ________ your brother.

14 스페인어는 이 셋 중 가장 어려운 언어이다. (difficult)

→ Spanish is ________ ________ ________ language of these three.

15 다음 대화를 읽고, 아침 식사를 자주 하는 순서대로 학생들의 이름을 나열하시오.

Teacher: How often do you eat breakfast?
Woody: I usually do.
Kelly: I often eat it.
Daniel: I sometimes do.
Alex: I always eat breakfast.

________ → ________ → ________ → ________

어려워요

16 다음 중 어법상 바르지 못한 것은?

① I will help always you.
② He is sometimes very sick.
③ My dad often cooks for me.
④ She usually takes a nap at noon.
⑤ Michael never washes his clothes.

[17-18] 다음 밑줄 친 부분을 바르게 고치시오.

17 Amanda can jump highly.

→ ____________

18 This candy has too many sugar.

→ ____________

서술형

[19-20] 다음 우리말과 일치하도록 괄호 안의 말을 바르게 배열하시오.

19 화면이 달력만큼 작다.
(the screen, small, as, as, a calendar, is)

→ ____________

20 그녀는 그녀의 반에서 가장 좋은 점수를 받았다.
(best, got, the, score, her class, she, in)

→ ____________

내신 완성 서술형

21 다음 밑줄 친 부분 중 어법상 틀린 것을 찾아 바르게 고치시오.

A: Do you go to bed ① late?
B: Yes. I ② usually go to bed at 1 a.m. I ③ always play online games before bed.
A: Do you get up ④ early?
B: No. So I ⑤ often am late for school.

____________ → ____________

[22-23] 다음 그림을 보고, 괄호 안의 단어를 이용하여 세 사람의 키를 비교하는 문장을 완성하시오.

22 Emily is ________ Brenda. (short)

23 Jim is ________ person of all. (tall)

24 다음 대화의 빈칸에 들어갈 말을 조건에 맞게 영작하시오.

A: ____________
B: I have flute lessons once a week.

조건 1: how와 often을 이용할 것
조건 2: 총 7단어로 작성할 것

→ ____________

WORD LIST

Grammar

□ lazy	형 게으른
□ fur	명 (동물의) 털
□ race	명 경주
□ carefully	부 주의하여
□ coin	명 동전
□ pray	동 기도하다
□ silent	형 조용한
□ pass away	돌아가시다
□ be busy with	…로 바쁘다
□ planet	명 행성
□ river	명 강
□ volleyball	명 배구
□ light	형 가벼운
□ wise	형 지혜로운
□ thin	형 얇은
□ lake	명 호수
□ careful	형 조심하는
□ novel	명 소설
□ playground	명 운동장
□ avenue	명 거리
□ weigh	동 무게가 …이다
□ heavy	형 무거운
□ second	명 (시간 단위의) 초
□ crowded	형 붐비는, 혼잡한
□ cheap	형 (값이) 싼
□ promise	명 약속

Reading

□ staircase	명 계단
□ top	명 맨 위 (부분), 꼭대기
□ climb	동 오르다
□ hard	형 어려운, 힘든
□ closed	형 문을 닫은, 폐쇄된
□ visitor	명 방문객
□ hundreds of	수백의
□ participant	명 참가자
□ quickly	부 빨리[빠르게]
□ seem	동 (…처럼) 보이다, …인 것 같다
□ other	대 다른 사람[것]
□ almost	부 거의
□ at least	적어도, 최소한
□ miss	동 놓치다
□ compare A with B	A와 B를 비교하다
□ score	명 득점, 점수
□ coach	명 코치
□ support	명 지지, 지원

Communication

□ check	동 확인하다
□ remind	동 상기시키다, 다시 한 번 알려 주다

Final Test

□ gather	동 모이다
□ plant	동 (나무 · 씨앗 등을) 심다
□ pick up	줍다
□ trash	명 쓰레기
□ ugly	형 못생긴, 추한
□ take a nap	낮잠을 자다
□ noon	명 정오

CHAPTER 09

to부정사

GET READY

I want **to know** your name.
(나는 너의 이름을 알고 싶어.)

It's time **to close** the store.
(가게를 닫을 시간이다.)

She ran **to catch** the train.
(그녀는 열차를 타기 위해 달렸다.)

to부정사는 「to+동사원형」의 형태이며, 문장에서 명사, 형용사, 부사 등 다양한 역할을 해요.

GRAMMAR FOCUS

A to부정사

「to+동사원형」 형태인 to부정사는 문장에서의 역할에 따라 명사적, 형용사적, 부사적 용법으로 나뉜다.

B 명사적 용법

to부정사는 명사처럼 문장에서 주어, 목적어, 보어의 역할을 한다.

1 주어 역할

'…하는 것은'으로 해석하며, 주어로 쓰인 to부정사는 단수 취급한다.

To exercise regularly is a good habit.

To understand this sentence is not easy.

내신 POINT PLUS

가주어(it)와 진주어(to부정사)

to부정사(구)가 주어인 경우, 주어 자리에 it을 쓰고 to부정사(구)는 뒤로 보내는 것이 일반적이다.
이때 it을 가주어, to부정사를 진주어라 하며 가주어 it은 따로 해석하지 않는다.

To play tennis is fun. → It is fun to play tennis. (테니스를 치는 것은 즐겁다.)
(To play tennis: 주어 / It: 가주어 / to play tennis: 진주어)

2 목적어 역할

'…하는 것을, …하기를'으로 해석한다. to부정사를 목적어로 취하는 동사는 want, like, need, decide, plan, hope, promise, agree, fail, start, begin 등이 있다.

I *want* **to be** alone now.

He *likes* **to watch** sad movies.

3 보어 역할

'…하는 것(이다)'라고 해석하며, 주어의 내용을 보충 설명한다.

Jen's wish is **to open** her own café.

My dream is **to invent** a time machine.

TIPS

to부정사의 부정형 「not[never] to-v」

to부정사의 부정형은 to부정사 앞에 not이나 never를 써서 나타낸다.
We agreed **to buy** a new computer. (우리는 새 컴퓨터를 사기로 동의했다.)
→ We agreed **not to buy** a new computer. (우리는 새 컴퓨터를 사지 않기로 동의했다.)
She promised **to return**. (그녀는 돌아오기로 약속했다.)
→ She promised **never to return**. (그녀는 절대 돌아오지 않기로 약속했다.)

Check-Up

A 다음 문장에서 밑줄 친 부분의 역할을 쓰시오.

1 <u>To read</u> many books is my goal. ________

2 She began <u>to sing</u> in a soft voice. ________

3 It is exciting <u>to meet</u> new people. ________

4 My plan is <u>to visit</u> Canada this winter. ________

B 다음 괄호 안에서 알맞은 말을 고르시오.

1 He wants (go / to go) to the festival.

2 It is a good idea (ask / to ask) for help.

3 Morrie's hobby is to (collect / collects) postcards.

4 They failed (getting / to get) good grades in school.

C 다음 밑줄 친 부분을 바르게 고치시오.

1 It is unhealthy to <u>ate</u> fast food. → ________

2 <u>That</u> is scary to ride a roller coaster. → ________

3 He planned <u>propose</u> to his girlfriend. → ________

4 Her job is to <u>teaching</u> English to students. → ________

D 다음 우리말과 일치하도록 괄호 안의 단어를 이용하여 문장을 완성하시오.

1 나의 숙제는 보고서를 쓰는 것이다. (write)

→ My homework is ________ ________ a report.

2 기타를 연주하는 것은 재미있다. (play)

→ It is interesting ________ ________ the guitar.

3 그녀는 늦지 않을 것을 약속했다. (be)

→ She promised ________ ________ ________ late.

4 그들은 Susan을 파티에 초대하기로 결심했다. (invite)

→ They decided ________ ________ Susan to the party.

WORDS

A
goal 명 목표
voice 명 목소리
plan 명 계획

B
collect 동 모으다, 수집하다
postcard 명 그림엽서
grade 명 성적, 학점

C
unhealthy 형 건강에 좋지 못한
propose 동 제안하다; *청혼하다

D
invite 동 초대하다

C 형용사적 용법

to부정사는 형용사처럼 앞에 있는 명사나 대명사를 수식하기도 하며, '…할, …하는'으로 해석한다.

We have a lot of things **to do**.

He didn't have time **to have** lunch.

I have something **to say** about this problem.

TIPS

「(대)명사+to-v+전치사」

to부정사의 수식을 받는 (대)명사가 to부정사 뒤에 오는 전치사의 목적어인 경우, 전치사를 생략해서는 안 된다.
There is *a chair* **to sit on**. (앉을 의자가 하나 있다.) (← sit on a chair)
There is a chair to sit. (x)
We're looking for *a house* **to live in**. (우리는 살 집을 찾고 있다.) (← live in a house)
I need *someone* **to talk to**. (나는 대화할 사람이 필요하다.) (← talk to someone)

D 부사적 용법

to부정사는 부사처럼 동사, 형용사, 다른 부사를 수식하기도 한다. 이때 문맥에 따라 목적, 감정의 원인, 결과 등의 의미를 나타낸다.

1 목적: '…하기 위해서'

I studied hard **to pass** the exam.
She went to the library **to borrow** books.
He woke up early **to take** the first bus.

TIPS

「in order to-v」

목적을 나타내는 to부정사는 그 의미를 더 분명히 하기 위해 「in order to-v」로 바꿔 쓸 수 있다.
They went out **in order to walk** around. (그들은 걸어 다니기 위해 밖으로 나갔다.)

2 감정의 원인: '…해서, …하게 되어'

to부정사가 happy, sad, glad, sorry, surprised 등 감정을 나타내는 형용사 뒤에 쓰일 때는 그 감정의 원인을 나타낸다.
I am *happy* **to hear** the test results.
She was *sad* **to leave** her hometown.

3 결과: '(…해서) ~하다'

She grew up **to be** a poet.
The man lived **to be** 100 years old.

Check-Up

A 다음 문장에서 밑줄 친 부분의 용법을 보기 에서 골라 쓰시오.

보기 형용사적 용법　　부사적 용법 (결과)　　부사적 용법 (감정의 원인)

1 I am pleased to work with you. ___________
2 Evan grew up to be a pilot. ___________
3 We want something to drink. ___________

WORDS

A
pleased 형 기쁜
pilot 명 조종사

B 다음 괄호 안에서 알맞은 말을 고르시오.

1 I have many friends to (play / play with).
2 She dressed up to (attend / attending) a wedding.
3 Do we have enough money (to buy / buying) the sofa?
4 Clara sent a message in order (say / to say) goodbye to him.

B
dress up 격식을 차려입다
attend 동 참석하다
say goodbye 작별 인사를 하다

C 다음 괄호 안의 단어를 빈칸에 알맞은 형태로 쓰시오.

1 I have a question ___________ you. (ask)
2 They left for Busan ___________ their parents. (visit)
3 He was surprised ___________ the loud sirens. (hear)
4 She eats lots of fresh vegetables ___________ healthy. (stay)

C
leave for …로 떠나다
surprised 형 놀란
siren 명 사이렌

D 다음 우리말과 일치하도록 괄호 안의 단어를 이용하여 문장을 완성하시오.

1 나는 두려울 것이 없다. (nothing, fear)
→ I have ___________ ___________ ___________.
2 그녀는 90세까지 살았다. (live, be)
→ She ___________ ___________ ___________ 90 years old.
3 그들은 서로를 만나서 기뻤다. (glad, meet)
→ They were ___________ ___________ ___________ each other.
4 우리는 콘서트홀에 입장하기 위해 빨리 달렸다. (enter)
→ We ran fast ___________ ___________ ___________ ___________ the concert hall.

D
fear 동 두려워하다
each other 서로

Grammar Practice

A 다음 괄호 안에서 알맞은 말을 고르시오.

1 He wanted (to take / taking) a nap.

2 To learn foreign languages (is / are) difficult.

3 I took notes in order (not to / to not) forget.

4 Do you need someone to (study / study with)?

5 I'm sorry (bother / to bother) you at this hour.

B 다음 빈칸에 들어갈 말을 보기 에서 골라 알맞은 형태로 쓰시오.

보기 be cancel get read apologize

1 His goal is __________ a better job.

2 Sally grew up __________ a musician.

3 It is important __________ for mistakes.

4 She called the hotel __________ the reservation.

5 Let's buy a newspaper __________ on the subway.

C 다음 밑줄 친 부분을 바르게 고치시오.

1 It is dangerous to <u>driving</u> fast. → __________

2 Do you have a spoon <u>with to eat</u>? → __________

3 Wendy hoped <u>meeting</u> the movie star. → __________

4 Betty drank coffee in order <u>stay</u> up late. → __________

D 다음 우리말과 일치하도록 괄호 안의 단어를 이용하여 문장을 완성하시오.

1 그들은 경기에서 져서 슬펐다. (sad, lose)

→ They were __________ __________ __________ the game.

2 나는 회의를 준비할 충분한 시간이 없었다. (time, prepare)

→ I didn't have enough __________ __________ __________ for the meeting.

WORDS

A
nap 명 낮잠
foreign language 외국어
bother 동 신경 쓰이게 하다, 귀찮게 하다

B
cancel 동 취소하다
apologize 동 사과하다
mistake 명 실수
reservation 명 예약

C
dangerous 형 위험한
stay up 깨어 있다

내신 완성 Grammar Practice

1 다음 빈칸에 들어갈 말이 바르게 짝지어진 것은?

- He likes ________ to classical music.
- I don't have anything ________ about.

① listen - worry
② listen - to worry
③ listens - to worry
④ to listen - worry
⑤ to listen - to worry

2 다음 밑줄 친 부분의 쓰임이 보기 와 같은 것은?

보기 Nancy turned on the TV <u>to watch</u> the news.

① His dream is <u>to become</u> a vet.
② There are some shoes <u>to wear</u>.
③ They agreed <u>to change</u> their plan.
④ I opened the curtains <u>to look</u> outside.
⑤ It is really fun <u>to play</u> baseball with them.

3 다음 중 어법상 <u>틀린</u> 것을 <u>모두</u> 고르시오. (2개)

① Jack decided to forgive her.
② He has babies to take care of.
③ I failed to get a driver's license.
④ It is impossible to not be late for school.
⑤ She took an airplane in order to went to Paris.

4 다음 우리말과 일치하도록 괄호 안의 말을 바르게 배열하시오.

(1) Frank는 뱀을 봐서 놀랐다. (see, surprised, to, was)
→ Frank ____________________ a snake.

(2) 매일 아침 7시에 일어나는 것이 나의 습관이다. (is, to, it, get up, my habit)
→ ____________________ at 7 a.m. every morning.

WORDS

1
classical music 고전 음악

2
vet 명 수의사

3
forgive 동 용서하다
driver's license 면허증
impossible 형 불가능한

4
snake 명 뱀

서술형에 나오는 WRITING

A **다음 우리말과 일치하도록 괄호 안의 말을 바르게 배열하시오.**

1 그의 직업은 벼를 재배하는 것이다.
(is, grow, job, his, to, rice)
→ ______________________________

2 우리는 세탁할 많은 옷이 있다.
(wash, have, clothes, to, we, a lot of)
→ ______________________________

3 여기서 다이빙하는 것은 안전하지 않다.
(not, to, is, dive, safe, it, here)
→ ______________________________

B **다음 우리말과 일치하도록 괄호 안의 말을 이용하여 문장을 완성하시오.**

1 나는 작은 화분에 씨앗들을 심기로 계획했다. (plan, plant seeds)
→ ______________________________ in the small pot.

2 물을 낭비하는 것은 좋지 않다. (good, waste water)
→ It is not ______________________________.

C **다음 그림을 보고, 괄호 안의 말과 to부정사를 이용하여 문장을 완성하시오.**

1

(the kitchen, do the dishes)
He went to ______________________________.

2

(shocked, see the price)
The girl was ______________________________.

1

The Producer of *The Smiths*

My name is Matt. I'm a big fan of your TV show, *The Smiths*. It is really fun, and I never miss an episode. But I have something ① to tell you about yesterday's episode.
It was about an overweight boy. Every girl hated the boy and said bad things about him. He had no friends ② to talk to. I was very angry ③ to see it. I'm also overweight. But I have many friends, and they all like me. It is wrong ④ to make fun of overweight people. I hope not ⑤ to watch another episode like this.

Matt from Texas

1 위 글을 쓴 목적으로 알맞은 것은?

① TV쇼의 제작자를 칭찬하기 위해
② TV쇼의 재방송을 요청하기 위해
③ TV쇼 주인공 교체를 제안하기 위해
④ TV쇼의 내용에 불만을 제기하기 위해
⑤ TV쇼의 인기 하락 원인을 지적하기 위해

2 위 글의 ①~⑤ 중 다음 보기 의 밑줄 친 부분과 쓰임이 같은 것은?

보기 They felt happy to come back home.

① ② ③ ④ ⑤

WORDS producer 명 생산자; *제작자 miss 동 놓치다 episode 명 에피소드, 1회 방송분 overweight 형 1 __________
hate 동 2 __________ make fun of …를 놀리다

2

A poor boy had nothing **to eat**. He decided **to ask** for food at the nearest house and knocked on the door. Surprisingly, a young girl came out, invited the boy in, and gave him a ham sandwich.

Twenty years later, the young girl grew up **to be** a woman. But she was terribly ill. Her doctors tried everything, but she kept getting sicker. Finally, her family asked a famous doctor **to treat** her. It took several months, but he cured her! When the woman went to his hospital pay her bill, she was shocked **to find** something out. Everything was free! Instead of a bill, the nurse gave her a note. It said, "Your bill was paid for with a sandwich twenty years ago."

1 **Which is the best title for the passage?**

① Searching for Free Hospitals
② Giving Prizes to Good Doctors
③ Selling Sandwiches to Poor Children
④ Looking for the Best Sandwich Maker
⑤ Repaying a Sandwich with a Free Cure

2 **Correct the underlined word.**

→ ______________

WORDS **poor** 형 가난한 **knock** 동 두드리다 **surprisingly** 부 놀랍게도 **terribly** 부 몹시 **ill** 형 [1] __________
treat 동 대하다; *치료하다 **several** 형 몇몇의 **cure** 동 [2] __________ **pay** 동 지불하다 **bill** 명 청구서, 계산서; 청구 금액
instead of ··· 대신에 문제 **prize** 명 상 **repay** 동 (돈, 은혜 등을) 갚다

A 좋아하는 것 묻고 답하기

A: **What's your favorite** color**?**
(네가 가장 좋아하는 색은 뭐니?)

B: **My favorite** color **is** orange. **What** color **do you like** best**?**
(내가 가장 좋아하는 색은 주황색이야. 너는 무슨 색을 가장 좋아해?)

A: **I like** blue best.
(나는 파란색을 가장 좋아해.)

상대방에게 좋아하는 것을 물을 때는 'What is your favorite ...?'이나 'What ... do you like?'라고 말할 수 있다. 이에 대해 'My favorite ... is ~' 혹은 'I like[love] ...'로 대답할 수 있다.

EXPRESSION PLUS

A: **Do you like** sports**?** (너는 스포츠를 좋아하니?)
B: Yes. They are exciting. (응. 그것들은 흥미진진해.)

A: **What do you like to do** in summer**?** (너는 여름에 뭐 하는 것을 좋아하니?)
B: **I like to** swim in the sea. (나는 바다에서 수영하는 것을 좋아해.)

Check-Up

[1-2] 다음 대화의 빈칸에 들어갈 말로 알맞은 것을 고르시오.

1
A: ______________________________
B: I like to play the guitar.

① Why do you like to dance?
② What will you do on Saturday?
③ What subject do you like best?
④ What's your favorite kind of music?
⑤ What do you like to do in your free time?

2
A: What's your favorite snack?
B: ______________________________

① I love snacks.
② I like potato chips best.
③ It's not my favorite snack.
④ I don't have breakfast.
⑤ My favorite place is the cafeteria.

WORDS

1
kind 명 종류

2
cafeteria 명 카페테리아, 구내식당

B 상기시켜 주기

A: When will you leave the classroom?
(너 언제 교실을 나갈 거니?)

B: I'll leave soon.
(나는 곧 나갈 거야.)

A: **Remember to** turn the light off.
(전등 끄는 거 기억해.)

상대방에게 잊지 말아야 할 내용을 상기시킬 때는 'Remember to-v ...' 또는 'Don't forget to-v ...'라고 말할 수 있다.

EXPRESSION PLUS

A: I'll arrive home at around 9 p.m. (나는 저녁 9시쯤에 집에 도착할 거야.)
B: **Don't forget to** call me then. (그때 내게 전화하는 것을 잊지 마.)

A: **Never forget to** lock the door. (문을 잠그는 것을 절대 잊지 마.)
B: Okay, I won't. (응, 안 잊을게.)

Check-Up

1 다음 문장이 들어갈 위치로 가장 알맞은 곳은?

Don't forget to bring your bat.

A: What sport do you like best? (①)
B: I like baseball. (②) What about you?
A: (③) I love baseball, too! Let's play it together!
B: Great. (④)
A: Okay, I won't. (⑤)

2 다음 우리말과 일치하도록 괄호 안의 단어를 이용하여 빈칸에 알맞은 말을 쓰시오.

구명조끼를 입는 것을 기억해라. (wear)

→ __________ __________ __________ a life jacket.

WORDS

1
bat 명 (야구) 방망이

2
life jacket 구명조끼

FINAL TEST

1 다음 중 영어 단어와 우리말 뜻이 잘못 연결된 것은?

① collect - 모으다 ② cancel - 취소하다
③ prize - 가격 ④ terribly - 몹시
⑤ surprisingly - 놀랍게도

2 다음 빈칸에 들어갈 단어로 가장 알맞은 것은?

love : hate = rich : ________

① ill ② poor
③ pleased ④ impossible
⑤ unhealthy

3 다음 대화의 밑줄 친 문장과 바꿔 쓸 수 있는 것은?

A: What's your favorite movie?
B: I like *Romeo & Juliet*.

① What do you think?
② What do you like to do?
③ What movie did you see?
④ Do you like *Romeo & Juliet*?
⑤ What movie do you like best?

4 다음 중 짝지어진 대화가 어색한 것은?

① A: Do you like tennis?
B: No. It's too hard for me.
② A: Who's your favorite actor?
B: I love Tom Holland.
③ A: What do you like to do at home?
B: I like the kitchen.
④ A: I'm going to go to the pool.
B: Remember to bring your swimsuit.
⑤ A: I'm planning to travel to Daegu.
B: Don't forget to visit the traditional market.

5 다음 문장과 같은 뜻이 되도록 빈칸에 알맞은 말을 쓰시오.

Remember to wash your hands.

→ Don't ________ ________ ________ your hands.

[6-7] 다음 빈칸에 들어갈 말로 알맞은 것을 고르시오.

6 They agreed ________ the war.

① end ② ends
③ to end ④ ended
⑤ ending

7 We need more chairs ________.

① sit ② sat
③ to sit ④ to sit on
⑤ sitting

[8-10] 다음 우리말과 일치하도록 빈칸에 들어갈 알맞은 말을 고르시오.

8 그들은 바나나를 사기 위해 가게에 갔다.
→ They went to the store ________ bananas.

① buy ② bought
③ to buy ④ buying
⑤ to buying

9 그녀는 자라서 유명한 요리사가 되었다.

→ She grew up ________ a famous chef.

① be ② to be
③ being ④ to being
⑤ was

10 지킬 기본 규칙들이 있다.

→ There are basic ____________.

① to rules follow ② to follow rules
③ rules to follow ④ rules follow to
⑤ follow rules to

11 다음 우리말을 영어로 바르게 옮긴 것은?

네 이야기를 믿는 것은 어렵다.

① Believe your story is hard.
② Your story is hard believe.
③ It is hard to believe your story.
④ To believe your story it is hard.
⑤ I am hard to believe your story.

[12-14] 다음 우리말과 일치하도록 to부정사와 괄호 안의 말을 이용하여 문장을 완성하시오.

12 나는 나를 도와줄 사람을 찾고 있다. (person, help)

→ I'm looking for a ________ ________ ________ me.

13 우리는 포기하지 않기로 약속했다. (give up)

→ We promised ________ ________ ________ ________.

14 그는 성공하기 위해 최선을 다했다. (succeed)

→ He tried his best ________ ________ ________ ________.

! 어려워요

[15-16] 다음 밑줄 친 부분의 쓰임이 나머지 넷과 다른 것을 고르시오.

15 ① I like to watch cartoons.
② It is time to make a choice.
③ My goal is to read 100 books.
④ It is fun to travel to other countries.
⑤ Kate decided to tell me everything.

16 ① It is my job to answer the phone.
② It is the fastest way to the airport.
③ It is important to make good friends.
④ It is dangerous to play with fire.
⑤ It will be a great honor to meet the president.

! 자주 나와요

17 다음 보기 의 밑줄 친 부분과 쓰임이 다른 것은?

보기 There's no place to put this table.

① I have a clock to sell.
② I found a pen to write with.
③ She gave me something to drink.
④ He came to Korea to learn Korean.
⑤ Do you need someone to carry the box?

18 다음 보기 의 밑줄 친 부분과 쓰임이 같은 것은?

보기 They were glad to see their old teacher.

① It is difficult to use this app.
② He went out to look at the stars.
③ I am sorry to be late for the party.
④ I have many problems to solve.
⑤ She wanted to be a fashion designer.

어려워요

19 다음 중 어법상 바르지 못한 것은?

① I tried never to fail a test again.
② We hurried in order to be on time.
③ Nathan couldn't find a house to live.
④ Jane and I promised to meet today.
⑤ They were excited to catch a big fish.

서술형

[20-21] 다음 우리말과 일치하도록 괄호 안의 말을 바르게 배열하시오.

20 그들의 계획은 환경을 보호하는 것이다.
(to, is, the environment, protect, plan)

→ Their ______________________.

21 나는 그 소식을 듣기 위해 오래 기다렸다.
(waited, to, the news, a long time, hear)

→ I ______________________.

내신 완성 서술형

22 다음 문장을 보기 처럼 바꿔 쓰시오.

보기 To make curry was easy.
→ It was easy to make curry.

To finish the work isn't possible.
→ ______________________

[23-24] 다음 두 문장을 보기 처럼 한 문장으로 바꿔 쓰시오.

보기 I saved money.
I wanted to buy a car.
→ I saved money to buy a car.

23 He will go to the library.
He should return some books.

→ ______________________

24 She set her alarm.
She needed to get up early.

→ ______________________

WORD LIST

Grammar

☐ goal	명 목표
☐ voice	명 목소리
☐ collect	동 모으다, 수집하다
☐ postcard	명 그림엽서
☐ unhealthy	형 건강에 좋지 못한
☐ propose	동 제안하다; 청혼하다
☐ invite	동 초대하다
☐ pleased	형 기쁜
☐ pilot	명 조종사
☐ dress up	격식을 차려입다
☐ attend	동 참석하다
☐ say goodbye	작별 인사를 하다
☐ leave for	…로 떠나다
☐ surprised	형 놀란
☐ siren	명 사이렌
☐ fear	동 두려워하다
☐ each other	서로
☐ nap	명 낮잠
☐ foreign language	외국어
☐ cancel	동 취소하다
☐ apologize	동 사과하다
☐ mistake	명 실수
☐ reservation	명 예약
☐ dangerous	형 위험한
☐ stay up	깨어 있다
☐ classical music	고전 음악
☐ forgive	동 용서하다
☐ driver's license	면허증
☐ impossible	형 불가능한

Reading

☐ producer	명 생산자; 제작자
☐ miss	동 놓치다
☐ overweight	형 과체중의
☐ hate	동 몹시 싫어하다
☐ make fun of	…를 놀리다
☐ poor	형 가난한
☐ knock	동 두드리다
☐ surprisingly	부 놀랍게도
☐ terribly	부 몹시
☐ ill	형 아픈
☐ treat	동 대하다; 치료하다
☐ cure	동 낫게 하다
☐ pay	동 지불하다
☐ bill	명 청구서, 계산서; 청구 금액
☐ prize	명 상

Communication

☐ cafeteria	명 카페테리아, 구내식당
☐ bat	명 (야구) 방망이
☐ life jacket	구명조끼

Final Test

☐ swimsuit	명 수영복
☐ traditional	형 전통의, 전통적인
☐ succeed	동 성공하다
☐ cartoon	명 만화, 만화영화
☐ make a choice	선택하다
☐ honor	명 명예; 영광
☐ president	명 대통령, 회장
☐ save	동 구하다; (돈을) 모으다, 저축하다

CHAPTER 10

동명사

GET READY

Climbing the mountain was hard.
(등산을 하는 것은 힘들었다.)

I enjoy **watching** sports.
(나는 운동 경기를 보는 것을 즐긴다.)

My favorite activity is **cooking**.
(내가 가장 좋아하는 활동은 요리하는 것이다.)

동명사는 「동사원형+ing」의 형태로, 명칭대로 동사와 명사의 성질을 동시에 지녔어요. to부정사와 마찬가지로 동명사도 명사처럼 주어, 목적어, 보어의 역할을 해요.

GRAMMAR FOCUS

A 동명사

「동사원형+ing」 형태의 동명사는 문장에서 명사처럼 주어, 목적어, 보어 역할을 한다.

1 주어 역할

'…하는 것은'으로 해석하며, 주어로 쓰인 동명사(구)는 단수 취급한다.

Playing chess with you is fun.

Finding the building wasn't easy.

2 목적어 역할

'…하기를, …하는 것을'로 해석하며, 동사나 전치사의 목적어 역할을 한다.

1) 동사의 목적어

I *like* **collecting** pictures of cute animals.

They *started* **playing** the musical instruments.

2) 전치사의 목적어

She is good *at* **writing** mystery stories.

TIPS

동명사의 부정형 「not[never] v-ing」

동명사의 부정형은 동명사 앞에 not이나 never를 써서 나타낸다.

Not telling the truth is bad. (진실을 말하지 않는 것은 나쁘다.)

He regretted **never taking** care of his health. (그는 그의 건강을 전혀 돌보지 않은 것을 후회했다.)

3 보어 역할

'…하는 것(이다)'으로 해석하며, 주어의 내용을 보충 설명한다.

His hobby was **painting** flowers.

My goal is **getting** good grades on math tests.

MORE EXPRESSIONS

자주 쓰이는 동명사 표현

- go v-ing …하러 가다
- feel like v-ing …하고 싶다
- keep (on) v-ing 계속 …하다
- cannot[can't] help v-ing …하지 않을 수 없다
- spend+시간[돈]+v-ing …하는 데 시간[돈]을 쓰다
- stop … from v-ing …가 ~하는 것을 막다[방지하다]

He will **go fishing** on Friday. (그는 금요일에 낚시하러 갈 것이다.)

I **couldn't help taking** a break. (나는 쉬지 않을 수 없었다.)

She didn't **feel like talking** to him. (그녀는 그와 말하고 싶지 않았다.)

We **spent an hour fixing** our machine. (우리는 우리의 기계를 수리하는 데 한 시간을 썼다.)

Check-Up

A 다음 문장에서 밑줄 친 부분의 역할을 쓰시오.

1 Thank you for <u>inviting</u> me. ____________
2 His dream is <u>becoming</u> a doctor. ____________
3 She enjoyed <u>talking</u> with foreigners. ____________
4 <u>Wearing</u> sunglasses can protect your eyes. ____________

WORDS

A
foreigner 명 외국인
protect 동 보호하다

B 다음 괄호 안에서 알맞은 말을 고르시오.

1 Reading newspapers (is / are) very helpful.
2 (Raise / Raising) sheep requires special skills.
3 We should stop (use / using) so much shampoo.
4 They are interested in (to learn / learning) Korean.
5 She will finish (do / doing) her homework soon.

B
helpful 형 도움이 되는
raise 동 기르다
require 동 요구하다

C 다음 밑줄 친 부분을 바르게 고치시오.

1 <u>To taking</u> notes is a good habit. → ____________
2 Joe's goal is <u>exercise</u> every day. → ____________
3 We spent 30 minutes <u>feed</u> the baby cats. → ____________
4 <u>Turning not</u> off the heater can be dangerous. → ____________

C
take notes 메모하다
feed 동 먹이를 주다
heater 명 난방기, 히터

D 다음 우리말과 일치하도록 괄호 안의 말을 이용하여 문장을 완성하시오.

1 그녀는 인도 카레를 먹고 싶었다. (feel, eat)
→ She ________ ________ ________ Indian curry.
2 그는 내일 아침에 조깅하러 갈 것이다. (go, jog)
→ He will ________ ________ tomorrow morning.
3 수업에 늦지 않는 것이 첫 번째 규칙이다. (be, late)
→ ________ ________ ________ for class is the first rule.
4 나는 외출하는 대신 집에 머물렀다. (instead of, go out)
→ I stayed home ________ ________ ________ ________.

D
instead of … 대신에

B 동명사와 to부정사

동사에 따라 목적어로 동명사나 to부정사를 취하거나, 둘 다 취할 수 있다.

1 동명사를 목적어로 취하는 동사

예 enjoy, finish, avoid, give up, keep, mind, quit 등
They **finished playing** mobile games.
You can't **avoid taking** the science test tomorrow.

2 to부정사를 목적어로 취하는 동사

예 want, need, wish, decide, hope, ask, expect, plan, promise, agree 등
Amy **wanted to raise** iguanas.
He **decided to enter** the speech contest.

3 동명사와 to부정사 둘 다 목적어로 취하는 동사

1) 의미 차이가 거의 없는 동사: like, love, hate, begin, start, continue 등
I **love taking**[**to take**] walks along the beach.
The boy **began crying**[**to cry**] loudly.

2) 의미 차이가 있는 동사: remember, forget, try 등

① 「**remember / forget to-v**」: (미래에) …할 것을 기억하다 / 잊다
She **remembered to write** a birthday card for him.
Don't **forget to bring** your umbrella.

② 「**remember / forget v-ing**」: (과거에) …한 것을 기억하다 / 잊다
I **remember hearing** her voice.
They **forgot closing** the window.

③ 「**try to-v**」: …하려고 노력하다 / 「**try v-ing**」: (시험 삼아) …해 보다
He **tries to keep** in shape.
Jennifer **tried using** the new printer.

내신 POINT PLUS

「stop v-ing」와 「stop to-v」
「stop v-ing」는 '…하는 것을 멈추다'는 의미이다. 반면, 「stop to-v」는 '…하기 위해 멈추다'의 의미이며, 이때 to부정사는 목적을 나타내는 부사적 용법의 to부정사이다.
The penguins **stopped walking**. (펭귄들이 걷는 것을 멈췄다.)
She **stopped to buy** some coffee. (그녀는 커피를 사기 위해 멈췄다.)

Check-Up

A 다음 괄호 안에서 알맞은 말을 고르시오.

1 They hoped (riding / to ride) horses.

2 He enjoyed (going / to go) surfing for a while.

3 Do you mind (turning / to turn) on the radio?

4 She expected (setting / to set) a world record.

5 Bernard plans (leaving / to leave) the company soon.

WORDS

A
surf 동 파도타기[서핑]를 하다
for a while 한동안
set a record 기록을 세우다
company 명 회사

B 다음 괄호 안의 동사를 빈칸에 알맞은 형태로 쓰시오.

1 I gave up __________ the race. (run)

2 She promised __________ the man's life. (save)

3 They finished __________ their room at 4 p.m. (clean)

4 My father quit __________ five years ago. (smoke)

5 The royal family wished __________ a castle in our town. (build)

B
save 동 구하다
royal 형 왕실의
castle 명 성

C 다음 두 문장이 같은 뜻이 되도록 빈칸에 알맞은 말을 쓰시오.

1 The man started to burn paper.
→ The man __________ __________ paper.

2 They like watching action movies.
→ They __________ __________ __________ action movies.

C
burn 동 (불이) 타오르다; *태우다

D 다음 우리말과 일치하도록 괄호 안의 단어를 이용하여 문장을 완성하시오.

1 Nancy는 충분한 수면을 취하려고 노력한다. (get)
→ Nancy __________ __________ __________ enough sleep.

2 나는 오늘 아침에 우유를 배달할 것을 잊었다. (deliver)
→ I __________ __________ __________ milk this morning.

3 그는 딸에게 인형을 사 줄 것을 기억했다. (buy)
→ He __________ __________ __________ his daughter a doll.

4 James는 표지판을 읽기 위해 걷는 것을 멈췄다. (walk)
→ James __________ __________ to read the sign.

D
enough 형 충분한
sign 명 신호; *표지판

Grammar Practice

A 다음 괄호 안에서 알맞은 말을 고르시오.

1 John is tired of (eat / eating) hamburgers.

2 She couldn't help (to laugh / laughing) at his joke.

3 We are expecting (to find / finding) our bag there.

4 Do you remember (to take / taking) a trip last year?

5 Lying down after meals (is / are) not good for your health.

B 다음 밑줄 친 부분을 바르게 고치시오.

1 Tina avoided <u>to touch</u> snakes. → ________

2 We decided <u>going</u> to Thailand. → ________

3 <u>Send</u> this package is impossible. → ________

4 What was your reason for <u>calling not</u> me? → ________

5 He was thinking about <u>sell</u> his old CD player. → ________

C 다음 괄호 안의 단어를 빈칸에 알맞은 형태로 쓰시오.

1 A: I have a headache.
B: Don't forget ________ medicine. (take)

2 A: The woman finally stopped ________. (sing)
B: Right. It is very quiet now.

3 A: Did he come to Tokyo last night?
B: No. He tried ________ a train ticket but he failed. (buy)

D 다음 두 문장을 한 문장으로 바꿀 때 빈칸에 알맞은 말을 쓰시오.

1 I sent him a text message. But I forgot that I did.
→ I forgot ________ him a text message.

2 Peter studied history. He continued for two hours.
→ Peter continued ________ ________ history for two hours.

WORDS

A
be tired of …에 싫증 나다
joke 명 농담
lie down 눕다

B
Thailand 명 태국
package 명 꾸러미, 소포
reason 명 이유

C
take medicine 약을 복용하다
finally 부 마침내
fail 동 실패하다

D
continue 동 계속하다

내신 완성 Grammar Practice

1 다음 빈칸에 들어갈 말로 알맞지 않은 것은?

She ________ walking her puppies in the park.

① kept ② wished
③ began ④ enjoyed
⑤ finished

2 다음 대화의 빈칸에 들어갈 말이 바르게 짝지어진 것은?

- A: Do you mind ________ the door?
  B: No. I can open it.
- A: Why did you stop ________ the game?
  B: Because I was sleepy.

① open - watching ② to open - to watch
③ to open - watching ④ opening - to watch
⑤ opening - watching

3 다음 중 어법상 바르지 못한 것은?

① I was afraid of going to the dentist.
② They planned to visit their grandparents.
③ Sora felt like having a slice of pizza.
④ Not protecting the forest is dangerous.
⑤ Frank and Amy went shop at the mall.

4 다음 우리말과 일치하도록 괄호 안의 단어를 바르게 배열하시오.

(1) Mina는 머핀 굽는 것을 잘한다. (at, good, is, baking)
→ Mina ________________________ muffins.

(2) 나는 그를 위한 선물을 사는 데 많은 돈을 썼다.
(lots, buying, money, spent, of)
→ I ________________________ gifts for him.

WORDS

1
walk 동 걷다; *(동물을) 산책시키다

2
sleepy 형 졸린

3
forest 명 숲, 삼림
mall 명 쇼핑몰

서술형에 나오는 WRITING

A **다음 우리말과 일치하도록 괄호 안의 말을 바르게 배열하시오.**

1 나는 지하철에서 그를 만났던 것을 기억했다.
(him, I, meeting, on the subway, remembered)
→ ______________________________

2 에스컬레이터 위에서 뛰는 것은 안전하지 않다.
(is, on, safe, running, not, the escalator)
→ ______________________________

B **다음 우리말과 일치하도록 괄호 안의 말을 이용하여 문장을 완성하시오.**

1 그는 길에서 사진을 찍기 위해 멈췄다. (stop, take a picture)
→ ______________________ on the road.

2 우리는 조언을 요청하지 않을 수 없었다. (help, ask for)
→ ______________________ some advice.

3 그들은 계속해서 별들에 대해 이야기했다. (keep, talk)
→ ______________________ about the stars.

C **다음 그림을 보고, 괄호 안의 단어를 이용하여 문장을 완성하시오. (과거시제로 작성할 것)**

1 Mike ______________________ a hot dog. (start, eat)

2 Anna ______________________ some snacks. (decide, buy)

3 Lily ______________________ her wallet. (forget, bring)

1

Peanut butter is delicious. But it is also useful. Did you know peanut butter is good for leather? **Rubbing** peanut butter on leather shoes (A) make your shoes shiny. This is because peanut butter contains natural oils. It can remove old stickers, too. Just rub some on the sticker and wait 40 minutes. The sticker will come off easily.

Peanut butter also makes ice cream cones less messy! Suppose you decide **to enjoy** an ice cream cone on a hot day. Of course, the ice cream will melt quickly. Before **adding** the ice cream, put a little peanut butter in the bottom of the cone. It will stop melted ice cream from (B) drip out. And when you eat the cone, there will be a special treat at the end!

1 **위 글에서 땅콩버터의 활용 방법으로 언급되지 않은 것은? (2개)**

① 가죽 구두를 반짝이게 해 준다.
② 음식이 상하는 것을 방지해 준다.
③ 생선 냄새가 퍼지는 것을 막아 준다.
④ 오래된 스티커를 쉽게 제거하게 해 준다.
⑤ 녹은 아이스크림이 흐르는 것을 막아 준다.

2 **위 글의 밑줄 친 (A)와 (B)를 알맞은 형태로 바꿔 쓰시오.**

(A) __________ (B) __________

WORDS

useful 형 유용한 **leather** 명 가죽 **rub** 동 문지르다, 비비다 **contain** 동 [1] __________ **natural** 형 자연[천연]의
remove 동 없애다, 제거하다 **messy** 형 지저분한, 엉망인 **suppose** 동 가정하다 **melt** 동 [2] __________
bottom 명 맨 아래 (부분) **drip** 동 뚝뚝 흐르다 **treat** 명 특별한 것[선물]

2

People can use their cell phones everywhere. So phone booths are becoming useless. Interestingly, two French artists decided (A) turning / to turn the booth into a special box. They made a phone booth aquarium!

Here's their way of (B) making / to make it. ***Sealing** the door and cracks tightly is the first step. This keeps water from **leaking** out. **Filling** the booth with clean water is the second step. (C) Add / Adding fish to the booth is the final step. Now, the old phone booth is an aquarium. People can visit and enjoy **seeing** the beautiful fish. And there's one more thing to see: the old telephone. The artists left it inside for fun!

*seal: 밀폐하다

1 **Which is the best title for the passage?**

① The First Telephone Booth
② A New Type of Cell Phone
③ Aquariums with a Variety of Fish
④ The Most Famous Aquarium in the World
⑤ A Beautiful Change: Phone Booth to Aquarium

2 **Choose the grammatically correct words in (A)~(C) and write them below.**

(A) __________ (B) __________ (C) __________

WORDS
everywhere 부 어디에서나 **phone booth** 공중전화 부스 **useless** 형 __________ **interestingly** 부 흥미롭게도 **aquarium** 명 수족관 **crack** 명 (갈라진) 금; *(좁은) 틈 **tightly** 부 단단히, 꽉 **step** 명 발걸음; *단계 **leak** 동 새다 **leave** 동 떠나다; *그대로 두다 (left - left) **for fun** 재미로 문제 **a variety of** 다양한

A 제안하고 답하기

A: Dad, **how about** going out for lunch**?**
(아빠, 점심에 외식하는 게 어때요?)

B: **Sounds good.** Where do you want to go?
(좋지. 어디로 가고 싶니?)

A: **Let's** go to a Chinese restaurant.
(중국 음식점으로 가요.)

B: **Okay.**
(그러자.)

상대방에게 제안할 때는 'How about v-ing ...?'나 'Let's+동사원형 ...' 등의 표현을 쓸 수 있다. 상대방의 제안을 받아들일 때는 'Sounds good.' 또는 'Okay.' 등으로 대답할 수 있다.

EXPRESSION PLUS

1 제안하기
- **What about** waiting a little more**?** (조금 더 기다리는 게 어떠니?)
- **Why don't you** wear rain boots**?** (장화를 신는 게 어떠니?)

2 대답하기
- Great! (정말 좋아!) / That's a good idea. (그거 좋은 생각이야.)
- I'm sorry, but I can't. (미안하지만, 그럴 수 없어.) / Maybe next time. (다음에 하자.)

Check-Up

1 다음 대화의 빈칸에 들어갈 말로 알맞지 않은 것은?

A: How about staying here tonight?
B: ______________________

① Great!　② I don't live here.
③ That's a good idea.　④ I'm sorry, but I can't.
⑤ That sounds good.

2 다음 대화의 빈칸에 들어갈 말로 알맞은 것은?

A: There is nothing to eat in the refrigerator.
B: ______________________

① No, thank you.　② That sounds great.
③ Maybe next time.　④ Why don't you cook for him?
⑤ Let's go out to get some food.

WORDS

2
refrigerator 명 냉장고

B 소망 묻고 답하기

A: **Would you like to** watch a basketball game together**?**
(너는 농구 경기를 함께 보고 싶니?)

B: **Yes, I'd like to.** When is the game?
(응, 그러고 싶어. 경기가 언제야?)

A: There is one on Sunday.
(일요일에 (경기가) 하나 있어.)

'…하고 싶니?'의 의미로 상대방에게 원하는 것을 물을 때 'Would you like to-v ...?'라고 말할 수 있다. 본인이 하고 싶은 것을 말할 때는 'I'd like to-v ...' 등으로 표현할 수 있다.

EXPRESSION PLUS

A: **Do you want to** take a trip**?** (너는 여행을 가고 싶니?)
B: **Yes, I do.** (응, 그러고 싶어.) / **No, I don't.** (아니, 그러고 싶지 않아.)

A: **What would you like to** do**?** (너는 무엇을 하고 싶니?)
B: I'd like to play with my nephew. (나는 조카와 놀고 싶어.)

TIPS 「would like to-v」는 '…하고 싶다'의 의미로, 「(주어)'d like to-v」로 축약해서 쓸 수 있다. 부정문은 「wouldn't like to-v」로 나타낸다.
I **wouldn't like to** invite Jack. (나는 Jack을 초대하고 싶지 않아.)

Check-Up

1 다음 우리말과 일치하도록 괄호 안의 단어를 이용하여 문장을 완성하시오.

A: 너는 그 동아리에 가입하고 싶니? (want, join)
B: Yes, I do.

→ ________ ________ ________ ________ ________ the club?

2 다음 괄호 안의 단어를 이용하여 대화를 완성하시오.

A: Would you like to ride the roller coaster?
B: No. ________ ________ ________ ________ ________ the wild animals. (feed)

WORDS

1
join 동 가입하다

2
wild animal 야생동물

FINAL TEST

1 다음 중 영어 단어와 우리말 뜻이 잘못 연결된 것은?

① save - 구하다
② rub - 문지르다
③ raise - 기르다
④ remove - 더하다
⑤ bottom - 맨 아래

2 다음 우리말과 일치하도록 괄호 안의 단어를 이용하여 문장을 완성하시오.

나는 이 드레스에 싫증 난다.

→ I ________ ________ ________ this dress. (tired)

3 다음 대화의 빈칸에 들어갈 말로 알맞은 것은?

A: Do you want to go to Jeju-do this summer?
B: ____________________

① Yes, I can.
② No, you may not.
③ Yes. It goes well with you.
④ No. I'd like to go to Spain.
⑤ No, I'm not. How about you?

4 다음 중 짝지어진 대화가 어색한 것은?

① A: Why don't you call her?
B: Maybe next time.
② A: What about riding bikes?
B: That's a good idea.
③ A: How about taking a shower?
B: Okay.
④ A: What would you like to do?
B: I'd like to relax at home.
⑤ A: Do you want to open the box?
B: I'm sorry to hear that.

5 밑줄 친 ①~⑤ 중 대화의 흐름과 어울리지 않는 것은?

A: ①How about trying on this red cap?
B: ②I don't like the color.
A: ③Then why don't you try that black one?
B: ④You did a good job! ⑤All right.

[6-8] 다음 빈칸에 들어갈 말로 알맞은 것을 고르시오.

6 Mario is proud of ________ a medal.

① get
② got
③ getting
④ to get
⑤ to getting

7 I expected ________ Ted's house.

① visit
② visited
③ visiting
④ to visit
⑤ to visiting

8 He didn't feel like ________ for his company anymore.

① work
② worked
③ working
④ to work
⑤ be working

! 자주 나와요

[9-10] 다음 빈칸에 들어갈 말로 알맞지 <u>않은</u> 것을 고르시오.

9 I ________ to cross the river bridge soon.

① plan ② wish
③ want ④ enjoy
⑤ hope

10 Mr. Brown ________ painting the wall yesterday.

① began ② started
③ finished ④ gave up
⑤ decided

11 다음 빈칸에 들어갈 말이 바르게 짝지어진 것은?

- You can't avoid ________ the question.
- Karl promised ________ a good grade.

① answer - receive
② to answer - receiving
③ to answer - to receive
④ answering - receiving
⑤ answering - to receive

[12-14] 다음 밑줄 친 부분이 어법상 바르면 O를 쓰고, 틀리면 바르게 고치시오.

12 David loves <u>to listen</u> to hip-hop music.

→ ________

13 She stopped <u>run</u> to check the time.

→ ________

14 Do you mind <u>to change</u> the channel?

→ ________

! 어려워요

15 다음 밑줄 친 부분의 쓰임이 보기 와 같은 것은?

보기 My role is <u>informing</u> people about our new products.

① Dark clouds are <u>moving</u> in.
② They continued <u>singing</u> songs.
③ Her hobby is <u>growing</u> vegetables.
④ Mark tried <u>driving</u> his car in the park.
⑤ I'm thinking of <u>taking</u> a trip tomorrow.

[16-17] 다음 괄호 안의 단어를 빈칸에 알맞은 형태로 쓰시오.

16 It's raining. You should remember ________ a raincoat. (wear)

17 I'm bored. I want to go ________. (skate)

어려워요

18 다음 중 어법상 바르지 못한 것은?

① Not be with her was my mistake.
② Her job is treating sick animals.
③ Pressing the button is the first step.
④ We are sorry for breaking your vase.
⑤ He planned to have a birthday party.

자주 나와요

19 다음 우리말을 영어로 바르게 옮긴 것은?

나는 창문을 닦았던 것을 잊어버렸다.

① I forgot clean the window.
② I forgot to clean the window.
③ I forgot cleaning the window.
④ I forgot to cleaning the window.
⑤ I forgot to be cleaning the window.

서술형

[20-21] 다음 우리말과 일치하도록 괄호 안의 단어를 바르게 배열하시오.

20 나는 울지 않을 수 없었다.
(help, I, crying, couldn't)

→ ______________________

21 그 수학 문제를 푸는 것은 어렵다.
(difficult, the math, solving, problem, is)

→ ______________________

내신 완성 서술형

22 다음 우리말과 일치하도록 괄호 안의 단어를 이용하여 영작하시오.

그는 계속 드럼을 연주했다. (keep, play)

→ ______________ the drums.

23 다음 밑줄 친 부분 중 어법상 틀린 것을 찾아 바르게 고치시오.

A: What do you like to do in your free time?
B: I like ① to swim in the pool.
A: Are you good at ② swimming?
B: Yes. How about going ③ swimming together?
A: Sorry, I can't ④ swim. ⑤ Swim is not easy for me.

________ → ________

24 다음 문장을 보기 처럼 바꿔 쓰시오.

보기 I imagined becoming a king.
→ I imagined not becoming a king.

Leaving the town was a good choice.
→ ______________________

WORD LIST

Grammar

□ foreigner	명 외국인
□ protect	동 보호하다
□ helpful	형 도움이 되는
□ raise	동 기르다
□ require	동 요구하다
□ take notes	메모하다
□ feed	동 먹이를 주다
□ for a while	한동안
□ set a record	기록을 세우다
□ save	동 구하다
□ royal	형 왕실의
□ castle	명 성
□ burn	동 (불이) 타오르다; 태우다
□ sign	명 신호; 표지판
□ be tired of	…에 싫증 나다
□ joke	명 농담
□ reason	명 이유
□ take medicine	약을 복용하다
□ finally	부 마침내
□ fail	동 실패하다
□ continue	동 계속하다
□ mall	명 쇼핑몰

Reading

□ useful	형 유용한
□ leather	명 가죽
□ rub	동 문지르다, 비비다
□ contain	동 …이 들어 있다
□ natural	형 자연[천연]의
□ remove	동 없애다, 제거하다
□ messy	형 지저분한, 엉망인
□ suppose	동 가정하다
□ melt	동 녹다
□ bottom	명 맨 아래 (부분)
□ treat	명 특별한 것[선물]
□ everywhere	부 어디에서나
□ useless	형 쓸모없는
□ interestingly	부 흥미롭게도
□ aquarium	명 수족관
□ tightly	부 단단히, 꽉
□ step	명 발걸음; 단계
□ leak	동 새다
□ leave	동 떠나다; 그대로 두다
□ for fun	재미로
□ a variety of	다양한

Communication

□ refrigerator	명 냉장고
□ wild animal	야생동물

Final Test

□ relax	동 휴식을 취하다
□ grade	명 성적, 학점
□ inform	동 (특히 공식적으로) 알리다
□ product	명 상품, 제품
□ press	동 누르다
□ vase	명 꽃병
□ choice	명 선택

CHAPTER 11

전치사와 접속사

GET READY

We met **at** *the restaurant*.
(우리는 식당에서 만났다.)

We had *pasta* **and** *pizza*.
(우리는 파스타와 피자를 먹었다.)

After *we had lunch*, we visited the gift shop.
(점심을 먹은 후에, 우리는 선물 가게를 방문했다.)

the restaurant 앞에 쓰인 at은 전치사이고, pasta와 pizza를 연결하고 있는 and와 we had lunch 앞의 After는 접속사예요. 전치사는 '앞에 위치하는 말'이라는 뜻으로, 명사나 대명사 앞에 쓰여 의미를 더하는 역할을 해요. 접속사는 앞뒤 말들을 연결하는 역할을 해요.

A 전치사

전치사는 명사나 대명사 앞에 쓰여 장소, 시간 등의 의미를 나타낸다.

1 장소를 나타내는 전치사

1) at(…에), **in**(…에, … 안에)

I saw you **at** the park. (장소의 한 지점)
Patrick lives **in** New York. (도시, 국가 등 넓은 장소)
Who is **in** the meeting room? (공간의 내부)

2) on(… 위에), **over**(… 위에), **under**(… 아래에)

A cat is lying **on** the chair. (표면 위)
A lamp hangs **over** the bed. (표면에서 떨어진 위)
There are some benches **under** the bridge. (표면에서 떨어진 아래)

3) in front of(… 앞에), **behind**(… 뒤에), **next to**(… 바로 옆에)

Olivia is standing **in front of** the building.
The boys were hiding **behind** the curtain.
She always sits **next to** me.

4) between A and B(A와 B 사이에)

My car is **between** a truck **and** a bus.

2 시간을 나타내는 전치사

1) in, **at**, **on**(…에)

in	오전/오후, 월, 계절, 연도	**in** the morning/the afternoon/the evening **in** spring/summer/fall/winter	**in** April/July **in** 2020/the 1990s
at	구체적 시각, 하루의 때	**at** 4:40/six o'clock **at** lunchtime/night	
on	날짜, 요일, 특정한 날	**on** March 11 **on** New Year's Day/my birthday	**on** Monday/Friday

He visited Korea **in** 2017.
You can go home **at** two o'clock.
Everyone looks happy **on** Christmas Day.

2) before(… 전에), **after**(… 후에), **for**(… 동안)

I wash my hands **before** meals.
We will practice ballet **after** school.
He took a break **for** ten minutes.

Check-Up

A 다음 그림을 보고, 괄호 안에서 알맞은 말을 고르시오.

1 The girl is sitting (behind / in front of) the sofa.
2 The dog is sleeping (under / next to) the sofa.
3 A clock is hanging (on / over) the sofa.

B 다음 밑줄 친 부분을 바르게 고치시오.

1 It is very dry on winter. → ________
2 The musical starts exactly in 5:30. → ________
3 Henry will spend his vacation at Italy. → ________

C 다음 빈칸에 들어갈 말을 보기 에서 골라 쓰시오.

보기 at on in between over

1 He is putting the books ________ the shelf.
2 I waited for my friend ________ the bus stop.
3 The bank is ________ the school and the hospital.
4 They opened the box. There was a cup ________ it.

D 다음 우리말과 일치하도록 괄호 안의 말을 이용하여 문장을 완성하시오.

1 그녀는 점심 식사 후에 음악을 들었다. (lunch)
→ She listened to music ________ ________.
2 우리는 30분 동안 얼음 위에서 스케이트를 탔다. (thirty minutes)
→ We skated on the ice ________ ________ ________.
3 너는 공연 전에 휴대폰을 꺼야 한다. (the show)
→ You should turn off your cell phone ________ ________ ________.

WORDS

A
hang 동 걸리다

B
dry 형 마른; *건조한
exactly 부 정확히

C
shelf 명 선반

D
skate 동 스케이트를 타다

B 접속사

1 등위 접속사

등위 접속사는 문법적으로 대등한 단어, 구, 절을 연결하는 말로, and(그리고), but(그러나), or(또는), so(그래서) 등이 있다.

Tom **and** *I* are good friends.

This dress is *pretty* **but** *expensive*.

You can *stay home* **or** *go out*.

I lost my bag, **so** *I went to the lost and found*.

2 종속 접속사

종속 접속사는 절과 절을 연결한다. 종속 접속사가 이끄는 절은 종속절, 종속절이 연결되는 절은 주절이라고 한다.

She always takes the subway **when** she goes to work.
주절 / 종속절

1) 시간을 나타내는 종속 접속사: when(…할 때), **before**(… 전에), **after**(… 후에), **while**(… 하는 동안), **as**(…할 때, …함에 따라)

When I was young, I didn't like vegetables.

Alex takes a shower **before** he goes to bed.

Sarah enjoyed her free time **after** she took a test.

We practiced singing **while** you were taking a break.

As I grew older, I became more forgetful.

TIPS

시간을 나타내는 부사절의 시제
시간을 나타내는 접속사가 이끄는 부사절에서는 미래시제 대신 현재시제를 쓴다.
He'll drink juice **when** the movie **ends**. (영화가 끝나면 그는 주스를 마실 것이다.)

2) 이유를 나타내는 종속 접속사: because(… 때문에)

I wore a thick coat **because** it was cold.

3) 명사절을 이끄는 종속 접속사: that(…라는 것)

접속사 that은 문장에서 주어, 목적어, 보어로 쓰이는 명사절을 이끈다. that절이 주어로 쓰일 때는 주로 「It(가주어) ... that(진주어)」 형태로 쓰며, 목적어로 쓰이는 명사절을 이끄는 that은 생략 가능하다.

That she is smart is true. → It is true **that** she is smart. (주어)

I believe (**that**) we can win the game. (목적어)

The news is **that** Chris is missing. (보어)

Check-Up

A 다음 빈칸에 접속사 and, but, or, so 중 알맞은 것을 골라 쓰시오. (한 번씩만 쓸 것)

1 What would you like, milk __________ tea?

2 Fast food is tasty __________ unhealthy.

3 He stretched his legs __________ arms together.

4 Lisa didn't bring her wallet, __________ she went back home.

B 다음을 연결하여 문장을 완성하시오.

1 Selena was sad •	• ⓐ that he won the award.
2 I took medicine •	• ⓑ after I had breakfast.
3 It is shocking news •	• ⓒ because her cat was sick.
4 We should stay inside •	• ⓓ while the heavy rain is passing by.

C 다음 우리말과 일치하도록 빈칸에 알맞은 말을 쓰시오.

1 우리가 서로를 돕는 것이 필요하다.

→ It is necessary __________ we help each other.

2 시간이 지남에 따라, 그는 더욱 화가 났다.

→ __________ time went by, he became angrier.

3 우리는 그 자전거를 고치거나 새것을 살 것이다.

→ We'll fix the bike __________ buy a new one.

D 다음 빈칸에 들어갈 말을 보기 에서 골라 쓰시오. (한 번씩만 쓸 것)

보기 before when because and that

1 I wanted to be a teacher __________ I was a child.

2 __________ you start swimming, you should warm up.

3 He ate a sandwich __________ drank a glass of milk.

4 I think __________ she forgave her friend.

5 Jenny got wet __________ she didn't have an umbrella.

WORDS

A
tasty 형 맛있는
stretch 동 뻗다

B
award 명 상
medicine 명 약
shocking 형 충격적인
pass by 지나가다

C
necessary 형 필요한, 필수의
go by (시간이) 지나가다
fix 동 고정시키다; *수리하다

D
warm up 준비 운동을 하다
forgive 동 용서하다
(forgave - forgiven)
wet 형 젖은

Grammar Practice

A 다음 괄호 안에서 알맞은 말을 고르시오.

1 I moved to this city (in / on) 2015.
2 Summer vacation begins (in / on) July 15.
3 Which place do you like more, the park (and / or) the mall?
4 David wears glasses (because / that) he has bad eyesight.

WORDS

A
glasses 명 안경
eyesight 명 시력

B 다음 빈칸에 들어갈 말을 보기 에서 골라 쓰시오.

보기 so that behind over as

1 Some birds are flying ________ the sea.
2 I hope ________ all of my friends are happy.
3 The moon disappeared ________ the clouds.
4 Tony was late, ________ he apologized to everyone.

B
disappear 동 사라지다
apologize 동 사과하다

C 다음 밑줄 친 부분을 바르게 고치시오.

1 Were you busy on the morning? → ________
2 My family gathers in New Year's Day. → ________
3 The truth is while he doesn't have money. → ________
4 I will help you after I will finish my work. → ________
5 We can play games or reading comic books. → ________

C
gather 동 모이다
truth 명 사실
comic book 만화책

D 다음 그림을 보고, 빈칸에 알맞은 전치사를 쓰시오.

pet shop gym bookstore café

1 The gym is ________ the pet shop ________ the bookstore.
2 There is a café ________ ________ the bookstore.

내신 완성 Grammar Practice

1 다음 빈칸에 들어갈 말이 바르게 짝지어진 것은?

- I was standing there ________ half an hour.
- He whistled ________ he was cleaning his house.

① at - so
② at - while
③ at - that
④ for - while
⑤ for - that

2 다음 빈칸에 들어갈 말이 나머지 넷과 다른 것은?

① We believe ________ you can recover.
② I was sleeping ________ you called me.
③ The fact is ________ he is a great dancer.
④ Did you hear ________ she had an accident?
⑤ It is strange ________ she didn't come on the field trip.

3 다음 (A)~(C)의 괄호 안에 들어갈 말이 바르게 짝지어진 것은?

(A) The festival begins (at / on) midnight.
(B) We will order the food when he (arrives / will arrive).
(C) I love making food (and / but) cookies.

	(A)	(B)	(C)
①	at	arrives	and
②	at	arrives	but
③	at	will arrive	and
④	on	arrives	but
⑤	on	will arrive	and

4 다음 우리말과 일치하도록 괄호 안의 단어를 바르게 배열하시오.

(1) 우체국은 경찰서 앞에 있다. (front, the police station, of, in)
→ The post office is ________________________.

(2) 그가 나의 이름을 아는 것은 불가능하다. (is, it, that, impossible)
→ ________________________ he knows my name.

WORDS

1
half 명 반, 절반
whistle 동 휘파람을 불다

2
recover 동 (건강이) 회복되다
fact 명 사실
field trip 현장 학습

3
festival 명 축제
order 동 주문하다

4
police station 경찰서
post office 우체국

서술형에 나오는 WRITING

A 다음 우리말과 일치하도록 괄호 안의 말을 바르게 배열하시오.

1 나는 그 소문이 사실이라는 것을 알았다.
(knew, true, I, the rumor, that, was)
→ ______________________________

2 호랑이가 자고 있을 때, 수의사는 그것을 치료했다.
(as, cured, the vet, was, it, sleeping, the tiger)
→ ______________________________

B 다음 그림을 보고, 보기 에서 알맞은 말을 골라 문장을 완성하시오.

보기
sat on
lay down over
read books over
set up a tent under

Bob and Silvia went to a park on Sunday.

1 They ______________ the grass.
2 They ______________ the tree.

C 다음은 Tony의 오늘 계획표이다. 표를 보고, 보기 처럼 괄호 안의 접속사를 이용하여 문장을 완성하시오.

Time	Activity
9:30 a.m.	read comic books
10 a.m.	do my art homework
12:30 p.m.	meet James
3 p.m.	go to the library
5 p.m.	prepare dinner

보기 Tony will meet James before he goes to the library. (before)

1 Tony will do his art homework ______________. (after)
2 Tony will go to the library ______________. (before)

1

Some dinosaurs ate meat, **and** others ate plants. But did you know **that** one meat-eating dinosaur ________________ **as** it got older? It was the *Limusaurus*, a small dinosaur that lived about 160 million years ago.

According to a study, it had sharp teeth **when** it was young. So it probably consumed both plants **and** meat. But **as** it turned into an adult, it lost all of its teeth. So scientists think **that** adults could only eat plants. "This happened **because** adults didn't want to compete for food with their young," one of them said. Surprisingly, the *Limusaurus* experienced more than 70 other changes to its body (older, it, while, grew).

1 위 글의 빈칸에 들어갈 말로 가장 알맞은 것은?

① ate its species
② fought its young
③ looked much younger
④ turned into a vegetarian
⑤ disliked plants and meat

! 서술형

2 위 글의 괄호 안의 단어를 바르게 배열하시오.

→ ________________________________
(older, it, while, grew)

WORDS dinosaur 명 공룡 million 형 백만의 sharp 형 1 __________ young 형 어린 명 (동물의) 새끼 probably 부 아마 consume 동 소모하다; *먹다 turn into …이 되다, …로 변하다 adult 명 어른; *다 자란 동물 compete for …를 위해 싸우다[경쟁하다] experience 동 2 __________ 문제 species 명 종(種) vegetarian 명 채식주의자

2

Sarah **and** an artist sat **in** his studio. The artist couldn't see her ___(A)___ he was sitting **behind** a curtain. Sarah talked about her face. For example, she said, "I think **that** I have a big jaw. And there are many *freckles **on** my cheeks." Then the artist painted her **on** his canvas.

After a while, he painted her again. But this time, another woman described Sarah. She said, "She has a beautiful forehead **and** deep blue eyes." ___(B)___ the artist finished, Sarah compared the two pictures. She liked the second picture better **because** she looked more attractive in it. So, what do you think of yourself? Maybe you are more beautiful than you think!

*freckle: 주근깨

1 Which is the best title for the passage?

① See Your Own Beauty
② Spend Your Time Painting
③ Draw the Faces of Strangers
④ Compare Pictures of Yourself
⑤ Look in the Mirror More Often

2 Which is the best pair for blanks (A) and (B)?

	(A)		(B)		(A)		(B)
①	but	-	When	②	when	-	While
③	while	-	Before	④	because	-	After
⑤	before	-	Because				

WORDS
studio 명 스튜디오, 화실 **curtain** 명 커튼, 막 **for example** 예를 들어 **jaw** 명 턱 **cheek** 명 볼, 뺨 **canvas** 명 화폭
after a while 잠시 후에 **describe** 동 [1] ________ **forehead** 명 이마 **compare** 동 비교하다 **attractive** 형 매력적인
문제 **stranger** 명 낯선 사람

A 길 묻고 답하기

A: **How can I get to** City Hall**?**
(시청에 어떻게 가나요?)

B: It's nearby. **Walk straight two blocks.**
It's across from G Tower.
(가까이 있어요. 두 블록을 곧장 걸어가세요. 그것은 G Tower 맞은편에 있어요.)

A: Thank you very much!
(정말 감사합니다!)

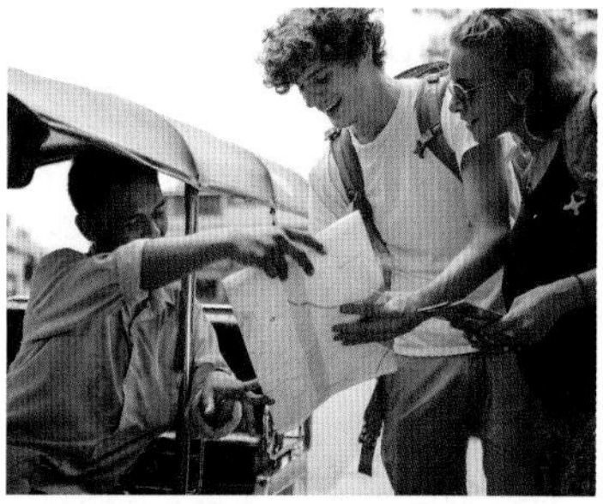

길을 물을 때는 'How can I get[go] to ...?'라고 물을 수 있다. 길을 안내할 때는 straight(곧장, 똑바로), across from(…의 맞은편에) 등 방향이나 위치를 나타내는 말을 사용한다.

EXPRESSION PLUS

1 길 묻기
- **Where can I find** the restaurant**?** (그 식당을 어디에서 찾을 수 있나요?)
- **Do you know the way to** the gallery**?** (미술관으로 가는 길을 아세요?)
- **Can you show me the way to** the airport**?** (공항으로 가는 길을 알려 주시겠어요?)

2 길 안내하기
- **Cross the street.** (길을 건너세요.)
- **It's on your** right. (그것은 당신의 오른편에 있습니다.)
- **You should take** the subway. (당신은 지하철을 타야 합니다.)

Check-Up

1 다음 대화의 빈칸에 들어갈 말로 알맞지 않은 것은?

A: How can I get to the bookstore?
B: ______________________

① Cross the street.
② You should take a bus.
③ I got it at the bookstore.
④ Turn right at the corner.
⑤ Walk straight one block.

2 다음 중 길을 묻는 표현을 모두 고르시오. (2개)

① Are you going to the bank?
② Where did you go yesterday?
③ What's your favorite building?
④ Do you know the way to the park?
⑤ Where can I find the movie theater?

WORDS

1
corner 명 모퉁이

2
theater 명 극장

B 약속 시간·장소 정하기

A: **Where shall we meet?**
(우리 어디서 만날까?)
B: At the shopping mall. **When shall we meet?**
(쇼핑몰에서. 우리 언제 만날래?)
A: **Can you make it by** 6 p.m.**?**
(오후 6시까지 올 수 있니?)
B: Okay. See you then.
(응. 그때 보자.)

약속 시간을 정할 때는 'What time / When shall we meet?', 장소를 정할 때는 'Where shall we meet?'이라고 말할 수 있다. 약속 시간을 제안할 때는 'Can you make it by+시간?'이라고 말할 수 있다.

EXPRESSION PLUS

A: **When do you want to meet?** (언제 만나고 싶니?)
B: **Let's meet at** 4 o'clock! (4시에 만나자!)

A: **Where do you want to meet?** (어디서 만나고 싶니?)
B: **How about** Seoul Station**?** (서울역은 어때?)

Check-Up

1 다음 문장이 들어갈 위치로 가장 알맞은 곳은?

When shall we meet?

A: Let's go to a basketball game. (①)
B: That's a good idea. (②)
A: How about 11 a.m.? (③)
B: Okay. (④) Where do you want to meet?
A: (⑤) Let's meet in front of the National Museum.

WORDS

1
national 형 국가의; *국립의

2 다음 괄호 안의 단어를 이용하여 대화를 완성하시오.

A: When do you want to meet?
B: ________ ________ ________ ________
by 8:30 p.m.? (make)
A: Sure.

FINAL TEST

1 다음 중 영어 단어와 우리말 뜻이 잘못 연결된 것은?

① truth - 사실　② recover - 회복되다
③ stretch - 뻗다　④ gather - 모이다
⑤ compare - 경험하다

2 다음 빈칸에 들어갈 단어로 가장 알맞은 것은?

old : young = dry : ________

① wet　② young
③ sharp　④ tasty
⑤ attractive

3 다음 대화의 빈칸에 들어갈 말로 알맞은 것은?

A: Amy and I are going to go hiking. Do you want to join us?
B: Sure. ________________
A: Let's meet at 5 p.m.

① Do you have the time?
② Where shall we meet?
③ How can you make it?
④ What time shall we meet?
⑤ Would you like to come over?

4 대화가 자연스럽게 이어지도록 (A)~(D)를 바르게 배열하시오.

(A) Where shall we meet?
(B) How about Dream Park?
(C) You should take the subway.
(D) Okay. But how can I get there?

______ → ______ → ______ → ______

자주 나와요

5 다음 중 짝지어진 대화가 어색한 것은?

① A: When shall we meet?
B: Can you make it by 2 p.m.?
② A: Where is your home?
B: It's across from the hair shop.
③ A: When do you want to meet?
B: Let's meet at Star Theater.
④ A: Let's have lunch together.
B: Okay. Where shall we meet?
⑤ A: Do you know the way to Grand Gym?
B: Yes. Walk straight three blocks.

[6-8] 다음 우리말과 일치하도록 할 때, 빈칸에 들어갈 말로 알맞은 것을 고르시오.

6 어렸을 때, 나는 고양이 한 마리가 있었다.

→ ________ I was young, I had a cat.

① For　② That
③ When　④ After
⑤ Because

7 우리는 산책하기 전에 아침을 먹었다.

→ We had breakfast ________ we took a walk.

① but　② after
③ while　④ before
⑤ because

8 그는 축구를 하는 동안 다리가 부러졌다.

→ He broke his leg ________ he was playing soccer.

① so ② and
③ that ④ after
⑤ while

9 다음 대화의 빈칸에 들어갈 말로 알맞지 않은 것은?

A: Where are my pants?
B: They are ________ the table.

① on ② for
③ under ④ next to
⑤ in front of

[10-11] 다음 대화의 빈칸에 들어갈 말이 바르게 짝지어진 것을 고르시오.

10 A: What do you like to do ________ summer?
B: I like to swim ________ the pool.

① in – on ② in – in
③ on – over ④ on – under
⑤ at – behind

11 A: Which do you want for dinner, chicken ________ pizza?
B: Pizza, please!
A: Okay. I'll call you when dinner ________ ready.

① or – be ② or – is
③ or – will be ④ and – is
⑤ and – will be

12 다음 빈칸에 공통으로 들어갈 말로 알맞은 것은?

- Charles felt tired ________ he worked all day.
- I turned down the music ________ it was too loud.

① or ② that
③ over ④ between
⑤ because

[13-14] 다음 지도를 보고, 알맞은 전치사를 이용하여 대화를 완성하시오.

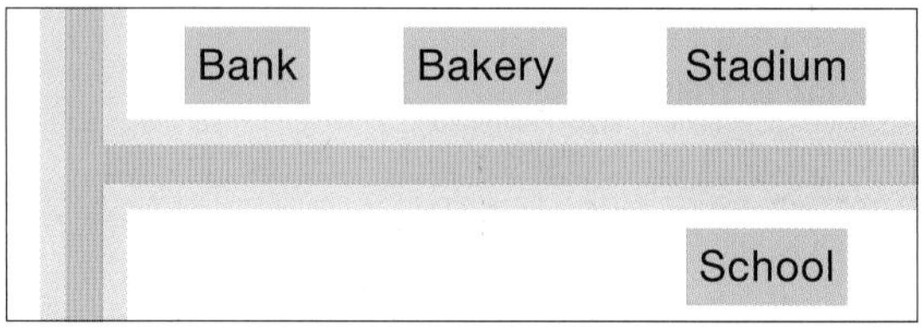

13 A: Is the stadium across from the bakery?
B: No. It is ________ ________ the bakery.

14 A: Where is the bakery?
B: It is ________ the bank ________ the stadium.

자주 나와요

15 다음 빈칸에 들어갈 말이 나머지 넷과 다른 것은?

① I believe ________ I'm smart.
② Please knock ________ you come in.
③ It isn't true ________ she can speak Chinese.
④ You may know ________ he likes Linda.
⑤ His idea is ________ we should clean our rooms.

어려워요

16 다음 밑줄 친 부분 중 어법상 바르지 못한 것을 모두 고르시오. (2개)

① It is windy and cold outside.
② We have to take a bus or walking.
③ After we pack our bags, we'll leave.
④ A little boy followed behind me.
⑤ Jenna closed her shop late in night.

[17-18] 다음 밑줄 친 부분을 바르게 고치시오.

17 There is a big mirror at the wall.

→ ____________

18 The opera will last on three hours.

→ ____________

[19-20] 다음 보기 와 괄호 안의 단어를 이용하여 문장을 완성하시오.

보기 at on in over

19 My classmates gave me some gifts ____________. (the morning)

20 My teacher wrote me a birthday card ____________. (lunchtime)

내신 완성 서술형

[21-22] 다음 두 문장을 알맞은 접속사를 이용하여 한 문장으로 바꿔 쓰시오.

21 I had a toothache. So I went to the dentist's.

→ I went to the dentist's ____________
____________.

22 The math teacher came into the classroom. The class began.

→ The class began ____________
____________.

[23-24] 다음 초대장을 보고, 질문에 대한 대답을 완성하시오.

Come to Our School Concert!

- When: Feb 14, 1:30 p.m.
- Where: Victoria Hall
- Transportation: Bus number 167

23 A: What time does the concert begin?
B: It ____________

24 A: How can I get to Victoria Hall?
B: You should take ____________.

WORD LIST

Grammar

☐	hang	동 걸리다
☐	dry	형 마른; 건조한
☐	exactly	부 정확히
☐	shelf	명 선반
☐	tasty	형 맛있는
☐	stretch	동 뻗다
☐	award	명 상
☐	medicine	명 약
☐	shocking	형 충격적인
☐	pass by	지나가다
☐	necessary	형 필요한, 필수의
☐	warm up	준비 운동을 하다
☐	wet	형 젖은
☐	eyesight	명 시력
☐	disappear	동 사라지다
☐	apologize	동 사과하다
☐	gather	동 모이다
☐	truth	명 사실
☐	half	명 반, 절반
☐	whistle	동 휘파람을 불다
☐	recover	동 (건강이) 회복되다
☐	fact	명 사실
☐	field trip	현장 학습
☐	festival	명 축제
☐	order	동 주문하다
☐	police station	경찰서
☐	post office	우체국

Reading

☐	dinosaur	명 공룡
☐	sharp	형 날카로운
☐	probably	부 아마
☐	consume	동 소모하다; 먹다
☐	adult	명 어른; 다 자란 동물
☐	experience	동 경험하다
☐	species	명 종(種)
☐	vegetarian	명 채식주의자
☐	curtain	명 커튼, 막
☐	for example	예를 들어
☐	jaw	명 턱
☐	cheek	명 볼, 뺨
☐	after a while	잠시 후에
☐	describe	동 묘사하다
☐	forehead	명 이마
☐	compare	동 비교하다
☐	attractive	형 매력적인
☐	stranger	명 낯선 사람

Communication

☐	corner	명 모퉁이
☐	theater	명 극장
☐	national	형 국가의; 국립의

Final Test

☐	pants	명 바지
☐	pool	명 수영장
☐	ready	형 준비가 된
☐	stadium	명 경기장
☐	follow	동 따라가다[오다]
☐	toothache	명 치통

CHAPTER 12

여러 가지 문장의 종류

GET READY

Look at the moon.
(달을 봐라.)

What a great idea it is!
(그것은 참 멋진 생각이구나!)

You are thirsty, **aren't you?**
(너는 목이 말라, 그렇지 않니?)

동사원형으로 문장을 시작해서 상대방에게 명령할 수 있고, 의문사로 시작하는 감탄문을 이용해 감정을 표현하기도 해요. 또한 부가 의문문을 문장 뒤에 붙여서 말한 내용을 확인하거나 동의를 구할 수 있어요.

A 명령문과 감탄문

1 명령문

명령문은 상대방에게 명령, 권유, 부탁 등을 할 때 쓰는 문장이다.

1) 명령문의 형태와 의미

형태	의미	예
동사원형	…해라	**Be** confident. **Call** me, please. (※ 문장 앞, 뒤에 please를 붙이면 공손한 부탁을 나타낸다.)
Don't+동사원형	…하지 마라	**Don't be** afraid. **Do not go** over the speed limit.
Let's+동사원형	…하자	**Let's watch** this movie. **Let's do** our math homework.
Let's not+동사원형	…하지 말자	**Let's not talk** about him. **Let's not climb** the mountain today.

2) 명령문에 대한 대답

긍정 대답	Okay. / All right. / Sure. / No problem. / Why not?
부정 대답	I'm sorry, but I can't.

(※ 「Let's+동사원형」에 대한 대답은 Yes, let's. / No, let's not.으로도 할 수 있다.)

내신 POINT PLUS

「명령문, and / or ...」

「명령문, and ...」는 '~해라, 그러면 …할 것이다'를, 「명령문, or ...」는 '~해라, 그렇지 않으면 …할 것이다'를 나타낸다.

Push the button, **and** the door will open. (버튼을 눌러라, 그러면 문이 열릴 것이다.)

Study hard, **or** you'll fail the exam. (열심히 공부해라, 그렇지 않으면 너는 시험에 떨어질 것이다.)

2 감탄문

감탄문은 자신의 감정이나 느낌을 표현하는 문장으로, '참 …하구나!'라고 해석한다.

1) What으로 시작하는 감탄문: 「What(+a / an)+형용사+명사(+주어+동사)!」

명사가 복수형이거나 셀 수 없는 명사이면 부정관사 a/an을 쓰지 않으며, 「주어+동사」는 생략할 수 있다.

What a cute girl (you are)**!** (← You are a very cute girl.)

2) How로 시작하는 감탄문: 「How+형용사 / 부사(+주어+동사)!」

How 뒤에는 형용사와 부사가 올 수 있으며, 「주어+동사」는 생략할 수 있다.

How small (the world is)**!** (← The world is very small.)

Check-Up

A 다음 괄호 안에서 알맞은 말을 고르시오.

1 (How / What) fast they eat!
2 (Be / Don't) proud of yourself.
3 (How / What) long ears the rabbit has!
4 Take a deep breath, (and / or) you will feel better.
5 Slow down a little, (and / or) you'll fall off the horse.

WORDS

A
take a deep breath 심호흡하다
slow down 속도를 줄이다
fall off 떨어지다

B 다음 빈칸에 들어갈 말을 보기 에서 골라 쓰시오.

보기 Be Don't What How Let's

1 I'm tired. ________ take a break.
2 Look at that! ________ a high mountain!
3 This knife is very sharp. ________ careful.
4 We have enough time. ________ be hasty.
5 My friends gave me a birthday present. ________ sweet they are!

B
take a break 잠시 휴식을 취하다
sharp 형 날카로운, 뾰족한
hasty 형 서두른, 성급한
sweet 형 달콤한; *상냥한

C 다음 문장을 명령문으로 바꿀 때, 빈칸에 알맞은 말을 쓰시오.

1 You have to wait here until noon.
→ ________ ________ until noon.
2 You can't play the piano at night.
→ ________ ________ the piano at night.

C
noon 명 정오

D 다음 문장을 감탄문으로 바꿀 때, 빈칸에 알맞은 말을 쓰시오.

1 It is a very nice day.
→ ________ a nice day!
2 The passengers were very lucky.
→ ________ ________ the passengers were!
3 The program is very funny.
→ ________ ________ the program is!

D
passenger 명 승객

B 여러 가지 의문문

1 부가 의문문

부가 의문문은 평서문 뒤에 덧붙이는 의문문으로, 상대방에게 동의를 구하거나 말한 내용을 확인할 때 사용한다.
부가 의문문이 긍정형이면 '그렇지?'로, 부정형이면 '그렇지 않니?'로 해석한다.

1) 부가 의문문의 형태: 「동사+주어?」

형태	긍정문 뒤에는 부정 의문문	You *are* sleepy, **aren't you?**
	부정문 뒤에는 긍정 의문문	He *isn't* a police officer, **is he?**
주어	평서문의 주어 → 대명사 (※ this/that → it)	*Lisa and Aaron* didn't order a drink, **did they?** *This* is your laptop computer, **isn't it?**
동사의 종류	be동사 → be동사 조동사 → 조동사 일반동사 → 조동사 do	It *is* windy, **isn't it?** He *can't* eat spicy food, **can he?** Kate *works* in Minnesota, **doesn't she?**
동사의 시제	평서문 시제에 일치	You *went* jogging this morning, **didn't you?**
명령문	..., will you?	*Make* lunch now, **will you?**
Let's로 시작하는 명령문	..., shall we?	*Let's* travel around Taiwan, **shall we?**

2) 부가 의문문에 대한 대답: 대답하는 내용이 긍정이면 Yes, 부정이면 No로 답한다.

A: You don't live in Seoul, **do you?** B: **Yes, I do.** (서울에 살고 있음.)
No, I don't. (서울에 살지 않음.)

2 부정 의문문

부정 의문문은 동사의 부정형으로 시작하는 의문문으로, '…하지 않니?'라고 해석한다.

1) 부정 의문문의 형태

be동사의 의문문	Aren't/Isn't+주어 ...? Wasn't/Weren't+주어 ...?	**Aren't** you excited**?** **Wasn't** he a designer**?**
일반동사의 의문문	Don't/Doesn't+주어+동사원형 ...? Didn't+주어+동사원형 ...?	**Doesn't** she eat meat**?** **Didn't** you make this poster**?**
조동사의 의문문	Can't/Won't/Shouldn't+주어+동사원형 ...?	**Can't** Jim help you now**?**

2) 부정 의문문에 대한 대답: 대답하는 내용이 긍정이면 Yes, 부정이면 No로 답한다.

A: **Didn't** you understand me**?** B: **Yes, I did.** (이해했음.)
No, I didn't. (이해하지 않았음.)

3 선택 의문문

선택 의문문은 접속사 or를 써서 제시된 대상 중 하나를 선택하도록 요구하는 의문문이다.
선택 의문문에는 Yes나 No가 아닌 제시된 것들 중 하나를 골라 대답한다.

A: Is she *a teacher* **or** *a firefighter***?** B: She is *a firefighter*.

Check-Up

A 다음 괄호 안에서 알맞은 말을 고르시오.

1 (Isn't / Aren't) the man handsome?

2 You jump very high, (can't / don't) you?

3 Throw out the trash, (will / shall) you?

4 Oliver scored a goal, (doesn't / didn't) he?

5 Which do you prefer, the bus (or / and) the train?

WORDS

A
throw out 버리다
score a goal 득점하다, 골을 넣다
prefer 동 선호하다

B 다음 대화의 빈칸에 알맞은 말을 쓰시오.

1 A: Can't you use this color printer?
B: Yes, ________ ________.

2 A: Didn't Harry make a reservation?
B: ________, he didn't.

3 A: Isn't Jane going to come to the exhibition?
B: ________, she is.

B
make a reservation 예약하다
exhibition 명 전시회

C 다음 밑줄 친 부분을 바르게 고치시오.

1 She can drive a car, didn't she? → ________

2 Mike will get a new job, won't Mike? → ________

3 Let's donate our old clothes, will we? → ________

4 Wasn't she go back to Nepal last week? → ________

C
donate 동 기부[기증]하다

D 다음 문장을 괄호 안의 지시대로 바꿀 때, 빈칸에 알맞은 말을 쓰시오.

1 You keep a diary. (부정 의문문으로)
→ ________ ________ ________ a diary?

2 Amy's friends saw him this afternoon. (부가 의문문으로)
→ Amy's friends saw him this afternoon, ________ ________?

3 She will arrive here today or tomorrow. (선택 의문문으로)
→ ________ ________ arrive here ________ ________ ________?

D
keep a diary 일기를 쓰다
arrive 동 도착하다

Grammar Practice

A 다음 괄호 안에서 알맞은 말을 고르시오.

1 Don't (be / being) rude to your neighbors.
2 (Turns / Turn) off the radio in your room.
3 (How / What) exciting the school trip was!
4 He will stay at his uncle's house, (wasn't / won't) he?
5 Sit down, (or / and) people won't be able to see the screen.

B 다음 밑줄 친 부분을 바르게 고치시오.

1 What tiny a baby she is! → ____________
2 You fed the pigs, don't you? → ____________
3 Not let's go into that cave. → ____________
4 Which do you want, a pen and a pencil? → ____________
5 Help me with my homework, shall you? → ____________

C 다음 대화의 빈칸에 알맞은 말을 쓰시오.

1 A: Won't you join the bowling club?
B: __________, __________ __________. I already joined the tennis club.
2 A: Isn't he the writer of the drama?
B: __________, __________ __________. He's proud of his work.
3 A: Let's buy this perfume for mom's present.
B: __________, __________ __________. She bought it yesterday.

D 다음 우리말과 일치하도록 괄호 안의 단어를 이용하여 문장을 완성하시오.

1 테이블 위의 조각품을 만지지 마시오. (touch)
→ __________ __________ the sculpture on the table.
2 이 책을 읽어라, 그러면 너는 그의 연설을 이해하게 될 것이다. (understand)
→ Read this book, __________ __________ __________ __________ his speech.

WORDS

A
rude 형 무례한
neighbor 명 이웃 (사람)
screen 명 화면

B
tiny 형 아주 작은
cave 명 동굴

C
bowling 명 볼링
already 부 이미, 벌써
perfume 명 향수

D
sculpture 명 조각품
speech 명 연설, 담화

내신 완성 Grammar Practice

1 다음 빈칸에 들어갈 말이 바르게 짝지어진 것은?

- The robot can lift heavy things, ________ it?
- Is this mushroom soup ________ broccoli soup?

① is – or
② isn't – or
③ can – and
④ can't – and
⑤ can't – or

2 다음 중 짝지어진 대화가 어색한 것은?

① A: They aren't singing, are they?
B: No, they aren't. They are talking.
② A: Don't walk on the grass.
B: All right. I won't.
③ A: Doesn't Jeremy have a driver's license?
B: Yes, he does. He should get one this year.
④ A: Let's put the alarm clock next to the bed.
B: No, let's not. Let's put it on the floor.
⑤ A: Which color do you like better, green or blue?
B: I like green better.

3 다음 중 어법상 바른 것을 모두 고르시오. (2개)

① Can't she ski well?
② How beautiful the bride!
③ Bring your student ID card with you.
④ This is a useful medicine, isn't this?
⑤ Billy drove the truck yesterday, doesn't he?

4 다음 우리말과 일치하도록 괄호 안의 단어를 바르게 배열하시오.

(1) 그건 참 멋진 스카프구나! (a, scarf, cool, what)
→ ______________________ it is!

(2) 과거에 초점을 맞추지 말자. (not, focus on, let's)
→ ______________________ the past.

WORDS

1
lift 동 들어 올리다
mushroom 명 버섯

2
driver's license 운전 면허증
floor 명 바닥

3
bride 명 신부

4
scarf 명 스카프
cool 형 멋진
focus on …에 초점을 맞추다, 집중하다
past 명 과거

A 다음 우리말과 일치하도록 괄호 안의 말을 바르게 배열하시오.

1 그녀는 중국이나 일본 중 어느 나라에서 왔니?
(Japan, country, is, or, which, China, she, from)
→ ______________________________

2 그는 그의 고향을 방문할 거야, 그렇지 않니?
(will, his, he, he, hometown, won't, visit)
→ ______________________________

3 내게 사실을 말해라, 그렇지 않으면 나는 화가 날 것이다.
(the truth, be angry, or, tell, will, I, me)
→ ______________________________

B 다음 문장을 괄호 안의 지시대로 바꿔 쓰시오.

1 We look for something to eat. (Let's 명령문으로)
→ ______________________________

2 They had a Halloween party last night. (부정 의문문으로)
→ ______________________________

3 You take off your shoes in the hall. (부정 명령문으로)
→ ______________________________

C 다음 문장을 괄호 안의 단어를 이용하여 감탄문으로 바꿔 쓰시오. (주어와 동사는 생략하지 말 것)

1 The lighthouse was very bright. (How)
→ ______________________________

2 These socks are very long. (How)
→ ______________________________

3 She has a very big kitchen. (What)
→ ______________________________

1

Josh is often late for school. He was late again this morning. When Josh saw his teacher, he said, "**What an unlucky morning!**" His teacher asked, "What's your story this time?" Josh said, "I was waiting for the bus. Suddenly it started raining. But I didn't bring my umbrella." "**How unfortunate you are!**" said his teacher. Josh said, "So I tried *hitchhiking. Luckily, Nick's parents saw me, and they gave me a ride." "그들은 참 친절하시구나!" said his teacher. "But their car broke down. So I had to walk to school." After he finished, his teacher replied, "**What an amazing story!** But you already used it last month."

*hitchhike: 남의 차를 얻어 타다

1 위 글의 내용으로 유추할 수 있는 것은?

① Josh의 집은 학교에서 멀다.
② Josh는 거짓말을 하지 않는다.
③ 선생님은 Josh의 말을 믿지 않는다.
④ 선생님은 Josh를 용서해 줄 것이다.
⑤ Josh는 학교 가는 길에 친구를 만났다.

서술형

2 위 글의 밑줄 친 우리말을 다음 조건에 맞게 영작하시오.

조건 1 how로 문장을 시작할 것
조건 2 kind를 포함하여 4단어로 작성할 것

→ ______________________________

WORDS unlucky 형 운이 나쁜 suddenly 부 [1]__________ unfortunate 형 운이 나쁜 give A a ride A를 태워 주다 break down 고장 나다 reply 동 대답하다 amazing 형 [2]__________

2

Imagine that we had just six minutes of sunshine a month. It would be terrible, ___(A)___ it? Actually, this recently happened in Moscow, Russia. (①) But in December 2017, it only got six minutes of sunshine! (②) Every day was dark and cloudy. (③) It was the darkest month on record in Moscow. (④) The previous record was set in December 2000. (⑤) There were only three hours of sunshine that month. ___(B)___ it sound depressing? The weather definitely made the people of Moscow feel blue. According to a local newspaper, there was a big increase in the number of visits to *psychiatrists that month!

*psychiatrist: 정신과 의사

1 **Where would the following sentence best fit?**

Moscow usually gets about 18 hours of sunlight each December.

① ② ③ ④ ⑤

2 **Which is the best pair for (A) and (B)?**

(A)		(B)
① isn't	–	Doesn't
② would	–	Isn't
③ would	–	Doesn't
④ wouldn't	–	Isn't
⑤ wouldn't	–	Doesn't

WORDS sunshine 명 햇빛 terrible 형 [1] ________ recently 부 최근에 happen 동 발생하다
cloudy 형 흐린, 구름이 잔뜩 낀 previous 형 이전의 depressing 형 우울하게 만드는 definitely 부 분명히[틀림없이]
blue 형 파란; *우울한 local 형 지역의, 현지의 increase 명 [2] ________

A 칭찬하기

A: I cooked this spaghetti with tomato sauce.
(내가 이 토마토소스 스파게티를 요리했어.)

B: **Good for you!** It looks tasty.
(잘했어! 맛있어 보인다.)

A: **Thank you.** Would you like some?
(고마워. 좀 먹을래?)

B: Sure! Let's try it together.
(물론이지! 같이 먹어 보자.)

'잘했어!'의 의미로 상대방을 칭찬할 때 'Good for you!'라고 말할 수 있다. 칭찬에 대해서는 'Thank you.' 등으로 대답할 수 있다.

EXPRESSION PLUS

A: I won a medal in the singing contest. (나는 노래 대회에서 메달을 땄어.)
B: **You did a great job!** (너 정말 잘했구나!)

A: I washed the dishes with Jacob, Mom. (저 Jacob과 설거지를 했어요, 엄마.)
B: **Excellent!** (훌륭하구나!)

Check-Up

1 다음 대화의 밑줄 친 문장과 바꿔 쓸 수 있는 것은?

A: I watered the trees and plants every morning.
B: <u>Excellent!</u>

① You're welcome.
② Good for you!
③ You did it again!
④ Not bad, thank you.
⑤ Pleased to meet you.

WORDS
1
water 동 물을 주다

2 다음 괄호 안의 말을 이용하여 대화를 완성하시오.

A: I got an A on the math test!
B: You ________ ________ ________ ________!
(great job)

B 놀라움 표현하기

A: **I can't believe it!** I won first prize.
(믿을 수 없어! 내가 1등 상을 탔어.)

B: **What a surprise!**
(정말 놀랍다!)

A: My parents will be very happy.
(부모님이 매우 기뻐하실 거야.)

B: I'm happy for you.
(잘 됐다.)

어떤 일에 대해 놀라움을 표현할 때 'I can't believe it!'이나 'What a surprise!'라고 말할 수 있다.

EXPRESSION PLUS

A: I'm going to Paris next week. (나는 다음 주에 파리에 가.)
B: **That's really surprising!** (그거 정말 놀랍다!)

A: Sue will enter Harvard University. (Sue가 하버드 대학에 입학할 거야.)
B: **How amazing!** (정말 놀랍다!)

Check-Up

1 대화의 밑줄 친 문장과 바꿔 쓸 수 있는 것은?

A: This tower is 1,500 years old.
B: That's surprising!

① How terrible!
② Good for you!
③ What a surprise!
④ You're surprised.
⑤ You did a good job!

2 다음 대화의 밑줄 친 문장과 쓰임이 다른 것을 모두 고르시오. (2개)

A: This camera is 70 percent off.
B: What a surprise!

① Good for you!
② How amazing!
③ I can't believe it!
④ You did a good job!
⑤ That's really surprising!

WORDS

1
tower 명 탑

2
off 부 할인되어

FINAL TEST

1 다음 중 밑줄 친 부분의 의미가 바르지 못한 것은?

① I keep a diary in English.
일기를 쓰다

② Can you give me a ride home?
…를 태워 주다

③ Throw out the trash right now.
재활용하다

④ Let's take a break under this tree.
잠시 휴식을 취하다

⑤ The machine won't break down again.
고장 나다

2 다음 우리말과 일치하도록 빈칸에 알맞은 말을 쓰시오.

다음 번에는 무슨 일이 발생할까?

→ What will ________ next time?

3 다음 대화의 빈칸에 들어갈 말로 알맞은 것은?

A: I helped an old man on the subway.
B: ________________

① Thank you.
② No problem.
③ He's very kind.
④ We should do that.
⑤ You did a great job!

4 밑줄 친 ①~⑤ 중 대화의 흐름과 어울리지 않는 것은?

A: ①I can't believe it! ②I finished writing my book today!
B: ③Good for you! ④Did you read your book?
A: ⑤Thank you.

5 다음 대화의 빈칸에 들어갈 말로 알맞지 않은 것을 모두 고르시오. (2개)

A: This monkey can read alphabet.
B: ________________

① I can't believe it!
② What a surprise!
③ You did a good job.
④ What's wrong with you?
⑤ That's really surprising.

(!) 자주 나와요

6 다음 중 짝지어진 대화가 어색한 것은?

① A: Look! There's a rainbow!
B: How amazing!
② A: I did volunteer work last weekend.
B: Great job!
③ A: I won a medal on Science Day.
B: Excellent!
④ A: I scored a goal in the soccer game.
B: Good for you!
⑤ A: I passed the test!
B: Happy to see you again.

7 다음 대화의 빈칸에 들어갈 말로 알맞은 것은?

A: Which do you like better, singing ________ dancing?
B: I like dancing better.

① or
② so
③ for
④ but
⑤ and

8 다음 빈칸에 공통으로 들어갈 말로 알맞은 것은?

- ________ quick! We're late.
- It's very dark. ________ careful.

① Do ② Be
③ Not ④ Don't
⑤ Let's

[9-10] 다음 빈칸에 들어갈 말이 나머지 넷과 다른 것을 고르시오.

9 ① ________ a boring novel it is!
② ________ fast the express trains are!
③ ________ sweet strawberries they are!
④ ________ expensive houses these are!
⑤ ________ charming girls the sisters are!

10 ① You and James are brothers, ________ you?
② He and I ________ late for the train, are we?
③ The coins on the desk ________ his, are they?
④ You ________ going to leave tomorrow, are you?
⑤ They remembered his phone number, ________ they?

[11-12] 다음 빈칸에 알맞은 부가 의문문을 쓰시오.

11 Henry is 14 years old now, ________ ________?

12 You can fix a broken toy, ________ ________?

13 다음 밑줄 친 부분 중 어법상 바르지 못한 것은?

① Put your books into a bag, will you?
② Let's have dinner together, shall we?
③ Shouldn't we get back to work now?
④ Didn't Colin and his dad go to Rome?
⑤ Tom and you were good friends, aren't you?

! 어려워요

14 다음 중 어법상 바른 것은?

① What funny he is!
② What lovely day it is!
③ What good a player he is!
④ What a pretty doll has she!
⑤ What beautiful flowers these are!

! 자주 나와요

[15-16] 다음 대화의 빈칸에 알맞은 말을 쓰시오.

15 A: Don't you like Seojin?
B: ________, ________ ________.
He is so cute.

16 A: Can't we stop by a café?
B: ________, ________ ________.
We don't have much time.

자주 나와요

17 다음 중 짝지어진 대화가 어색한 것은?

① A: Let's get on the elevator.
B: No, let's not.
② A: Look at the sky! It's clear.
B: How blue it is!
③ A: Is Joe's car black or white?
B: Yes, it is black.
④ A: It'll be snowy tonight, won't it?
B: Yes. It'll snow.
⑤ A: Cut the bread into two pieces.
B: All right.

18 다음 우리말을 영어로 바르게 옮긴 것은?

너 어젯밤에 TV를 보지 않았니?

① Do you watch TV last night?
② Did you watch TV last night?
③ Don't you watch TV last night?
④ Didn't you watch TV last night?
⑤ Won't you watch TV last night?

서술형

[19-20] 다음 우리말과 일치하도록 괄호 안의 단어를 바르게 배열하시오.

19 너는 참 아름답게 노래하는구나!
(beautifully, sing, how, you)

→ ________________________

20 지하철을 타자, 그럴 거지?
(take, shall, the subway, we, let's)

→ ________________________

내신 완성 서술형

[21-22] 다음 두 문장을 and 또는 or를 이용하여 한 문장으로 바꿔 쓰시오.

21 Present the coupon. You'll get a discount.

→ ________________________
____

22 Buy the concert ticket now. You won't see your favorite singer tomorrow.

→ ________________________
____

[23-25] 다음은 영화관에서 지켜야 할 규칙을 나타낸 안내문이다. 안내문을 바르게 고쳐 쓰시오.

Sit down before the movie starts.

23 Turns off your cell phone.
24 Don't kicks the seat.
25 Do not to talk during the movie.

23 ________________________

24 ________________________

25 ________________________

WORD LIST

Grammar

- take a deep breath　심호흡하다
- slow down　속도를 줄이다
- fall off　떨어지다
- take a break　잠시 휴식을 취하다
- sharp　[형] 날카로운, 뾰족한
- passenger　[명] 승객
- throw out　버리다
- score a goal　득점하다, 골을 넣다
- prefer　[동] 선호하다
- make a reservation　예약하다
- exhibition　[명] 전시회
- donate　[동] 기부[기증]하다
- keep a diary　일기를 쓰다
- arrive　[동] 도착하다
- rude　[형] 무례한
- neighbor　[명] 이웃 (사람)
- screen　[명] 화면
- tiny　[형] 아주 작은
- cave　[명] 동굴
- already　[부] 이미, 벌써
- sculpture　[명] 조각품
- speech　[명] 연설, 담화
- lift　[동] 들어 올리다
- bride　[명] 신부
- focus on　…에 초점을 맞추다, 집중하다

Reading

- unlucky　[형] 운이 나쁜
- suddenly　[부] 갑자기
- give A a ride　A를 태워 주다
- break down　고장 나다
- reply　[동] 대답하다
- amazing　[형] 놀라운
- sunshine　[명] 햇빛
- terrible　[형] 끔찍한
- recently　[부] 최근에
- happen　[동] 발생하다
- cloudy　[형] 흐린, 구름이 잔뜩 낀
- previous　[형] 이전의
- depressing　[형] 우울하게 만드는
- definitely　[부] 분명히[틀림없이]
- blue　[형] 파란; *우울한
- local　[형] 지역의, 현지의
- increase　[명] 증가

Communication

- water　[동] 물을 주다
- tower　[명] 탑
- off　[부] 할인되어

Final Test

- machine　[명] 기계
- rainbow　[명] 무지개
- express train　급행열차
- stop by　잠시 들르다
- present　[동] 제시하다
- coupon　[명] 쿠폰, 할인권
- discount　[명] 할인
- kick　[동] (발로) 차다

MEMO

MEMO

MEMO

MEMO

MEMO

MEMO

MEMO

지은이

NE능률 영어교육연구소

NE능률 영어교육연구소는 혁신적이며 효율적인 영어 교재를 개발하고
영어 학습의 질을 한 단계 높이고자 노력하는 NE능률의 연구조직입니다.

능률중학영어 〈중1〉

펴 낸 이 주민홍
펴 낸 곳 서울특별시 마포구 월드컵북로 396(상암동) 누리꿈스퀘어 비즈니스타워 10층
㈜NE능률 (우편번호 03925)
펴 낸 날 2019년 1월 5일 개정판 제1쇄 발행
2023년 11월 15일 제13쇄
전 화 02 2014 7114
팩 스 02 3142 0356
홈페이지 www.neungyule.com
등록번호 제1-68호
I S B N 979-11-253-2449-2 53740
정 가 12,000원

NE 능률

고객센터

교재 내용 문의 : contact.nebooks.co.kr (별도의 가입 절차 없이 작성 가능)
제품 구매, 교환, 불량, 반품 문의 : 02-2014-7114
☎ 전화문의는 본사 업무시간 중에만 가능합니다.

중학 내신 완벽 대비 종합서

능률 중학영어

중1

정답 및 해설

NE 능률

중학 내신 완벽 대비 종합서

능률 중학 영어

중1

정답 및 해설

CHAPTER 01 인칭대명사와 be동사

GRAMMAR FOCUS

p. 8

A 인칭대명사와 be동사

1 Sarah는 수영 선수이다. 그녀는 빠르게 수영한다.
Ben은 화가이다. 그의 그림들은 멋지다.
나는 애완용 새가 있다. 나는 그것을 사랑한다.
내 가방은 작다. 그들의 것은 크다.

2 1) 나는 똑똑한 소년이다.
그는 지금 바쁘다.
그것은 그녀의 휴대 전화이다.
그들은 나의 반 친구들이다.

Check-Up

p. 9

A 1 I 2 He 3 hers 4 His 5 them
B 1 I'm 2 It's 3 She's 4 We're 5 You're
C 1 It 2 He 3 her 4 yours 5 Their
D 1 are 2 are 3 It 4 my 5 We

GRAMMAR FOCUS

p. 10

B be동사의 부정문과 의문문

1 나는 게으르지 않다.
너는 혼자가 아니다.
그는 체육관에 있지 않다.
그들은 나의 부모님이 아니다.

2 A: 저는 좋은 야구 선수인가요?
B: 응, 그래. / 아니, 그렇지 않아.
A: 너는 십 대이니?
B: 응, 그래. / 아니, 그렇지 않아.
A: 그들은 인기 있는 배우들이니?
B: 응, 그래. / 아니, 그렇지 않아.

Check-Up

p. 11

A 1 You are not 2 Are they 3 Is she
4 There aren't
B 1 he is 2 I'm not 3 they aren't[they're not]
C 1 It isn't 2 They aren't 3 She isn't
4 We aren't
D 1 There are 2 Is there 3 There is not

Grammar Practice

p. 12

A 1 Are 2 our 3 is 4 It 5 I am
B 1 their 2 his 3 are 4 is not 5 Its
C 1 Is she 2 It is 3 There is
D 1 ours, theirs 2 its

문제해설

A 1 주어가 복수명사이므로 be동사로 Are가 와야 한다.
2 명사 앞에는 소유 관계를 나타내는 소유격 our가 와야 한다.
4 날씨를 나타낼 때는 비인칭 주어 It을 쓴다.
5 「Are you(단수) ...?」에 대한 긍정 대답으로는 Yes, I am.이 알맞다.

B 2 '그의 것'이라는 의미인 소유대명사 his가 알맞다.
3 뒤에 복수명사가 이어지므로 be동사는 are가 알맞다.
4 주어가 3인칭 단수이고, '…에 없다'라는 의미이므로 is not이 알맞다.

D 1 각 빈칸에 '우리의 것'과 '그들의 것'이라는 의미의 소유대명사 ours와 theirs를 써야 한다.
2 '그것의'라는 의미를 나타내는 소유격 its를 쓴다.

내신 완성 Grammar Practice

p. 13

1 ⑤ 2 ⑤ 3 ④ 4 (1) Is there a bank
(2) is not mine (3) There are not many stars

문제해설

1 there 뒤에 복수명사가 이어지므로 첫 번째 빈칸에는 Are가 와야 한다.
두 번째 빈칸에는 '우리의 것'이라는 의미의 소유대명사 ours가 와야 한다.

2 ⑤ 두 번째 문장에서 주어가 He이므로 are를 is로 고쳐야 한다.

3 ④ It 뒤에는 be동사 is가 와야 한다. 나머지에는 모두 are[Are]가 와야 한다.

서술형에 나오는 WRITING

p. 14

A 1 He is their English teacher.
2 That T-shirt is not hers.
3 Are you from Italy?
B 1 Is your uncle 2 My car is not[isn't]
3 It is[It's] Saturday
C 1 His cap is 2 There are (four) baseballs

문제해설

C 1 주어 자리에 「소유격+명사」인 His cap을 쓰고, 주어가 3인칭 단수이므로 be동사로 is를 쓴다.
2 책상 아래에 4개의 야구공이 있으므로 「There are ...」 구문을 쓴다.

READING WITH GRAMMAR pp. 15~16

Reading 1 | **1** ⑤ **2** there are not six people
Words | [1] 가르치다 [2] 마지막의

해석 | Clara: 봐! 이건 나의 가족사진이야.
Jacob: 와, 너의 가족은 대가족이구나.
Clara: 응. 나의 가족에는 여섯 명이 있어.
Jacob: 이 남자분이 너의 아버지시니?
Clara: 응, 맞아. 아빠는 바리스타셔. 아빠는 카페에서 일하셔.
Jacob: 알겠어. 이 여자분은 너의 어머니셔?
Clara: 응, 맞아. 엄마는 중학교 선생님이셔. 엄마는 수학을 가르치셔.
Jacob: 오, 이 남자애들은 아주 비슷하다! 그들은 쌍둥이니?
Clara: 응, 맞아. 그들은 내 남동생들이야. 그들의 이름은 Jay와 Sam이야.
Jacob: 그리고 이 소녀는 너구나. 음…. 그런데, 사진에는 여섯 명이 있지 않네.
Clara: 마지막 구성원은 Max야. 여기 그가 있어. 그는 우리의 애완 고양이야!

구문해설

5행 Is **this** man your dad?

8행 Is **this** woman your mom?
▸ this는 '이 …'의 의미로, 가까이 있는 것을 가리킬 때 쓴다.

문제해설

1 ⑤ 애완 고양이가 있다고 했다.

2 '…가 있지 않다'를 나타내는 「There are not ...」 뒤에 six people을 쓴다.

Reading 2 | **1** ⑤ **2** (A) am (B) them
Words | [1] 사람

해석 | 너는 나를 아니? 나는 일본 삿포로에 살아. 내가 사람일까? 아니, 그렇지 않아. 전 세계 사람들이 2월에 나를 찾아와. 그들은 눈 축제를 위해서 오지. 그들은 얼음 성들을 봐. 그 성들은 높지만, 나는 키가 크지 않아. 예술가들이 그것들을 만들어. 하지만 누구나 나를 만들 수 있지!
그저 큰 눈덩이 두 개를 만들어 봐. 하나는 내 몸을 위한 것이고, 나머지 하나는 내 머리를 위한 거야. 내 눈은 단추야. 내 팔은 나뭇가지야. 그리고 내 코는 당근이지. 너는 이제 나를 알겠니? 당연히 너는 알지! 나는 눈사람이야!

구문해설

1행 I live **in** Sapporo, Japan.
▸ 도시, 국가 등 넓은 장소 앞에는 전치사 in을 쓴다.

2행 **People** from all around the world **visit** me *in* February.
▸ 문장의 주어는 People, 동사는 visit이며, from ... world는 People을 수식하는 형용사 역할을 하는 전치사구이다.
▸ 월(月) 앞에는 전치사 in을 쓴다.

5행 **One** is for my body, and **the other** is for my head.
▸ one ... the other ~: (둘 중) 하나는 …, 나머지 하나는 ~

8행 Of course you **do**!
▸ do는 앞 문장의 know me를 가리키는 대동사이다.

문제해설

1 글쓴이에 대해 사실이 아닌 것은?
① 그것은 일본에 산다.
② 사람들은 그것을 만들 수 있다.
③ 그것은 눈을 위한 단추가 있다.
④ 나뭇가지는 그것의 팔이다.
⑤ 그것의 코는 눈덩이로 만들어진다.
▸ ⑤ 그것의 코는 당근이라고 했다.

2 밑줄 친 (A)와 (B)를 바르게 고치시오.
▸ (A) 주어가 1인칭 단수 I이므로 be동사로 am을 써야 한다.
(B) '그들을'에 해당하는 목적격 them을 써야 한다.

내신에 나오는 COMMUNICATION

A 안부 묻고 답하기 p. 17

Check-Up | **1** ① **2** ⑤

문제해설

2 ⑤는 날씨를 묻는 표현이고, 나머지는 상대방의 안부를 묻는 표현이다.

B 소개하고 답하기 p. 18

Check-Up | **1** ⑤ **2** ②

문제해설

1 ⑤ Kate와 Dave는 처음 만나 인사를 하고 있으므로 빈칸에는 Kate를 소개하는 말이 들어가는 것이 자연스럽다.

2 ② 서로 자신을 소개하는 상황에서 What's up?이라고 안부를 묻는 것은 자연스럽지 않다.

FINAL TEST pp. 19~21

1 ② **2** good at **3** ④ **4** ③ **5** (C)→(B)→(A)
6 ⑤ **7** ④ **8** ② **9** ② **10** ④ **11** ② **12** ②
13 ③ **14** ③ **15** ⑤ **16** ③ **17** ① **18** ②
19 Her story is not fun. **20** Is this watch yours?
21 I am[I'm] not a figure skater. **22** Are his gloves on the floor? **23** Is, Yes, it is **24** Are, No, they aren't[they're not]

문제해설

1 ② alike는 '(아주) 비슷한'의 뜻이다.

2 be good at: …를 잘하다

3 ④ 자신을 소개할 때는 Let me introduce myself.라고 말한다.

4 A가 잘 지낸다고 대답하는 것으로 보아, 빈칸에는 안부를 묻는 표현인 ③이 와야 한다.

5 (C) 내 소개를 할게. 나는 Tom이야.
(B) 안녕, Tom. 내 이름은 Lina야.
(A) 만나서 반가워, Lina.

6 be동사 are가 쓰였으므로, 주어 자리에 3인칭 단수명사인 ⑤는 알맞지 않다.

7 be동사 is가 쓰였으므로, 주어 자리에 복수명사인 ④는 알맞지 않다.

8 ② 주어가 단수명사이므로 be동사로 is가 오고, 그 뒤에 '우리의 것'을 나타내는 소유대명사 ours가 와야 한다.

9 ② 주어 that actor와 he는 3인칭 단수이므로 빈칸에 공통으로 들어갈 말은 is이다.

10 주어 your parents는 복수명사이므로 첫 번째 빈칸에는 be동사 Are가 와야 한다.
두 번째 빈칸에는 3인칭 복수명사를 대신해서 가리키는 말인 they가 와야 한다.

11 주어가 you and Maria인 의문문에 대한 대답이므로 첫 번째 빈칸에는 we가 와야 한다.
두 번째 빈칸에는 '그녀의 것'이라는 의미의 소유대명사 hers가 와야 한다.

13 ③의 his는 소유대명사이고 나머지는 모두 소유격이다.

14 ③의 It은 '그것'을 의미하는 인칭대명사이고 나머지는 모두 비인칭 주어이다.

15 ⑤에는 be동사 is가, 나머지에는 모두 Are[are]가 와야 한다.

16 ③ them을 '그들의 것'이라는 의미의 소유대명사 theirs로 고쳐야 한다.

17 ② yours → your, ③ him → he, ④ are → is, ⑤ her → hers로 고쳐야 한다.

18 ② 의문문의 주어가 2인칭 복수대명사 you이므로 Yes, we are.라고 대답해야 한다.

21 be동사의 부정문은 「주어+be동사+not ...」의 형태로 쓴다.

22 be동사의 의문문은 「be동사+주어 ...?」의 형태로 쓴다.

23 주어가 3인칭 단수이므로 A의 빈칸에는 Is를 쓴다. A의 질문에 대한 긍정 대답은 Yes, it is.이다.

24 주어가 3인칭 복수이므로 A의 빈칸에는 Are를 쓴다. A의 질문에 대한 부정 대답은 No, they aren't[they're not].이다.

CHAPTER 02 일반동사

GRAMMAR FOCUS p. 24

A 일반동사의 현재형

2 1) 나는 너를 사랑해.
너는 멋진 셔츠를 가지고 있다.
우리는 함께 퀴즈쇼를 본다.
그들은 그 도시 주위에 나무를 심는다.
많은 사람들이 Holmes Bakery에서 빵을 산다.
2) 그는 매일 물을 여덟 잔 마신다.
나의 애완동물은 공을 매우 잘 잡는다.
그녀는 일요일에 교회에 간다.
아기가 매우 크게 운다.
Smith 씨는 네 명의 아이들이 있다.

Check-Up p. 25

A 1 wake 2 like 3 stop 4 flies 5 washes
B 1 sell 2 has 3 plays 4 finishes 5 write
C 1 sets 2 tries 3 goes 4 swim
D 1 study 2 worries 3 opens 4 eat

GRAMMAR FOCUS p. 26

B 일반동사의 부정문과 의문문

1 1) 나는 모바일 게임을 하지 않는다.
우리는 그 뉴스를 믿지 않는다.
그들은 안경을 쓰지 않는다.
2) 그 시장은 주말에 닫지 않는다.
내 개는 큰 소리로 짖지 않는다.
선미는 일기 예보를 확인하지 않는다.

2 1) A: 너는 그 드라마를 보니?
B: 응, 그래. / 아니, 그렇지 않아.
A: 그의 아이들은 치즈를 좋아하니?
B: 응, 그래. / 아니, 그렇지 않아.
2) A: 네 고모는 런던에 사시니?
B: 응, 그래. / 아니, 그렇지 않아.

Check-Up p. 27

A 1 Do 2 doesn't 3 Does 4 don't
B 1 I do 2 it does 3 they don't
C 1 I don't live 2 Do they prepare
3 She doesn't visit 4 Does Alex grow
D 1 Does he have 2 don't use
3 Do you save 4 don't eat

Grammar Practice p. 28

A 1 flies 2 don't[do not] 3 Do 4 teaches
5 doesn't[does not]
B 1 helps 2 has 3 doesn't[does not] miss
4 makes 5 don't[do not] live
C 1 runs 2 O 3 O 4 listen
5 don't[do not]
D 1 We do not send 2 Do they stay

문제해설

A 1 「자음+y」로 끝나는 동사의 3인칭 단수 현재형은 y를 i로 고치고 -es를 붙여 만든다.
2 주어가 1인칭 복수이므로 don't[do not]를 써서 부정문을 만든다.
3 주어가 3인칭 복수이므로 의문문은 Do로 시작한다.
4 -ch로 끝나는 동사의 3인칭 단수 현재형은 뒤에 -es를 붙여 만든다.
5 주어가 3인칭 단수이므로 doesn't[does not]를 써서 부정문을 만든다.

B 2 have의 3인칭 단수 현재형은 has이다.

내신 완성 Grammar Practice p. 29

1 ⑤ 2 ④ 3 ② 4 doesn't, plays the violin

문제해설

1 주어가 3인칭 단수이므로 learn 앞에 doesn't를 써서 부정문을 만든다.
brush는 -sh로 끝나는 동사이므로 3인칭 단수 현재형은 brushes이다.

2 ④는 '…를 하다'라는 의미의 일반동사이고, 나머지는 의문문이나 부정문을 만들 때 쓰는 조동사이다.

3 ⓒ 주어가 복수이므로 doesn't는 don't가 되어야 한다.
ⓔ 의문문에서는 주어 뒤에 동사원형을 써야 하므로 watches는 watch가 되어야 한다.

4 일반동사의 의문문에 대한 부정 대답에서 주어가 3인칭 단수인 she이므로 첫 번째 빈칸에는 doesn't가 들어가야 한다.
두 번째 빈칸에는 동사 play의 3인칭 단수 현재형인 plays를 써서 문장을 완성한다.

서술형에 나오는 WRITING p. 30

A 1 Do you take a shower
2 James does not clear
B 1 don't[do not] skip art class
2 goes hiking in the spring
C 1 reads books 2 rides a bike 3 watches TV

문제해설

A 1 주어가 you인 일반동사의 의문문은 「Do you+동사원형 ...?」의 어순으로 쓴다.

B 1 주어가 3인칭 단수에서 1인칭으로 바뀌었으므로 doesn't를 don't[do not]로 바꿔 써야 한다.
2 주어가 3인칭 복수에서 3인칭 단수로 바뀌었으므로 동사 go를 goes로 바꿔 써야 한다.

READING WITH GRAMMAR pp. 31~32

Reading 1 | 1 ② 2 they don't[do not] listen carefully
Words | [1]숙제 [2]이해하다

해석 | 안녕하세요, 저는 조언이 필요해요! 저는 너무 바빠요. 제게는 일주일에 두 번 영어 수업, 일주일에 세 번 피아노 수업이 있고, 매일 밤 숙제가 있어요. 저는 밤늦게까지 잠자리에 들지 않아요. 그리고 저는 절대 제 친구들을 만날 수 없어요. 물론 저는 수업을 빼먹고 싶어요. 하지만 제가 뒤처질까 봐 두려워요. 그건 너무 스트레스예요.
모두 제가 행복하고 평범한 학생이라고 생각해요. 하지만, 가끔 저는 제 방에서 혼자 운답니다. 저는 종종 제 친구들에게 이것에 대해 말해요. 그러나 그들은 주의 깊게 듣지 않아요. 그들은 그저 "하지만 너는 학교에서 공부를 잘하잖아."라고 말해요. 당신은 제 문제를 이해하시나요? 제가 어떻게 해야 할까요?

구문해설

4행 And I **never** get to meet my friends.
▶ never는 '절대 …않다'라는 의미의 부사이다.

5행 But **I'm afraid** (**that**) I'll fall behind.
▶ I'm afraid (that)은 '(유감이지만) …이다, …가 두렵다'라는 의미이다.

7행 **Everyone thinks** (*that*) I'm a happy, normal student.
▶ Everyone(모두)은 단수 취급하므로 뒤에 3인칭 단수 동사 thinks가 왔다.
▶ thinks의 목적어 역할을 하는 명사절을 이끄는 접속사 that이 생략되어 있다.

문제해설

1 ② 글쓴이는 수업이 많고 매일 밤 숙제가 있는 등 학업이 너무 바쁜 것이 고민이라고 했다.

2 주어가 복수인 they이므로, doesn't를 don't[do not]로 고쳐야 한다.

Reading 2 | 1 ⑤ 2 ⑤
Words | [1]공기 [2]보호하다

해석 | Amy: 너 무슨 일 있니? 기분이 안 좋아 보여.
Charlie: 나는 이 감자 칩 봉지에 화가 나. 이 안에 공기가 너무 많아.
Amy: 공기? 봉지 안에 있는 가스 말이니?

Charlie: 응, 맞아. 그 가스가 봉지 전체를 거의 가득 채우고 있어. 그래서 감자 칩이 많지 않아. 이건 말이 안 돼!
Amy: 이해해, Charlie. 하지만 그건 그냥 공기가 아니야. 그건 질소 가스야.
Charlie: 질소 가스? 회사가 과자를 질소 가스로 채운 거야?
Amy: 응, 맞아. 그리고 그 가스가 안에 있는 감자 칩을 보호하지.
Charlie: 그 가스는 안전하니?
Amy: 응, 그래. 그건 냄새, 맛, 또는 색깔이 없어.
Charlie: 휴 …. 알았어. 하지만 나는 감자 칩을 원해, 가스 말고!

구문해설

1행 **What's the matter** with you**?**
▸ What's the matter?: 무슨 일 있니?

4행 It has too **much** air in it.
▸ much는 '많은'이라는 뜻의 수량형용사로 셀 수 없는 명사 앞에 온다.

9행 It doesn't **make sense**!
▸ make sense: 타당하다, 말이 되다

문제해설

1 질소 가스에 대해 사실이 아닌 것은?
① 그것은 봉지를 거의 가득 채운다.
② 그것은 감자 칩을 보호한다.
③ 그것은 냄새가 나지 않는다.
④ 그것은 맛이 나지 않는다.
⑤ 그것은 흰색이다.
▸ ⑤ 질소 가스는 색이 없다고 했다.

2 어법상 바르지 못한 것은?
▸ ⑤ 주어가 1인칭이므로 동사원형 want를 써야 한다.

내신에 나오는 COMMUNICATION

A 외모 묘사하기

p. 33

Check-Up | 1 ③ 2 What, look like, is handsome

문제해설

1 ③ 개의 외모에 대해 묻고 있으므로 그것은 그의 개라고 대답하는 것은 적절하지 않다.

B 음식 권하고 답하기

p. 34

Check-Up | 1 ③ 2 ④, ⑤

문제해설

2 A: 바닐라 아이스크림 좀 먹을래?
B: 응. 고마워.
▸ 밑줄 친 문장은 상대방에게 음식을 권하는 표현으로, ④와 ⑤로 바꿔 쓸 수 있다.

FINAL TEST

pp. 35~37

1 ③ 2 advice 3 ③ 4 ③ 5 (C) → (B) → (A)
6 ② 7 ④ 8 ② 9 ④ 10 ④ 11 ⓔ 12 ⓐ
13 ⓓ 14 ⑤ 15 ② 16 ② 17 don't bake cookies
18 doesn't come from 19 ③ 20 Do they work
21 Does she know 22 cook 23 washes
24 Does, Yes, he does 25 Do, No, they don't

문제해설

1 ③ huge는 '거대한'의 뜻이다.

3 A: Kevin은 어떻게 생겼니?
B: ____________
▸ 외모가 어떤지 물었으므로 짙은 머리를 가지고 있다는 ③이 대답으로 적절하다.

4 A: 딸기 케이크를 좀 드시겠어요?
B: ____________ 저는 배불러요.
▸ 뒤에 배가 부르다는 말이 이어지는 것으로 보아, 문맥상 거절의 표현인 ③이 적절하다.

5 네 애완동물은 어떻게 생겼니?
(C) 내 애완동물은 작고 흰색이야.
(B) 그것은 곱슬곱슬한 털을 가졌니?
(A) 아니, 그렇지 않아.

6 A: 엄마, 좋은 냄새가 나는데요!
B: 크림소스 스파게티를 먹겠니?
A: (저는 스파게티를 좋아하지 않아요.) 네, 주세요. 저는 배가 고파요.
B: 아이스티도 좀 마시겠니?
A: 네. 저는 목이 말라요.

7 ④ enjoy의 3인칭 단수형은 enjoys이다.

8 ② dry의 3인칭 단수형은 dries이다.

9 동사가 3인칭 단수 현재형이므로 주어로 복수인 ④는 알맞지 않다.

11 주어가 3인칭 단수인 일반동사의 의문문이므로, 적절한 대답은 ⓔ이다.

12 주어가 2인칭 단수인 일반동사의 의문문이므로, 적절한 대답은 ⓐ이다.

13 주어가 3인칭 복수인 일반동사의 의문문이므로, 적절한 대답은 ⓓ이다.

14 주어가 3인칭 단수인 일반동사의 의문문이고 문맥상 부정 대답이 와야 하므로 ⑤가 적절하다.

15 ① Do → Does, ③ cleans → clean, ④ move → moves, ⑤ doesn't → don't로 고쳐야 한다.

16 보기와 ①, ③, ④, ⑤는 일반동사의 의문문과 부정문에 쓰인 조동사이며, ②는 '…를 하다'라는 의미의 일반동사이다.

19 ③ 의문문의 주어가 you and Mia이므로 Yes, we do.라고 대답해야 한다.

20 주어가 3인칭 복수(they)인 일반동사의 의문문은 「Do they+동사원형 ...?」의 형태로 쓴다.

21 주어가 3인칭 단수(she)인 일반동사의 의문문은 「Does she+동사원형 ...?」의 형태로 쓴다.

[22-23] A: 우리 엄마는 매일 저녁을 만드셔.
B: 너희 아빠도 요리를 하시니?
A: 아니, 그렇지 않아. 하지만 아빠는 저녁 식사 후에 설거지를 하셔.

22 일반동사의 의문문에서는 주어 뒤에 동사원형이 와야하므로 cooks를 cook으로 고쳐야 한다.

24 주어가 3인칭 단수이므로 일반동사의 의문문은 Does로 시작하며, 긍정 대답은 Yes, he does.이다.

25 주어가 복수이므로 일반동사의 의문문은 Do로 시작하며, 부정 대답은 No, they don't.이다.

CHAPTER 03 동사의 시제

GRAMMAR FOCUS p. 40

A 과거시제

1 1) 그는 어제 매우 아팠다.
너는 2016년에 초등학생이었다.
2) 그날 밤 그 집은 비어 있지 않았다.
그들은 그 소식에 기뻐하지 않았다.
3) A: 그녀는 학교에 늦었니?
B: 응, 그랬어. / 아니, 그렇지 않았어.
A: 우리는 그때 보스턴에 있었니?
B: 응, 그랬어. / 아니, 그렇지 않았어.

2 1) 나는 나의 과학 숙제를 끝냈다.
그녀는 지난주에 한국에 왔다.
2) 나는 오늘 아침에 신문을 읽지 않았다.
3) A: Bill은 콘서트에 갔니?
B: 응, 그랬어. / 아니, 그렇지 않았어.

Check-Up p. 41

A 1 were 2 was 3 Did 4 drank 5 didn't
B 1 had 2 went 3 lived 4 was
C 1 open 2 Was 3 moved 4 Did
D 1 I didn't work 2 He wasn't afraid
3 Were they busy 4 Did the lady visit

GRAMMAR FOCUS p. 42

B 진행형

1 1) 나는 내 방을 청소하고 있다.
2) 그 아기는 지금 울고 있지 않다.
3) A: Jenny와 Ken은 음악을 듣고 있니?
B: 응, 그래. / 아니, 그렇지 않아.

2 1) 그 소년은 벤치에 앉아 있었다.
2) 그들은 컴퓨터 게임을 하고 있지 않았다.
3) A: 너는 한 시간 전에 자고 있었니?
B: 응, 그랬어. / 아니, 그렇지 않았어.

Check-Up p. 43

A 1 shopping 2 writing 3 lying
B 1 is running 2 was not holding
3 Was Olivia drawing
C 1 were helping 2 am not going
3 Was Jake moving
D 1 Yes, they were 2 No, he isn't[he's not]

GRAMMAR FOCUS p. 44

C 미래시제

1 1) 내일은 맑을 것이다.
나는 이번에 시험에 합격할 것이다.
2) 그들은 제시간에 도착하지 않을 것이다.
그 아이는 다시 거짓말을 하지 않을 것이다.
3) A: 너는 오늘 밤에 집에 있을 거니?
B: 응, 그럴 거야. / 아니, 그러지 않을 거야.
A: Cindy는 새 우비를 살 거니?
B: 응, 그럴 거야. / 아니, 그러지 않을 거야.

2 1) 우리는 소풍을 갈 것이다.
그는 방과 후에 배드민턴을 칠 것이다.
2) 나는 내 마음을 바꾸지 않을 것이다.
그들은 그들의 차를 팔지 않을 것이다.
3) A: 너는 저 모자를 쓸 거니?
B: 응, 그럴 거야. / 아니, 그러지 않을 거야.
A: 그녀는 연극 동아리에 가입할 예정이니?
B: 응, 그럴 거야. / 아니, 그러지 않을 거야.

Check-Up p. 45

A 1 will check 2 to plant 3 contact 4 isn't
B 1 will not[won't] 2 take 3 to study
4 Henry going
C 1 will be 2 Will we meet
3 is not going to go
D 1 will wash 2 will call 3 won't forget

Grammar Practice
p. 46

A 1 looking 2 visit 3 cut 4 am not
B 1 took 2 hit 3 ate
C 1 won't miss 2 invited 3 going to open
4 is frying
D 1 Will Sally be 2 David wasn't taking

문제해설

A 1 be동사와 함께 쓰여 현재진행형을 나타내는 구문이므로 looking으로 고쳐야 한다.
2 조동사 will 뒤에는 동사원형을 써야 한다.
3 동사 cut의 과거형은 cut이다.
4 be going to의 부정문은 be동사 뒤에 not을 써서 나타낸다.

C 1 미래를 나타내는 next week이 쓰였고 부정문이므로 「will not[won't]+동사원형」이 되어야 하며, 빈칸이 두 개이므로 won't miss로 쓴다.
2 last Friday가 쓰였으므로 과거형 invited를 쓴다.
3 soon이 쓰였으므로 「be going to+동사원형」으로 쓴다.
4 현재진행형 의문문에 대한 대답이므로 현재진행형으로 쓴다.

내신 완성 Grammar Practice
p. 47

1 ④ 2 ⑤ 3 ② 4 (1) Are you going to play tennis
(2) They were not dancing

문제해설

1 ④ 각각의 빈칸에는 wake와 set의 과거형인 woke, set이 와야 한다.

2 ① jog → jogging, ② are knowing → know, ③ are → be, ④ gathered → gather로 고쳐야 한다.

3 ② 현재진행형 의문문에 과거시제로 대답하는 것은 어색하다.

서술형에 나오는 WRITING
p. 48

A 1 Nancy was wearing a long coat.
2 Are they going to help their uncle?
3 I will not throw away the cup.
B 1 Billy is going to return home
2 Did you have a good time
3 She didn't[did not] finish the painting
C 1 bought a pair of jeans
2 is reading a novel at home
3 will[is going to] visit his grandparents

문제해설

B 1 '…할 것이다'라는 미래의 계획은 be going to로 나타낸다.
2 일반동사 과거형의 의문문은 「Did+주어+동사원형 ...?」으로 쓴다.
3 일반동사 과거형의 부정문은 「주어+didn't[did not]+동사원형 ...」으로 쓴다.

READING WITH GRAMMAR
pp. 49~50

Reading 1 | 1 ⑤ 2 Did
Words | [1] 도착하다

해석 | 학교는 4시에 끝났다. Jenna는 그녀의 공책들을 가방에 넣고 학교에서 달려 나왔다. 그녀는 신이 났다. 미국에 계신 삼촌이 오고 계셨다! "우리 삼촌이 나에게 선물을 가져다주실 거야."라고 그녀는 생각했다. "삼촌이 맛있는 미국 간식을 가져오실까? 삼촌이 재미있는 미국 장난감을 가져오실까?"라고 그녀는 궁금해했다.

Jenna는 그녀의 집에 도착했다. 삼촌이 소파에 앉아 계셨다! 그는 그녀를 만나서 행복해했고 그녀를 꼭 안아주었다. Jenna는 기뻐서 뛰었다. "미국에서 뭔가를 가져오셨어요? 특별한 선물을 가져오셨어요?"라고 그녀가 물었다. "미안한데."라고 삼촌이 대답했다. "나는 나만 데려왔어!" Jenna는 웃었다. "그것은 미국에서 온 완벽한 선물이네요."라고 그녀가 말했다.

구문해설

1행 Jenna **put** her notebooks **in** her bag and *ran out of* the school.
▸ put A in B: A를 B에 넣다
▸ run out of: …에서 달려 나오다
3행 ..., "My uncle will **bring me a gift**."
▸ bring A B: A에게 B를 가져다주다
7행 He was happy **to see** her and ....
▸ to see는 감정의 원인을 나타내는 부사적 용법의 to부정사이며, '…해서 (~한)'로 해석한다.

문제해설

1 ⑤ 삼촌은 자기 자신만 미국에서 데려왔다고 했다.

2 일반동사 과거형의 의문문은 「Did+주어+동사원형 ...?」의 형태이므로, 빈칸에는 모두 Did가 들어가야 한다.

Reading 2 | 1 ⑤ 2 won't be
Words | [1] 환경 [2] 받다

해석 | 여러분은 모험을 좋아하십니까? 여러분은 새로운 행성에서의 삶을 꿈꾸십니까? 그렇다면 여기 여러분을 위한 기회가 있습니다. 우리는 화성 프로젝트에 참여할 지원자를 선정할 예정입니다. 그들 중 4명은 2024년에 화성으로 떠날 것입니다.

하지만 그곳의 환경은 완전히 다를 것입니다. 그리고 화성에서의 여러분의 삶은 힘들 것입니다. 그래서, 우리는 인내심 있는 사람들을 찾을 예정입니다. 또한, 여러분은 화성에서 몇몇 임무를 수행할 것입니다. 그러므로, 우리는 용감한 사람들이 필요합니다. 출발 전에, 여러분은 몇 년간 훈련을 받을 것입니다. 여러분은 생존 기술에 대해서 배우게 될 것입니다. 여러분은 화성으로 가는 첫 번째 인류 파견단에 참가하시겠습니까? 신중하게 생각하십시오. 지구로 돌아오는 표는 없을 것입니다.

구문해설

3행 Four of **them** will leave for Mars in 2024.

▶ them은 앞 문장의 volunteers를 가리킨다.

9행 **Before** the departure, you will receive training for several years.

▶ Before는 '… 전에'의 의미로, 시간을 나타내는 전치사이다.

문제해설

1 위 글의 제목으로 가장 알맞은 것은?
① 유용한 생존 기술들
② 화성: 붉은 행성
③ 유명한 우주 과학자들
④ 화성에서의 환경
⑤ 화성에서 새로운 인생을 시작하세요!
▶ 화성에 파견되어 새로운 삶을 시작할 지원자를 모집하는 내용이므로 ⑤가 제목으로 적절하다.

2 밑줄 친 부분을 바르게 고치시오.
▶ won't 뒤에는 동사원형을 써야 하므로 are를 be로 고쳐야 한다.

내신에 나오는 COMMUNICATION

A 의도·계획 묻고 답하기 p. 51

Check-Up | **1** (1) ⓒ (2) ⓑ (3) ⓐ
2 Are you planning to have

문제해설

2 '…할 계획이니?'는 「Are you planning to ...?」로 나타낼 수 있다.

B 행동·동작 묘사하기 p. 52

Check-Up | **1** ④ **2** ①

문제해설

1 ④는 앞으로의 계획을 나타내고, 나머지는 모두 현재의 동작을 나타낸다.

2 A: 그는 지금 무엇을 하고 있니?
B: ____________
▶ 현재의 동작을 묻고 있으므로 청바지를 입고 있다는 내용의 ①이 대답으로 적절하다.

FINAL TEST pp. 53~55

1 ④ **2** ③ **3** ⑤ **4** ③ **5** (B) → (A) → (D) → (C)
6 ③ **7** ① **8** ② **9** ⑤ **10** ⑤ **11** ③, ④
12 have **13** to rent **14** ④ **15** ③ **16** ④ **17** ②
18 ② **19** Were you cooking meat **20** Did Jack study for the test **21** I was washing my hair in the bathroom. **22** reading a newspaper **23** Is Brian[he] making spaghetti **24** Will Brian[he] write in his diary

문제해설

1 ① 쇼핑몰 ② 극장 ③ 박물관 ⑤ 경기장
▶ ④ dessert는 '디저트, 후식'의 의미이다.

2 William은 ____________ 사람이다.
① 용감한 ② 특별한 ③ 큰 소리로 ④ 완벽한 ⑤ 참을성 있는
▶ 빈칸에는 사람의 성격이나 특징을 묘사하는 형용사가 와야 하므로 ③은 적절하지 않다.

3 A: ____________
B: 나는 집에서 쉴 거야.
▶ ⑤ 집에서 쉴 것이라고 대답하고 있으므로, 빈칸에는 계획을 묻는 질문이 들어가야 한다.

5 (B) 너는 무엇을 하고 있니?
(A) 나는 가방을 싸고 있어.
(D) 왜? 너는 여행 갈 계획이니?
(C) 응. 나는 해변에 갈 계획이야!

6 ③ 동사 say의 과거형은 said이다.

7 ① 일반동사 과거형의 의문문은 「Did+주어+동사원형 ...?」의 형태로 쓴다.

9 ⑤ 다음 금요일에 일어날 일이므로 빈칸에는 모두 미래를 나타내는 조동사 Will[will]이 들어가야 한다.

10 ⑤ 주어가 3인칭 단수인 현재진행형 의문문이므로 첫 번째 빈칸에는 working이 들어가야 하고, 두 번째 빈칸에는 부정 대답을 나타내는 isn't가 들어가야 한다.

12 일반동사 과거형의 부정문이므로 did not 뒤에 동사원형인 have를 써야 한다.

13 「be동사+주어+going to+동사원형 ...?」 구문이 쓰인 것이므로, rent 앞에 to가 와야 한다.

14 ④는 주어의 의지를 나타내는 반면, 나머지는 모두 미래에 대한 예측을 나타낸다.

15 ③ 일반동사 have가 소유의 의미를 나타낼 때는 진행형으로 쓸 수 없으므로, is having을 has로 고쳐야 한다.

17 우리 가족은 일주일 전에 호수에 갔다. 우리 아빠는 텐트를 치셨다. 나는 고기를 잡았다. 하지만 오후에 비가 왔다. 그리고 멈추지 않았다. 아빠는 "하늘이 맑아지지 않을 거야. 집으로 가자."라고 말씀하셨다. 나는 정말로 슬펐다!
▶ ② put의 과거형은 put이다.

18 ② be동사 was가 쓰인 과거진행형 의문문이므로 긍정 대답은 Yes, she was.라고 해야 한다.

22 A: Brian은 오전 10시에 편지를 읽고 있었니?
B: 아니, 그렇지 않아. 그는 신문을 읽고 있었어.

23 A: 지금 Brian은[그는] 스파게티를 만들고 있니?
B: 응, 그래.

24 A: 저녁 8시 50분에 Brian은[그는] 일기를 쓸 거니?
B: 응, 그럴 거야.

CHAPTER 04 조동사

GRAMMAR FOCUS ························ p. 58

A 조동사 can, may

2 1) 그녀는 스파게티를 요리할 수 있다.
나는 날 수 없다.
A: 너는 그 상자들을 옮길 수 있니?
B: 응, 할 수 있어. / 아니, 못 해.
2) 너는 일정을 바꿔도 된다.
너는 계단에서 뛰면 안 된다.
A: 내가 이 지우개를 빌려도 될까?
B: 응, 돼. / 아니, 안 돼.

3 1) 곧 비가 올지도 모른다.
그 소문은 사실이 아닐지도 모른다.
2) 너는 지금 방을 나가도 된다.
우리는 여기에서 어떤 것도 먹으면 안 된다.
A: 제가 이 운동화를 신어 봐도 될까요?
B: 네, 돼요. / 물론이죠. / 물론이죠.
아니요, 안 돼요. / 죄송하지만, 안 돼요.

Check-Up ························ p. 59

A 1 May 2 he is 3 you can't[cannot]
4 you may not
B 1 to make 2 see 3 sleep 4 borrow
C 1 may not 2 Can you
D 1 Are you able to 2 are not able to
3 was able to

GRAMMAR FOCUS ························ p. 60

B 조동사 must, have to, should

1 학생들은 학교 규칙을 따라야 한다.
너는 도서관에서 큰 소리로 말하면 안 된다.
A: 내가 거기에 너와 함께 가야 하니?
B: 응, 그래야 해. / 아니, 그럴 필요 없어.

2 우리는 교복을 입어야 한다.
그녀는 첫 기차를 타야 한다.
나는 표를 일찍 예매해야 했다.
너는 서두를 필요가 없다.
A: 민수는 일요일에 일해야 하니?
B: 응, 그래야 해. / 아니, 그럴 필요 없어.

3 너는 진찰을 받는 것이 좋겠다.
우리는 물을 낭비하면 안 된다.
A: 내가 채소를 더 많이 먹어야 할까?
B: 응, 그래야 해. / 아니, 그러지 않아도 돼.

Check-Up ························ p. 61

A 1 pick up 2 learn 3 had to
4 doesn't have to 5 not be
B 1 you must 2 don't have to 3 they should
4 have to
C 1 must not 2 don't have to 3 should
D 1 have to 2 don't have to

Grammar Practice p. 62

A 1 mays → may 2 showed → show
3 can → could 4 has → have 5 Is → Are
B 1 don't have to 2 must not 3 should
C 1 don't have to cook 2 may not send
3 was able to take
D 1 She will be able to do
2 Does Jack have to speak

문제해설

A 1 조동사는 주어의 인칭과 수에 따라 형태가 변하지 않는다.
3 어젯밤 일이므로 can을 과거형 could로 고쳐야 한다.
4 주어가 3인칭 단수일 때 have to의 부정형은 doesn't have to이다.

B 1 날씨가 맑다고 했으므로, 우산을 가져갈 필요가 없다(don't have to)고 하는 것이 자연스럽다.
2 강이 매우 깊다고 했으므로, 그곳에 뛰어들지 말아야 한다(must not)고 금지하는 것이 자연스럽다.
3 너무 늦었다고 했으므로, 택시를 타는 것이 좋겠다(should)고 권유하는 것이 자연스럽다.

C 1 '…할 필요가 없다'는 「don't have to+동사원형」을 쓴다.
2 '…하지 않을지도 모른다'는 「may not+동사원형」을 쓴다.
3 '…할 수 있었다'는 「be동사의 과거형+able to+동사원형」을 쓴다.

D 1 미래의 능력은 will be able to로 나타낸다.
2 have to가 있는 문장의 의문문이고 주어가 3인칭 단수이므로 「Does+주어+have to ...?」의 형태로 쓴다.

내신 완성 Grammar Practice p. 63

1 ② 2 ③ 3 ④ 4 (1) Do I have to put (2) were not able to pass

문제해설

1 첫 번째 빈칸에는 허가를 나타내는 조동사 Can이 와야 한다. 두 번째 빈칸에는 충고를 나타내는 조동사 should가 와야 한다.

2 ① A: 제가 창문을 열어도 되나요?
B: 네, 돼요.
② A: 저희가 오래 기다려야 하나요?
B: 아니요, 그럴 필요 없어요.
④ A: 그가 새로운 직장을 구할 수 있게 될까?
B: 응, 그럴 거야.
⑤ A: 내 딸이 네 장난감을 가지고 놀아도 되니?
B: 네, 그래도 돼요.
▸ ③ must 의문문에 대한 부정 대답은 don't[doesn't] have to로 나타낸다.

3 ④ '…하는 것이 좋다'라는 의미로 권유나 충고를 나타낼 때는 조동사 should를 쓴다.

서술형에 나오는 WRITING p. 64

A 1 He should keep his promise.
2 She may not come to the event hall.
3 Are you able to drive a car?
B 1 He has to answer the question.
2 I am[I'm] not able to understand this movie.
3 May I listen to the radio now?
C 1 must not enter 2 must arrive early

문제해설

B 1 He는 3인칭 단수이므로 has to를 써야 한다.
2 be able to의 부정형은 be동사 뒤에 not을 쓴다.
3 조동사가 있는 의문문은 「조동사+주어+동사원형 ...?」의 형태로 쓴다.
C 1 must not을 이용하여 금지를 나타낸다.
2 must를 이용하여 의무를 나타낸다.

READING WITH GRAMMAR pp. 65~66

Reading 1 | 1 ④ 2 ②
Words | ¹ 위험 ² 예의 바른

해석 | 셀피를 찍는 것은 매우 재미있다. 그러나 당신은 그것들 때문에 곤란에 처할지도 모른다. 따라서 당신은 몇 가지 기본 규칙을 따라야 한다.
1. 안전하게 있어라! 어떤 셀피는 당신을 위험에 빠뜨릴지도 모른다. 상황을 상상해보자: 당신은 카메라를 들고 다리 가장자리에 서 있다. 그것은 멋져 보일지도 모른다. 그러나, 그것은 위험하기도 하다.
2. 당신은 어떤 장소들에서는 셀피를 찍어서는 안 된다. 이런 장소에는 공중화장실과 병원이 포함된다. 당신은 예의를 지켜야 한다.
3. 주의를 기울여라! 당신은 셀카봉을 사용할지도 모른다. 당신 주위 사람들을 잊지 마라. 당신은 셀카봉으로 누구도 치지 않아야 한다.
4. 당신은 다른 사람들과 같이 있는 셀피를 올리고 싶은가? 그러면, 당신은 그들에게 먼저 물어봐야 한다.

구문해설

1행 But you may **get in trouble** *because of* them.
▸ get in trouble: 곤란에 처하다
▸ because of는 '… 때문에'라는 뜻으로, 뒤에 대명사나 명사(구)가 와야 한다.
▸ them은 앞 문장의 selfies를 가리킨다.
4행 It may **look cool**.
▸ look+형용사: …하게 보이다
13행 Then, you should ask **them** first.
▸ them은 앞 문장의 other people을 가리킨다.

문제해설

1 ④ 셀피를 찍을 때와 올릴 때 주의할 점을 안내하는 글이다.
2 ② 문맥상 (A)와 (B)에는 '…일지도 모른다'라는 불확실한 추측을 나타내는 조동사 may가 와야 한다.

Reading 2 | 1 ② 2 ⑤
Words | ¹ 비슷한 ² 이상한

해석 | 착륙 전에, 조종사들은 공항에 있는 항공 교통 관제 센터에 보고를 해야 한다. 조종사들은 전 세계 각기 다른 국가 출신이다. 그래서 그들은 다양한 언어로 말한다. 의사소통을 위해, 그들은 하나의 언어, 즉 영어를 사용해야 한다.
하지만 글자에 문제가 있다. 조종사는 "이 비행기는 BE 449편입니다."라고 말할지도 모른다. 하지만 B는 P 혹은 V처럼 들릴지도 모른다. 그리고 E는 I처럼 들릴지도 모른다. 비슷한 소리는 듣는 사람들을 혼동시킬 수 있다! 그래서 조종사들은 '스펠링 알파벳'을 사용한다. 예를 들어, BE 449편의 경우, 조종사들은 (B를 위해) "bravo", (E를 위해) "echo", "4-4-9"라고 말해야 한다. IU 108편의 경우, 그들은 (I를 위해) "India", (U를 위해) "uniform", "1-0-8"이라고 말해야 한다. 이것들은 이상하게 들릴지도 모른다. 하지만 듣는 사람들은 각 글자를 이해할 수 있다!

구문해설

5행 But B may **sound like** P or V.
▸ sound like+명사: …처럼 들리다
11행 **These** may *sound strange*.
▸ These는 '이것들'이라는 의미의 지시대명사로, 앞에서 언급된 예들을 가리킨다.

▶ sound+형용사: …하게 들리다

문제해설

1 위 글의 제목으로 가장 알맞은 것은?
① 조종사의 삶
② 조종사 의사소통
③ 영어 글자의 문제점들
④ 공항의 새로운 언어
⑤ 조종사들이 가장 좋아하는 언어
▶ ② 세계 여러 나라 출신의 조종사들이 원활한 소통을 위해 사용하는 의사소통 방식을 설명하는 글이다.

2 어법상 바르지 못한 것은?
▶ ⑤ 주어가 복수이므로 is를 are로 고쳐야 한다.

내신에 나오는 COMMUNICATION

A 능력 묻고 답하기 p. 67

Check-Up | **1** ④ **2** ②

문제해설

1 ④ 과학을 잘하는지 물었으므로 '아니. 나는 과학자야.'라는 대답은 부자연스럽다.

2 조동사 can을 이용해 능력을 묻는 말에 대한 대답으로는 ②(아니, 나는 그것을 만들 수 없어.)가 적절하다.

B 조언·충고하기 p. 68

Check-Up | **1** (1) ⓐ (2) ⓒ (3) ⓑ
2 Why don't you drink

문제해설

2 '…하는 게 어때?'는 「Why don't you+동사원형 ...?」으로 나타낼 수 있다.

FINAL TEST pp. 69~71

1 ④ **2** ⑤ **3** ④ **4** ④ **5** (C)→(B)→(D)→(A)
6 ②, ⑤ **7** ② **8** ② **9** ④ **10** ② **11** ⓑ **12** ⓓ
13 ④ **14** ⑤ **15** ④ **16** may not be **17** was able to read **18** Should I exercise **19** ③ **20** ④
21 David will be able to paint the wall. **22** Lisa had to share a room with her sister. **23** They don't have to attend the meeting. **24** Do I have to call Joe later?

문제해설

1 ④ include는 '포함하다'라는 뜻이다.

2 noisy(시끄러운)와 quiet(조용한)는 반의어 관계로, different(다른)의 반의어가 될 수 있는 것은 ⑤ similar(비슷한)이다.

3 ④ 충고를 구하는 말에 「Why don't you+동사원형 ...?」을 이용해 대답하는 것이 자연스럽다.

4 A: 너는 100미터 달리기를 20초 안에 뛸 수 있니?
B: 아니, 못해. 너는 어때?
A: 나는 그걸 15초 안에 뛸 수 있어.
(나는 천천히 걸을 수 있어.)
B: 너는 정말 빨리 뛰는구나!

5 (C) 너 속상해 보여. 무슨 일 있니?
(B) 나는 한 시간 전에 내 카메라를 잃어버렸어.
(D) 너는 분실물 센터에 가 봐야 해.
(A) 조언 고마워.

6 ① A: 너는 스케이트를 탈 수 있니?
B: 응, 탈 수 있어.
③ A: 너는 쿠키를 구울 수 있니?
B: 아니, 못해.
④ A: 나는 두통이 있어. 내가 무엇을 해야 할까?
B: 약을 좀 먹는 게 어때?
▶ ② 테니스를 잘 못 친다면서 운동을 잘한다고 하는 것은 어색하다.
⑤ 잠을 잘 못 잔다고 조언을 구하는 말에, 자신도 늦게 잔다고 대답하는 것은 어색하다.

7 A: 너는 운전을 잘할 수 있니?
B: ____________ 나는 초보야.
▶ 문맥상 빈칸에는 운전을 잘 못한다고 대답하는 ②가 와야 한다.

8 A: 내가 네 휴대 전화를 써도 되겠니?
B: ____________ 여기 있어.
▶ 문맥상 빈칸에는 조동사 may를 이용하여 상대방이 휴대 전화를 써도 된다고 대답하는 ②가 오는 것이 알맞다.

9 ④ 의무를 나타내는 must는 have to로 바꿔 쓸 수 있다.

10 ② 허가를 나타내는 can은 may로 바꿔 쓸 수 있다.

11 저희가 메뉴판을 봐도 될까요? – ⓑ 물론이죠, 그래도 돼요.

12 제가 지금 가스를 꺼야 하나요? – ⓓ 아니요, 그럴 필요 없어요.

13 ④는 허가를 나타내며, 나머지는 모두 능력·가능을 나타낸다.

14 ⑤는 허가를 나타내며, 나머지는 모두 추측을 나타낸다.

15 ④ '갈 필요가 없다'의 의미이다.

19 ③ be able to는 조동사 can 대신 쓸 수 있는 말이므로 두 표현을 연달아 쓰지 않는다.

20 ④ 큰 소리로 말해도 되는지 묻는 말에 '물론이지, 그래도 돼.'라고 대답하며 다시 '우리는 조용히 해야 해.'라고 말하는 것은 어색하다.

21 능력을 나타내는 can의 미래형은 will be able to이다.

22 must의 과거형은 had to이다.

23 '…할 필요가 없다'는 don't have to로 나타낸다.

24 의무를 나타내고 Do로 시작하는 의문문은 「Do+주어+have to ...?」로 쓴다.

CHAPTER 05 문장의 형식

GRAMMAR FOCUS
p. 74

A 감각동사가 있는 문장

2 1) 그 소년들은 피곤해 보인다.
그 호수는 고요하고 평화로워 보인다.
2) 네 목소리는 멋지게 들린다.
그들의 계획은 완벽하게 들렸다.
3) 그 꽃들은 좋은 냄새가 났다.
이 신발은 지독한 냄새가 난다.
4) 초콜릿은 달콤한 맛이 난다.
그 샌드위치들은 맛있었다.
5) 나는 종종 행복하다고 느낀다.
Nick은 결과를 자랑스럽게 느꼈다.
이 수건은 (촉감이) 거칠다.

Check-Up
p. 75

A 1 bad 2 good 3 salt 4 sad
B 1 hungry 2 soft 3 healthy 4 interesting
C 1 tastes bitter 2 looked sick 3 felt nervous
D 1 smells delicious 2 tastes sour

GRAMMAR FOCUS
p. 76

B 수여동사가 있는 문장

2 나는 그녀에게 생일 선물을 주었다.
그는 우리에게 영어를 가르친다.
Sophia는 Logan에게 그녀의 사진들을 보여 주었다.
나의 부모님이 나에게 새 컴퓨터를 사 주셨다.

3 1) 그 군인이 나에게 편지를 보냈다.
2) Erik이 그 고객에게 치즈 케이크를 만들어 주었다.
3) Park 선생님은 그의 학생들에게 부탁을 했다.

Check-Up
p. 77

A 1 me, history 2 my notebook, you
3 a toy, her brother
4 his friend, a recipe book
B 1 him an email 2 me the pepper
3 them a question
C 1 to 2 of 3 for
D 1 to Aiden 2 for him
3 her friends candy bars
4 our family spaghetti

Grammar Practice
p. 78

A 1 to him 2 me 3 strange 4 sounds
B 1 feel 2 smell 3 make 4 lend
C 1 cute dolls for their children
2 a funny joke to his classmates
D 1 her son red gloves
2 a favor of the citizens
3 like strawberries

문제해설

A 1 수여동사 write가 쓰인 3형식 문장이므로, him 앞에 전치사 to를 써야 한다.
2 수여동사 bring이 쓰인 4형식 문장이므로, to me를 me로 고쳐야 한다.
3 감각동사의 보어로 형용사를 써야 하므로, strangely를 strange로 고쳐야 한다.
4 감각동사의 보어로 형용사(scary)가 쓰였으므로 전치사 like는 쓰지 않는다.

B 1 '졸리다고 느끼다'라는 의미가 되어야 하므로 feel을 쓴다.
2 '매운 냄새가 나다'의 의미가 되어야 하므로 smell을 쓴다.
3 '팬케이크를 만들어 주다'라는 의미가 되어야 하므로 make를 쓴다.
4 '내 것을 빌려주다'의 의미가 되어야 하므로 lend를 쓴다.

D 1 「make+간접목적어+직접목적어」의 어순이 되어야 한다.
2 「ask+직접목적어+of+간접목적어」의 어순이 되어야 한다.
3 「taste like+명사」의 형태가 되어야 한다.

내신 완성 Grammar Practice
p. 79

1 ②, ⑤ 2 ⑤ 3 ③ 4 (1) Sam sent me a text message. (2) I will cook a special dinner for my parents.

문제해설

1 ②, ⑤ 수여동사 get이 쓰인 문장은 「get+간접목적어+직접목적어」 또는 「get+직접목적어+for+간접목적어」의 어순이 알맞다.

2 ⑤ 수여동사 pass가 쓰인 3형식 문장에는 간접목적어 앞에 전치사 to를 쓴다.

3 ③에는 전치사 for가 와야 하고, 나머지에는 모두 전치사 to가 와야 한다.

서술형에 나오는 **WRITING** p. 80

A **1** Linda bought her friend lunch.
2 The waiter will bring the bill to you.
B **1** His mother made fresh orange juice for him.
2 The nurse gave medicine to the patients.
C **1** tastes delicious **2** smells bad
3 feels thirsty

문제해설

B 4형식 문장을 3형식 문장으로 전환할 때 동사 make가 쓰인 문장은 전치사 for를, 동사 give가 쓰인 문장은 전치사 to를 간접목적어 앞에 쓴다.

READING WITH GRAMMAR pp. 81~82

Reading 1 | **1** ⑤ **2** we bring the babies our hats
Words | [1] 구하다

해석 | Q: 저는 당신의 캠페인, 아프리카의 아기들을 위한 모자에 대해 들었습니다. 하지만 그것은 이상하게 들려요. 아프리카는 매우 덥잖아요! 우리가 정말 그 아기들에게 모자를 보내야 하나요?
A: 대답은 '네'입니다. 아프리카에서는, 수백만 명의 아기들이 생후 첫날 밤에 사망합니다. 놀랍게도, 그들은 추위로 인해 사망합니다. 왜일까요? 아프리카의 어떤 지역은, 밤에 매우 추워질 수 있습니다. 그리고 그 추운 기온은 (생후) 하루 된 아기들을 위협합니다. 그래서 저희는 캠페인을 시작했습니다. 저희는 짐바브웨와 에티오피아에 있는 아기들에게 털모자를 만들어 줍니다. 그리고 저희는 그 아기들에게 저희 모자를 가져다줍니다. 그 모자들이 아기들을 구하고 있습니다. 당신도 저희와 함께하실 수 있습니다. 뜨개질을 전혀 못하신다고요? 그렇다면 저희가 당신에게 뜨개질 수업을 해드리겠습니다!

구문해설

2행 **It**'s very hot in Africa!
▶ It은 날씨를 나타내는 비인칭 주어이다.

4행 In Africa, **millions of** babies die on the first night after birth.
▶ millions of: 수백만의

6행 ..., it can **get** very **cold** at night.
▶ get+형용사: …하게 되다, …해지다

10행 You can'**t** knit **at all**?
▶ not ... at all: 전혀 … 아니다

문제해설

1 ⑤ 털모자를 만들어 추위로 인해 사망하는 아프리카의 신생아들을 살리는 캠페인에 관한 내용이다.

2 수여동사 bring이 쓰인 3형식 문장은 「주어+bring+간접목적어+직접목적어」 어순의 4형식 문장으로 전환할 수 있다.

Reading 2 | **1** ③ **2** ④
Words | [1] 이유 [2] 대답하다

해석 | 친절한 괴물이 한 남자를 만났다. 그 남자는 춥고 배고파 보였다. 그는 자신의 손에 공기를 불어 넣고 있었다. 괴물이 그에게 이유를 물었다. 남자는 "저는 제 손을 더 따뜻하게 만들고 있어요."라고 말했다. 괴물은 그를 안쓰럽게 여겨서, 그를 집으로 데리고 갔다.
괴물은 남자에게 담요를 가져다주고 그에게 수프 한 그릇을 만들어 주었다. 남자는 고맙게 느꼈다. 그러고 나서 그는 수프에 공기를 불기 시작했다. 괴물은 남자에게 또 하나 질문을 했다. 괴물은 "당신은 수프를 더 따뜻하게 만들고 있나요?"라고 말했다. "아니요. 저는 그것을 더 차갑게 만들고 있어요."라고 남자는 대답했다. 괴물은 혼란스럽게 느꼈다. 괴물은 "당신은 같은 입에서 뜨거운 공기와 차가운 공기를 내뿜네요! 난 당신을 믿을 수 없어요!"라고 소리쳤다. 그리고 괴물은 남자를 자신의 집에서 쫓아냈다.

구문해설

6행 ..., "I am **making my hands warmer**."
▶ make+목적어+목적격보어(형용사): …를 ~하게 만들다

7행 The monster **felt sorry for** him, *so* it took him home.
▶ feel sorry for: …를 안쓰럽게[안됐다고] 여기다
▶ so는 '그래서'라는 의미의 접속사이다.

9행 It **brought** the man a blanket and **cooked** a bowl of soup for him.
▶ 동사 brought와 cooked가 접속사 and로 병렬 연결되어 있다.

11행 Then he **began blowing** air on the soup.
▶ begin+v-ing: …하기 시작하다

문제해설

1 괴물은 마지막에 어떻게 느꼈는가?
① 지루한 ② 피곤한 ③ 화난 ④ 신이 난 ⑤ 고맙게 생각하는
▶ 괴물은 남자의 말을 믿을 수 없다고 소리치며 그를 내쫓았으므로, 괴물의 심경으로 적절한 것은 ③이다.

2 어법상 바르지 못한 것은?
▶ ④ 수여동사 cook이 쓰인 3형식 문장에서 간접목적어 앞에 전치사 for를 쓴다.

내신에 나오는 **COMMUNICATION**

A 전화하기 1 p. 83

Check-Up | **1** ④ **2** ④

문제해설

2 Who's calling, please?는 전화를 건 사람이 누구인지 묻는 표현으로, ④ Who am I speaking to?와 바꿔 쓸 수 있다.

B 전화하기 2
p. 84

Check-Up | 1 ④ 2 (C) → (A) → (D) → (B)

문제해설

1 ④ 통화할 사람을 찾는 말에 메모를 남기겠느냐는 대답은 어색하다.

2 (C) 여보세요, 거기 Sean 있나요?
(A) 미안하지만, 그는 외출했어요.
(D) 제가 메모를 남겨도 될까요?
(B) 물론이죠, 그렇게 하세요.

FINAL TEST
pp. 85~87

1 ④ 2 ① 3 ① 4 ② 5 ③ 6 ④ 7 ② 8 ①
9 ① 10 ④ 11 ③ 12 ⑤ 13 ④ 14 ⑤
15 That cloud looks like a rabbit. 16 I will write her a poem. 17 ③ 18 ② 19 The music sounds strange. 20 My uncle taught us science.[My uncle taught science to us.] 21 ② a cushion her → a cushion for her[her a cushion] 22 Diego is cooking tacos for me. 23 The man asked a favor of his neighbor. 24 These shoes feel comfortable.

문제해설

1 ④ grateful은 '고마워하는'의 의미이다.

2 보기의 salty(짠), bitter(쓴), sour(신), spicy(매운)는 모두 ① taste(맛)를 나타내는 단어이다.

3 전화를 건 사람이 누구인지 묻는 말에 대한 대답으로 ①(저 Ian이에요.)이 적절하다.

4 ① A: 누구시죠?
B: 네 아빠다.
③ A: Johnson 씨와 통화할 수 있을까요?
B: 전데요.
④ A: 여보세요, Philip 있나요?
B: 네, 전데요.
⑤ A: 여보세요, Sue와 통화할 수 있을까요?
B: 그녀는 지금 여기 없어요.
▶ ② 메모를 남겨도 되는지 묻는 말에 '아니요, 괜찮아요.'라고 대답하는 것은 어색하다.

5 A: 여보세요. Peter와 통화할 수 있을까요?
B: 전데요. (그는 누구죠?)
A: 안녕, Peter. 나 Julia야. 너 뭐 하고 있니?
B: 나는 음악을 듣고 있어.

6 ④ 수여동사 buy가 쓰인 3형식 문장이므로 간접목적어(me) 앞에 전치사 for가 와야 한다.

7 ② 수여동사 show가 쓰인 3형식 문장이므로 간접목적어(the guests) 앞에 전치사 to가 와야 한다.

10 감각동사 sound의 보어로 명사가 쓰였으므로 첫 번째 빈칸에는 전치사 like가 와야 한다.
문맥상 '무섭게 느끼다'가 되어야 하므로 두 번째 빈칸에는 감각동사 feel이 알맞다.

11 문맥상 '짠맛이 나다'가 되어야 하므로 첫 번째 빈칸에는 감각동사 tastes가 적절하다.
수여동사 get이 쓰인 3형식 문장이므로 두 번째 빈칸에는 전치사 for를 써야 한다.

12 ⑤ 수여동사 tell이 쓰인 3형식 문장인 told my secret to the teacher로 쓰거나, 4형식인 told the teacher my secret으로 쓰는 것이 알맞다.

13 ④에는 수여동사 give가 쓰였으므로 전치사 to가 와야 하고, 나머지에는 모두 전치사 for가 와야 한다.

14 ⑤ 감각동사의 보어로는 형용사를 써야 하므로 부사 freshly를 형용사 fresh로 고쳐야 한다.

19 감각동사의 보어로는 형용사를 써야 하므로 부사 strangely를 형용사 strange로 고쳐야 한다.

20 수여동사 teach가 쓰인 문장은 4형식인 「teach + 간접목적어 + 직접목적어」 또는 3형식인 「teach + 직접목적어 + to + 간접목적어」의 어순으로 쓴다.

21 A: 너 바빠 보인다.
B: 곧 우리 엄마 생신이야. 그래서 나는 엄마에게 쿠션을 만들어 드리고 있어.
A: 그거 좋다.
▶ ② 수여동사 make가 쓰인 문장은 4형식인 「make + 간접목적어 + 직접목적어」 또는 3형식인 「make + 직접목적어 + for + 간접목적어」의 어순이 되어야 한다.

24 당신은 가게에 있다. 당신은 신발 한 켤레를 신어 보고 있다. 그것들은 편안하다. 그래서, 당신은 점원에게 "이 신발들은 편하게 느껴져요."라고 말한다.
▶ '편하게 느껴지다'는 feel comfortable로 나타낸다.

CHAPTER 06 의문사가 있는 의문문

GRAMMAR FOCUS
p. 90

A 의문사 who, what, which

1 2) 내 카드는 어디에 있어?
너는 언제 학교에 가니?
너는 무엇을 살 거니?
누가 드럼을 연주해?

2 A: 저 예쁜 소녀는 누구니? B: 그녀는 내 새로운 반 친구야.
A: 누가 이 햄버거를 먹었니? B: 내가 그랬어.

3 A: 이 동물은 무엇이니? B: 그건 북극곰이야.
A: 너는 공원에서 무엇을 했니? B: 나는 강아지를 산책시켰어.
A: 너희 엄마는 무슨 일을 하시니?
B: 엄마는 환자들을 치료하셔.

4 A: 어떤 것이 그녀의 자전거니? B: 노란 것이 그녀의 것이야.
A: 너는 아이스하키나 스키 중 어느 것을 더 좋아하니?
B: 나는 아이스하키를 더 좋아해.

Check-Up p. 91

A 1 Who 2 Which 3 What
B 1 Which 2 Who 3 What
C 1 ⓒ 2 ⓐ 3 ⓑ
D 1 What 2 Who 3 Which

GRAMMAR FOCUS p. 92

B 의문사 when, where, why, how

1 A: 크리스마스이브는 언제니? B: 12월 24일이야.
A: 너는 언제 아침을 먹니?
B: 나는 8시 30분에 아침을 먹어.

2 A: 나의 새 신발은 어디에 있니? B: 그것은 선반 위에 있어.
A: 너희 할머니는 어디에 사시니? B: 할머니는 보스턴에 사셔.

3 A: 너는 왜 팬케이크를 좋아하니?
B: 왜냐하면 그것은 맛이 있어.
A: 너는 왜 Mark에게 그렇게 화가 났니?
B: 왜냐하면 그가 나에게 거짓말을 했어.

4 A: 내가 어떻게 부산역에 갈 수 있니?
B: 너는 26번 버스를 타면 돼.
A: 오늘 날씨는 어떠니? B: 눈이 내리고 추워.

5 A: 너는 얼마나 많은 모자를 가지고 있니?
B: 나는 모자 일곱 개를 가지고 있어.
A: 그는 얼마나 많은 돈이 필요하니?
B: 그는 5달러가 필요해.
A: 이 반지는 얼마니? B: 그건 40달러야.
A: 그녀는 몇 살이니? B: 그녀는 14살이야.
A: 너는 얼마나 자주 캠핑을 가니?
B: 나는 일 년에 두 번 캠핑을 가.
A: 박물관까지는 얼마나 머니? B: 약 10킬로미터야.
A: 금문교는 얼마나 길어? B: 그건 2,737미터야.
A: 얼마나 오래 걸리니? B: 2시간 걸려.
A: 그 나무는 얼마나 크니? B: 그건 3미터야.

Check-Up p. 93

A 1 How 2 Where 3 How far 4 How many
B 1 ⓓ 2 ⓒ 3 ⓑ 4 ⓐ
C 1 How long 2 When 3 Why
D 1 How often 2 How much 3 When

Grammar Practice p. 94

A 1 How 2 What 3 Why
B 1 Where 2 How many 3 Which
C 1 Who won 2 Where did you see
D 1 What time did 2 What does she

문제해설

A 1 정말 재미있었다고 대답하고 있으므로 빈칸에는 콘서트가 어땠는지 묻는 How가 와야 한다.
2 장난감 자동차를 들고 있다고 대답하고 있으므로 빈칸에는 '무엇'에 해당하는 What이 와야 한다.
3 대답이 Because로 시작하고 있으므로 빈칸에는 이유를 묻는 Why가 와야 한다.

B 1 연습하는 장소에 대해 대답하고 있으므로 Why를 Where로 고쳐야 한다.
2 셀 수 있는 명사의 복수형(times)이 뒤따르므로 How much를 How many로 고쳐야 한다.
3 정해진 대상 중에서의 선택을 묻고 있으므로 What을 Which로 고쳐야 한다.

C 1 의문사가 주어인 경우 「의문사+동사 ...?」로 쓴다.
2 의문사가 있는 일반동사 과거시제 의문문은 「의문사+did+주어+동사원형 ...?」으로 쓴다.

D 1 시간을 묻는 What time을 쓰고, 일반동사의 과거시제 의문문이므로 조동사는 did를 쓴다.
2 생일 선물로 무엇을 원하는지 물어야 하므로 What을 쓰고, 주어가 she인 일반동사의 현재시제 의문문이므로 조동사 does를 쓴다.

내신 완성 Grammar Practice p. 95

1 ③ 2 ④ 3 ③ 4 (1) Who agrees with me
(2) What movie did you see

문제해설

1 한 시간 전이라는 대답이 이어지므로 첫 번째 빈칸에는 When(언제)이 와야 한다.
세종대왕이라는 대답이 이어지므로 두 번째 빈칸에는 Who(누구)가 와야 한다.

2 ④ 지갑 안에 무엇이 있는지 묻는 말에 어디에서 지갑을 샀는지 말하는 것은 어색하다.

3 ③에는 What이 와야 하는 반면, 나머지에는 모두 How가 와야 한다.

서술형에 나오는 WRITING

p. 96

A 1 Where can I get information?
2 How tall is your brother?
3 How often does she cook pasta?
B 1 Why do you read magazines?
2 Who made his gloves?
C 1 How long does it take
2 When does OJ8945 arrive

문제해설

C 1 1시간 5분이 걸린다고 대답하고 있으므로 '얼마나 걸리니?'를 How long을 이용해 쓴다.
2 10시 55분에 도착한다고 대답하고 있으므로 'OJ8945가 언제 도착하니?'를 When을 이용해 쓴다.

READING WITH GRAMMAR

pp. 97~98

Reading 1 | 1 ③ 2 How much is the tour?
Words | [1] 여행, 관광 [2] 즐기다

해석 | 여행사: Dubai Travel입니다. 어떻게 도와 드릴까요?
고객: 저는 다음 달에 두바이로 여행 갈 거예요. 어떤 종류의 관광 상품들이 있나요?
여행사: 낙타 관광과 두바이 시내 관광이 있어요.
고객: 낙타 관광이 흥미롭게 들리네요. 그건 뭐죠?
여행사: 낙타 농장에 가는 짧은 여행이에요. 당신은 거기에서 낙타를 타실 수 있어요. 그리고 모래 썰매도 즐기실 수 있어요.
고객: 그거 재미있게 들리네요! 그 관광은 얼마인가요?
여행사: 한 사람당 200달러예요.
고객: 관광은 몇 시에 시작하죠? 그리고 얼마나 오랫동안 하나요?
여행사: 저희는 오전 8시에 낙타 농장으로 떠나요. 그리고 온종일 걸려요.
고객: 좋아요. 제가 그 관광을 어떻게 예약하죠?
여행사: 저에게 성함을 알려주세요.

구문해설

9행 It's 200 dollars **per** person.
▶ per는 '…당'의 의미로, 부정관사 a로 바꿔 쓸 수 있다.
11행 We **leave for** the camel farm at 8 a.m.
▶ leave for: …로 떠나다

문제해설

1 ③ 관광 활동에 모래 썰매도 포함되어 있다.
2 가격을 물을 때는 How much를 쓴다.

Reading 2 | 1 ② 2 ②
Words | [1] 넓은

해석 | 전 세계에서 어떤 국가가 가장 많은 언어를 가지고 있을까? 답은 파푸아 뉴기니다. 그곳은 호주 근처의 작은 나라이다. 약 7백만 명의 사람들이 그 나라에 산다. 얼마나 많은 언어가 그곳에서 사용될까? 놀랍게도, 820개가 넘는다!
왜 파푸아 뉴기니에는 그렇게 많은 언어가 있을까? 높은 산, 울창한 숲, 그리고 넓은 강 때문에, 다른 지역에 사는 원주민들은 쉽게 만날 수 없었다. 수년 동안, 각 원주민 집단은 자신들만의 언어를 발달시켰다. 그렇다면 어떻게 방문자들은 파푸아 뉴기니 사람들과 의사소통할 수 있을까? 그들은 영어로 말할 수 있는데, 영어가 국가의 공식 언어 중 하나이기 때문이다!

구문해설

10행 **Because of** *high mountains*, *thick forests*, and *wide rivers*, ...
▶ Because of: … 때문에
▶ 명사구 high mountains, thick forests, wide rivers가 등위접속사 and로 병렬 연결되어 있다.
13행 Over many years, **each** native group developed its own language.
▶ each는 '각각의'라는 의미로, 뒤에 단수명사가 온다.
14행 They can speak English, because it's **one of the country's official languages**!
▶ one of the+복수명사: … 중 하나

문제해설

1 위 글의 제목으로 가장 알맞은 것은?
① 언어는 어떻게 발달하는가
② 많은 언어를 가진 국가
③ 파푸아 뉴기니의 역사
④ 파푸아 뉴기니의 원주민
⑤ 파푸아 뉴기니의 자연환경
▶ 파푸아 뉴기니가 세계에서 가장 많은 언어를 가진 나라임을 소개하며 그 이유를 설명하는 글이므로, 제목으로 가장 적절한 것은 ②이다.
2 빈칸 (A)와 (B)에 들어갈 말이 바르게 짝지어진 것은?
▶ (A) 820개가 넘는 언어가 있다는 대답이 이어지고 있으므로, 빈칸에는 셀 수 있는 명사의 수를 묻는 How many가 들어가야 한다.
(B) 이어지는 대답에서 왜 파푸아 뉴기니에 많은 언어가 있는지를 설명하고 있으므로, 빈칸에는 이유를 묻는 Why가 들어가야 한다.

내신에 나오는 COMMUNICATION

A 슬픔 · 실망의 원인 묻기

p. 99

Check-Up | 1 ③, ⑤ 2 What's bothering you

문제해설

1 A: 너 슬퍼 보여. ______________
B: 내가 가장 좋아하는 선생님이 다른 학교로 옮기셨어.
▶ 문맥상 슬픔의 원인을 묻는 말이 와야 하므로 ③(너 뭐하고 있니?), ⑤(너는 어느 것을 더 좋아하니?)는 적절하지 않다.

B 동정 · 유감 표현하기 p. 100

Check-Up | 1 ④ 2 (B) → (C) → (A)

문제해설

1 A: 가람이는 어제 다리가 부러졌어.
B: ______________
▶ 문맥상 동정이나 유감을 표현해야 하므로 ④(정말 좋다!)는 적절하지 않다.

2 (B) 무슨 일이니, Tom?
(C) 나는 버스에 내 노트북을 놓고 내렸어.
(A) 정말 안됐다!

FINAL TEST pp. 101~103

1 ④ 2 absent from 3 ④ 4 ② 5 (B) → (C) → (A)
6 ② 7 ③ 8 ② 9 ④ 10 ④ 11 Why
12 Who 13 How 14 (1) ⓒ (2) ⓐ (3) ⓓ
15 Which fruit 16 How much water
17 did happen → happened 18 you are → are you
19 ④ 20 ⑤ 21 ③ 22 Who 23 Which, math
24 What do you want 25 I'm sorry to hear that.

문제해설

1 ④ develop은 '발달시키다, 발달하다'의 의미이다.

2 be absent from: …에 결석하다

4 ② 상대방에게 동정이나 유감을 나타낼 때 쓰는 What a pity!는 That's too bad. 등으로 바꿔 쓸 수 있다.

5 (B) 나는 지난주에 감기에 걸렸어.
(C) 그것 참 유감이다. 지금은 상태가 어때?
(A) 지금은 나아졌어.

6 A: 무슨 안 좋은 일이 있니?
B: 나는 내 영어 교과서를 잃어버렸어!
A: (너는 영어를 좋아하니?) 그것 참 안됐구나!
B: 네 것을 빌릴 수 있을까?
A: 물론이지.

8 ② How many 뒤에는 셀 수 있는 명사의 복수형이 와야 하므로 셀 수 없는 명사인 salt(소금)는 알맞지 않다.

9 빈도를 묻는 질문에 대한 대답으로는 ④가 알맞다.

10 뒤에 색상을 언급하는 대답이 이어지고 있으므로 어떤 색을 원하는지 묻는 ④가 빈칸에 알맞다.

11 이유를 설명하는 대답이 이어지고 있으므로 빈칸에는 Why가 와야 한다.

12 그 남자가 누구인지 설명하는 대답이 이어지고 있으므로 빈칸에는 Who가 알맞다.

13 날씨 상태를 묘사하는 대답이 이어지고 있으므로 빈칸에는 상태를 묻는 How가 와야 한다.

14 (1) Sam은 여기에 어떻게 오니? – ⓒ 그는 지하철로 와.
(2) 이 요구르트는 얼마니? – ⓐ 그것은 800원이야.
(3) 너는 몇 시에 일어나니? – ⓓ 아침 6시쯤에.

17 의문사가 주어인 의문문으로, 의문사 뒤에 조동사 없이 바로 동사를 쓰는 형태가 되어야 하므로 did happen을 happened로 고쳐야 한다.

18 동사가 be동사인 의문문은 「의문사+be동사+주어 ...?」의 어순으로 쓴다.

19 ④의 How long은 '얼마나 오래'의 뜻이다.

20 ① A: 누가 그 비밀을 아니?
B: 아무도 몰라.
② A: 민호의 생일은 언제니?
B: 3월 16일이야.
③ A: 너는 어떤 종류의 음식을 좋아하니?
B: 나는 멕시코 음식을 좋아해.
④ A: 너희 아빠는 어디에서 일하시니?
B: 아빠는 우체국에서 일하셔.
▶ ⑤ 시장에 가는 이유를 묻는 말에 걸어간다고 대답하는 것은 어색하다.

21 ③ 의문사 what으로 시작하는 의문문이므로 she closes를 does she close로 고쳐야 한다.

22 Alice가 그럴 것이라고 대답하고 있으므로 빈칸에는 Who가 알맞다.

23 수학이나 영어 중 Paul이 토요일에 어떤 과목을 공부할지 물어야 하므로 첫 번째 빈칸에는 Which를 써야 한다.
토요일에 Paul은 수학을 공부할 계획이므로 두 번째 빈칸에는 math를 써야 한다.

24 중국 음식을 원한다고 대답하고 있으므로 빈칸에는 무엇을 원하는지 묻는 표현인 What do you want가 들어가야 한다.

25 상대방에게 유감을 표현할 때는 I'm sorry to hear that.이라고 할 수 있다.

CHAPTER 07 명사와 관사

GRAMMAR FOCUS p. 106

A 명사의 종류

1 접시에 사과와 복숭아 몇 개가 있다.
두 남자가 사무실에서 일하고 있다.

2 1) Alice는 유럽을 여행했다.
2) 좋은 소식이 있다.
3) 우리는 물 없이 살 수 없다.

Check-Up p. 107

A 1 tables 2 fish 3 tomatoes 4 hobbies
5 flies 6 dresses 7 wolves 8 mice
9 women 10 boxes
B 1 sister 2 salt 3 luck 4 seasons
C 1 cup 2 pieces 3 bottles 4 slice
D 1 Thieves 2 glasses 3 men 4 water

GRAMMAR FOCUS p. 108

B 관사

1 1) 너는 숟가락이 있니?
2) 그녀는 한 달 전에 일본에 갔다.
3) 나는 하루에 세 번 세수를 한다.
그 버스는 한 시간에 70킬로미터를 간다.

2 1) Jessie는 지난주에 시계를 하나 샀다. 그녀는 그 시계를 매일 착용한다.
2) 나에게 그 신문을 가져다줄래?
3) 저 사진에 있는 남자분은 나의 선생님이다.
4) 우리는 하늘에 있는 많은 별들을 보았다.
그녀는 바이올린을 연주하고 있다.

Check-Up p. 109

A 1 The 2 a 3 an 4 The
B 1 a 2 x 3 x 4 an 5 The
C 1 an angel 2 a week 3 breakfast
4 go to bed
D 1 the Internet 2 the ice cream
3 an[one] hour

Grammar Practice p. 110

A 1 the 2 bear 3 lunch
B 1 a → an 2 milks → milk 3 cup → cups
4 storys → stories
C 1 fish 2 a month 3 a bottle of water
D 1 three[some] potatoes 2 a piece of

문제해설

A 2 앞에 부정관사 a가 쓰였으므로 단수형 bear가 와야 한다.
3 식사 이름 앞에는 관사를 쓰지 않는다.

B 1 honest의 발음이 모음으로 시작되므로 앞에 부정관사 an이 와야 한다.
2 물질명사 milk는 단수형으로 써야 한다.
3 앞에 two or three가 쓰였으므로 cup을 복수형 cups로 고쳐야 한다.
4 story의 복수형은 stories이다.

C 2 부정관사로 '…마다'를 표현할 수 있으며, 뒤에 오는 month의 발음이 자음으로 시작되므로 a를 쓴다.
3 '… 한 병'은 a bottle of로 나타낸다.

내신 완성 Grammar Practice p. 111

1 ④ 2 ③ 3 ⑤ 4 (1) three times a year
(2) two slices of cheese

문제해설

1 ④ sheep의 복수형은 sheep이다.

2 보기와 ③은 '…마다, …당'의 의미이다. ①과 ②는 특정하지 않은 하나를, ④와 ⑤는 하나를 나타내는 부정관사이다.

서술형에 나오는 WRITING p. 112

A 1 saw her photo on the Internet
2 The men went out for dinner
B 1 Her children like the heroes
2 I traveled to London by bicycle
C 1 ordered four sandwiches
2 drank three cups of coffee
3 bought two bottles of water

문제해설

B 1 child와 hero의 복수형은 각각 children과 heroes이다. heroes는 수식어구 in the movie의 수식을 받는 명사이므로 앞에 정관사 the를 붙인다.
2 '자전거를 타고'는 by bicycle로 나타낸다.

READING WITH GRAMMAR pp. 113~114

Reading 1 | 1 ① 2 ⑤
Words | [1] 섞다

해석 | Joe의 요리 교실에 오신 것을 환영합니다! 오늘은 추워서, 우리는 뜨겁고 영양가 있는 것을 만들 거예요—미트볼이요! 우리는 간 쇠고기 500g, 빵가루 100g, 작은 양파 한 개, 달걀 한 개, 약간의 올리브유, 그리고 토마토소스 한 병을 가지고 있어요. 시작하겠습니다!

먼저, 쇠고기, 양파, 빵가루, 그리고 달걀을 큰 그릇에 섞으세요. 섞은 것을 작은 공 모양으로 만드세요. 이제 올리브유를 냄비에 넣으세요. 몇 분 동안 그것을 달구세요. 그다음에 냄비에서 미트볼을 구우세요. 미트볼에 토마토소스를 첨가하세요. 미트볼이 소스로 덮일 때까지 굴리세요. 그다음에 냄비에 뚜껑을 얹으세요. 마지막으로, 미트볼에 20분 동안 열을 가하세요. 이제, 여러분의 맛있는 음식을 즐기세요!

구문해설

1행 **It**'s cold today, so we'll make *something hot and*

nutritious—meatballs!

▸ It은 날씨를 나타내는 비인칭 주어이다.

▸ -thing으로 끝나는 대명사는 형용사가 뒤에서 수식한다.

8행 Heat it for **a few** minutes.

▸ a few는 복수명사 앞에 쓰인다.

10행 **Add** the tomato sauce **to** the meatballs.

▸ add A to B: A를 B에 첨가[추가]하다

문제해설

1 ① 미트볼 조리법

② 새로운 미트볼 기계

③ 미트볼 요리 경연 대회

④ 미트볼과 잘 어울리는 음식

⑤ 미트볼 요리: 건강에 좋은 음식

▸ 요리 교실에서 미트볼을 만드는 방법을 소개하고 있으므로 ①이 제목으로 적절하다.

2 ⑤ 앞에 언급된 명사를 다시 언급할 때는 정관사 the를 써야 한다.

Reading 2 | **1** ⑤ **2** ③

Words | **1** …에 닿다 **2** … 뒤에

해석 | 한 노인이 길을 따라 걷고 있었다. 그는 어느 집 앞에서 소년을 보았다. 그 소년은 초인종을 누르려고 애쓰고 있었다. 하지만, 그는 키가 매우 작았고 초인종은 너무 높이 있었다. 그래서 그는 그것에 닿을 수 없었다. 그 남자는 한동안 그를 바라보았다. 그러고 나서 그 남자는 그 소년에게 걸어서 다가갔다. 그 남자는 "도움이 필요하니, 꼬마야?"라고 물었다. "네, 부탁드려요."라고 그 소년은 대답했다. 그 신사는 소년 뒤에 서서 그를 위해 초인종을 눌렀다. "이제, 들어가도 된단다."라고 그가 미소를 띠며 말했다. 그러자 그 소년은 "할아버지, 우리는 뛰어야 해요!"라고 대답했다.

구문해설

3행 The boy was **trying to ring** the doorbell.

▸ try+to-v: …하려고 애쓰다

5행 So he couldn't reach **it**.

▸ it은 앞 문장의 the doorbell을 가리키는 대명사이다.

7행 Then the man **walked up to** the boy.

▸ walk up to: …에 걸어서 다가가다

10행 The gentleman **stood** behind the boy and **rang** the bell for him.

▸ 동사 stood와 rang이 접속사 and로 병렬 연결되어 있다.

문제해설

1 위 글의 분위기로 가장 알맞은 것은?

① 지루한 ② 축제의 ③ 감동적인 ④ 낭만적인 ⑤ 재미있는

▸ ⑤ 노인은 선의로 소년을 도와주었지만, 결국 소년의 장난에 도움을 준 것이었다는 재미있는 분위기의 글이다.

2 빈칸 (A)~(C)에 들어갈 말이 바르게 짝지어진 것은?

▸ ③ 특정하지 않은 하나를 나타낼 때는 부정관사를 쓰고, 앞에 나온 명사를 다시 언급할 때는 정관사를 쓴다.

내신에 나오는 COMMUNICATION

A 의견 묻고 답하기

p. 115

Check-Up | **1** (1) ⓒ (2) ⓑ (3) ⓐ **2** ⑤

문제해설

2 A: 나는 그 노래가 좋다고 생각해. 너는 어때?

B: ______________

▸ 노래에 대한 의견을 물었으므로 ⑤(내 의견으로는, 그건 환상적이야.)가 대답으로 알맞다.

B 동의하기

p. 116

Check-Up | **1** ③ **2** ②, ⑤

문제해설

1 A: 수학 시험은 매우 어려웠어.

B: 난 네 말에 동의해.

▸ 밑줄 친 문장처럼 상대방의 말에 동의하는 표현은 ③이다.

2 A: 나는 우리 교복이 멋지다고 생각해.

B: ____________ 그것은 멋지지 않아.

▸ A의 의견과 달리 B는 교복이 멋지지 않다고 했으므로, 빈칸에는 상대방의 의견에 동의하지 않을 때 쓰는 표현인 ②와 ⑤가 적절하다.

FINAL TEST

pp. 117~119

1 ② **2** turn off **3** ⑤ **4** ② **5** ④ **6** ③ **7** ⑤ **8** ⑤ **9** ② **10** ② **11** ② **12** three cities **13** two glasses of **14** a[per] year **15** ⑤ **16** ④, ⑤ **17** ④ **18** ① **19** peace **20** by train **21** We go to school **22** She had four pieces of **23** exercise nine hours a[per] week **24** Do you agree with me?

문제해설

1 ② east는 '동쪽'이라는 뜻이다.

2 '…를 끄다'라는 의미는 turn off로 나타낸다.

3 A: 너는 그 그림에 대해 어떻게 생각해?

B: ______________

▸ 그림에 대한 의견을 묻고 있으므로, 「I think that ...」으로 자신의 의견을 말하는 ⑤가 대답으로 가장 적절하다.

4 A: 너는 내 계획에 대해 어떻게 생각해?

B: 내 의견으로는, 그건 좋지 않은 생각이야.

▸ ② 상대방의 의견을 묻는 표현 「What do you think of ...?」는 「How do you feel about ...?」으로 바꿔 쓸 수 있다.

5 A: 너는 이 차에 대해 어떻게 생각해?

B: 나는 그것이 너무 비싸다고 생각해. 내 말에 동의하니?
A: 응, 동의해. 하지만 나는 그것이 멋진 차라고 생각해.
B: 나도 그렇게 생각해.

6 ① A: 이 티셔츠는 예뻐.
B: 나도 그렇게 생각해.
② A: 과학은 너무 어려워.
B: 나는 동의하지 않아. 그건 쉬워.
④ A: 이번 주말에 소풍을 가자.
B: 그거 좋은 생각이야.
⑤ A: 당신은 새로 온 직원에 대해 어떻게 생각하세요?
B: 그는 친절한 것 같아요.
▶ ③ 쇼에 대한 의견을 묻는 말에 동의한다는 대답은 어색하다.

7 ⑤ church의 복수형은 churches이다.

9 ② 주어(The geese)가 복수이며 빈칸 뒤에 v-ing가 쓰였으므로, 빈칸에는 be동사 are가 와야 한다.

10 Rob은 새 컴퓨터를 샀다. 그 컴퓨터는 싸지 않았다.
▶ ② 자음 소리 앞에서 특정하지 않은 하나를 나타낼 때는 부정관사 a를 쓰고, 앞에 언급된 명사를 다시 언급할 때는 정관사 the를 쓴다.

11 A: 설탕을 넣은 커피 한 잔을 마실 수 있을까요?
B: 물론이죠. 그 밖에 다른 건요?
A: 저는 케이크 한 조각도 원해요.
▶ ② 잔에 담긴 커피는 a cup of를, 조각 단위의 음식은 a piece of를 이용해 수량을 나타낸다.

15 ⑤는 '…마다, …당'의 의미이고, 나머지는 모두 하나를 나타낸다.

16 ④ 운동 경기 이름 앞에는 관사를 쓰지 않는다.
⑤ '1킬로그램당'의 의미이므로 부정관사 a가 와야 한다.

17 ④ life의 복수형은 lives이다.

18 ① 태양(sun)은 유일한 자연물이므로 A를 The로 고쳐야 한다.

19 추상명사 peace 앞에는 부정관사를 쓰지 않는다.

20 '…를 타고'라는 의미인 「by+교통수단」에서 교통수단 앞에는 관사를 쓰지 않는다.

24 A가 동의한다고 대답하는 것으로 보아 빈칸에는 동의하는지 묻는 표현인 Do you agree with me?가 들어가야 한다.

CHAPTER 08 형용사와 부사

GRAMMAR FOCUS
p. 122

A 형용사와 부사

1 1) 그는 오래된 차를 팔았다.
그 차는 오래되었다.
2) 식탁 위에 접시들이 조금 있다.
이 선풍기는 에너지를 거의 소비하지 않는다.

2 1) 그녀는 천천히 걷는다.
이 게임은 정말 재미있다.
나는 매우 열심히 공부했다.
다행히도, 그들은 경기에서 이겼다.

Check-Up
p. 123

A 1 lazy 2 fur 3 ran 4 Listen
B 1 much 2 friendly 3 few 4 silently
5 Sadly
C 1 ① 2 ② 3 ②
D 1 ⓑ, ⓓ 2 ⓐ, ⓒ, ⓓ 3 ⓑ, ⓓ 4 ⓐ, ⓒ, ⓓ

GRAMMAR FOCUS
p. 124

B 비교 구문

2 1) Sarah는 그녀의 언니만큼 친절하다.
그는 Justin만큼 노래를 잘 부른다.
2) 그녀의 눈은 네 것보다 더 어둡다.
소고기는 돼지고기보다 더 비싸다.
3) 이것은 세계에서 가장 높은 탑이다.
가장 신나는 부분은 퍼레이드였다.

Check-Up
p. 125

A 1 than 2 longest 3 as 4 most
B 1 lighter 2 wise as 3 more beautiful
4 the oldest
C 1 better 2 thin 3 warmer 4 tallest
D 1 earlier than 2 as big as 3 the deepest

Grammar Practice
p. 126

A 1 a little 2 carefully 3 youngest
4 as gloomy
B 1 easily 2 harder 3 few[lot of]
4 the largest 5 often writes
C 1 late 2 sweeter 3 busiest 4 closest
D 1 the heaviest 2 faster than

문제해설

A 1 셀 수 없는 명사(money) 앞에는 a little이 알맞다.
2 동사를 수식하는 부사 carefully가 알맞다.
3 「the+최상급+in+장소나 범위를 나타내는 단수명사」 구문이 쓰인 것이므로 youngest가 알맞다.

4 원급 비교 표현은 「as+원급+as」이므로 as gloomy가 알맞다.

B 1 동사를 수식하는 부사 easily로 고쳐야 한다.
2 hard 뒤에 than이 있으므로 비교급인 harder를 써야 한다.
3 뒤에 셀 수 있는 명사의 복수형(potatoes)이 쓰였으므로 little을 few 또는 lot of로 고쳐야 한다.
4 최상급을 나타낼 때는 앞에 the를 써야 한다.
5 빈도부사는 일반동사 앞에 위치한다.

D 1 Joanna가 세 명 중 제일 무거우므로 「the+최상급」 형태로 쓴다.
2 Andrew가 Billy보다 더 빨리 달리므로 「비교급+than」 형태로 쓴다.

내신 완성 Grammar Practice p. 127

1 ⑤ 2 ④ 3 ④ 4 (1) usually brush my teeth (2) can always check the weather

문제해설

1 homework는 셀 수 없는 명사이므로 첫 번째 빈칸에는 much를 쓴다.
최상급 비교 표현에서 비교 대상이 되는 복수명사 앞이므로 두 번째 빈칸에는 전치사 of를 쓴다.

2 ④ 부츠는 60달러이고 스카프는 40달러이므로 부츠가 스카프보다 더 비싸다.

3 ④ 명사를 수식하는 것은 형용사이므로 부사 warmly를 형용사 warm으로 고쳐야 한다.

서술형에 나오는 WRITING p. 128

A 1 I am often angry
2 He made lots of mistakes
B 1 never eats breakfast
2 always walks her dog
3 usually draws pictures
C 1 more popular than 2 as popular as
3 the most popular

문제해설

A 1 빈도부사는 be동사 뒤에 쓴다.

C 1 Sam은 Emma보다 더 많은 표를 받았으므로 more popular than을 쓴다.
2 Emma와 Scarlet은 동일하게 표를 받았으므로 as popular as를 쓴다.
3 Sam이 가장 많은 표를 받았으므로 the most popular를 쓴다.

READING WITH GRAMMAR pp. 129~130

Reading 1 | 1 ③ 2 more quickly than other runners
Words | [1] 오르다

해석 | 세계에서 가장 긴 계단을 보고 싶은가? 그렇다면 스위스에 있는 니젠산을 방문해 보아라. 그 계단은 산 정상까지 올라가 있다. 그것은 길이가 3.4km이고, 11,674개의 단으로 이루어졌다. 그것은 많은 계단이다! 정상까지 오르는 것은 힘들다. 그것은 일곱 번 이상 엠파이어 스테이트 빌딩을 오르는 것과 같다.

일 년 중 대부분, 그 계단은 방문객들에게 폐쇄되어 있다. 그러나, 그것은 매년 6월에 하루 동안 개방된다. 그날에는, 특별한 계단 경주인 Niesenlauf가 개최된다. 수백 명의 참가자가 다른 주자들보다 더 빠르게 계단을 오르려고 노력한다. 기록상 가장 빠른 시간은 1시간 2분이었다!

구문해설

3행 **Climbing** to the top **is** hard.
▶ 동명사 주어는 단수 취급하므로 단수동사 is가 쓰였다.

4행 It is **the same as** climbing the Empire State Building *more than* seven times.
▶ the same as: …와 마찬가지로
▶ more than: …보다 많이, …이상(의)

7행 On that day, **the Niesenlauf, a special staircase race**, *is held*.
▶ the Niesenlauf와 a special staircase race는 동격이다.
▶ 경주가 '개최되는' 것이므로, 수동태 is held가 쓰였다.

8행 Hundreds of participants **try to climb** the staircase ....
▶ try+to-v: …하려고 애쓰다

문제해설

1 ③ 매년 6월에 하루 동안만 개방된다고 했다.

2 '…보다 더 ~하게'는 「비교급+than」으로 나타낸다.

Reading 2 | 1 ③ 2 (A) sadder (B) better
Words | [1] (…처럼) 보이다, …인 것 같다 [2] 놓치다

해석 | Q: 어제, 저는 TV로 올림픽 메달 시상식을 보고 있었습니다. 금메달리스트는 세상에서 가장 행복한 사람처럼 보였습니다. 동메달리스트도 매우 행복해 보였습니다. 하지만, 은메달리스트는 다른 사람들보다 더 슬퍼 보였습니다. 왜 그녀는 동메달리스트보다 더 행복하게 느끼지 않았을까요?
A: 메달리스트들은 그들의 사고방식 때문에 행복하거나 행복하지 않게 느낍니다. 은메달리스트는 "나는 거의 이겼었어. 나는 금메달리스트보다 더 잘될 수 있었어."라고 생각할 수도 있습니다. 그리고 동메달리스트는 "적어도 나는 메달을 땄잖아! 나는 그걸 거의 놓칠 뻔했어."라고 생각할 수도 있습니다. 다시 말해서, 은메달리스트는 그들 자신을 우승자들과 비교합니다. 하지만, 동메달리스트는 그들 자신을 메달을 따지 못한 이들과 비교합니다. 그것이 동메달리스트들이 은메

달리스트들보다 더 행복하게 느끼는 이유입니다.

구문해설

2행 The bronze medalist **seemed** very **happy**, too.
▶ seem+형용사: …해 보이다

6행 The medalists feel **happy or unhappy** *because of* their attitude.
▶ 형용사 happy와 unhappy가 접속사 or로 병렬 연결되어 있다.
▶ because of는 '… 때문에'라는 뜻으로, 뒤에 명사(구)가 온다.

9행 **In other words**, silver medalists compare *themselves* with the winners.
▶ in other words: 다시 말해서
▶ 주어와 목적어가 동일인이므로, 재귀대명사 themselves가 쓰였다.

13행 **That's why** bronze medalists feel happier than silver medalists.
▶ That's why ...: 그것이 …하는 이유이다

문제해설

1 위 글의 빈칸에 들어갈 말로 가장 알맞은 것은?
① 우승자
② 그들의 점수
④ 올림픽 대회
⑤ 그들의 코치들의 지원
▶ 마음가짐에 따라 메달리스트들의 감정이 달라진다는 내용이 뒤에 이어지고 있으므로, 빈칸에 알맞은 말은 ③ '그들의 사고방식'이다.

2 (A)와 (B)를 어법상 바른 형태로 쓰시오.
▶ (A)와 (B) 뒤에 than이 왔으므로 각각 비교급인 sadder와 better로 써야 한다.

내신에 나오는 *COMMUNICATION*

A 습관 묻고 답하기 p. 131

Check-Up | **1** ① **2** What do you usually do

문제해설

1 A: 너는 얼마나 자주 네 이메일을 확인하니?
B: ______________________
▶ 빈도를 물어보는 말에 대해 횟수로 대답하는 ①이 적절하다.

2 '너는 주로 무엇을 하니?'는 「What do you usually do ...?」로 나타낸다.

B 요청하고 답하기 p. 132

Check-Up | **1** ② **2** Can you remind me

문제해설

1 A: 부탁 좀 들어줄래?
B: ______________________
▶ 부탁하는 말에 대한 대답으로는 ②(그래. 뭔데?)가 적절하다.

FINAL TEST pp. 133~135

1 ③ **2** ② **3** ④ **4** ④ **5** (D)→(B)→(C)→(A)
6 ⑤ **7** ① **8** ④ **9** ① **10** ④ **11** ③ **12** ①
13 thinner than **14** the most difficult **15** Alex → Woody → Kelly → Daniel **16** ① **17** high
18 much **19** The screen is as small as a calendar.
20 She got the best score in her class. **21** ⑤ often am → am often **22** shorter than **23** the tallest **24** How often do you have flute lessons?

문제해설

1 open(열려 있는)과 closed(닫힌)는 반의어 관계로, light(가벼운)의 반의어는 ③ heavy(무거운)이다.

2 ② at least는 '적어도, 최소한'의 뜻이다.

3 일 년에 두 번이라는 횟수로 대답하고 있으므로 빈칸에는 빈도를 묻는 ④가 와야 한다.

4 거절하는 말로 대답하고 있으므로, 빈칸에는 부탁하는 표현인 ④가 와야 한다.

5 (D) 부탁 좀 들어줄래?
(B) 물론이지. 뭔데, Steven?
(C) 음악 소리 좀 줄여줘.
(A) 그래, 그럴게.

6 ① A: 나무들을 심어 줘.
B: 알겠어, 그럴게.
② A: 부탁 좀 들어줄래?
B: 그래. 문제없어.
③ A: 쓰레기를 좀 주워 줄래?
B: 미안하지만 못해.
④ A: 너는 저녁 7시에 주로 무엇을 하니?
B: 나는 주로 저녁을 먹어.
▶ ⑤ 채소를 얼마나 자주 먹는지 묻는 말에 바쁘다고 대답하는 것은 어색하다.

7 ① fast는 형용사와 부사의 형태가 같다.

8 ④ ugly의 비교급과 최상급은 uglier와 ugliest이다.

9 ① 빈칸 앞뒤로 as가 있는 것으로 보아 원급 비교 표현이므로, strong이 와야 한다.

10 우유는 셀 수 없는 명사이므로 첫 번째 빈칸에는 a little이나 much가 와야 한다.
달걀은 셀 수 있는 명사이므로 두 번째 빈칸에는 a few가 와야 한다.

11 첫 번째 빈칸에는 주어를 보충 설명하는 형용사 sad가 와야 한다.

두 번째 빈칸에는 문장 전체를 수식하는 부사 luckily가 와야 한다.

12 ①은 원급 비교 표현이 쓰였으므로 빈칸에 as가 와야 하며, 나머지는 형용사의 비교급이 쓰였으므로 than이 와야 한다.

15 빈도부사를 빈도순으로 나열하면 always(항상) → usually(보통) → often(자주) → sometimes(때때로) 순이다.

16 ① 빈도부사는 조동사 뒤, 일반동사 앞에 위치하므로 will always help로 고쳐야 한다.

17 동사 jump를 수식하는 부사는 high(높이)가 되어야 한다. 부사 highly는 '대단히, 매우'라는 의미이다.

18 sugar는 셀 수 없는 명사이므로 many 대신 much를 써야 한다.

21 ⑤ 빈도부사는 be동사 뒤에 위치한다.

24 A: ______________________
B: 나는 일주일에 한 번 플루트 레슨이 있어.
▶ 일주일에 한 번이라고 횟수로 대답하고 있으므로 빈도를 묻는 표현인 「How often do you ...?」로 쓴다.

CHAPTER 09 to부정사

GRAMMAR FOCUS p. 138

B 명사적 용법

1 규칙적으로 운동하는 것은 좋은 습관이다.
이 문장을 이해하는 것은 쉽지 않다.

2 나는 지금 혼자 있기를 원한다.
그는 슬픈 영화 보는 것을 좋아한다.

3 Jen의 바람은 그녀 자신의 카페를 여는 것이다.
내 꿈은 타임머신을 발명하는 것이다.

Check-Up p. 139

A 1 주어 2 목적어 3 (진)주어 4 보어
B 1 to go 2 to ask 3 collect 4 to get
C 1 eat 2 It 3 to propose 4 teach
D 1 to write 2 to play 3 not to be 4 to invite

GRAMMAR FOCUS p. 140

C 형용사적 용법

우리는 할 일이 많다.
그는 점심을 먹을 시간이 없었다.
나는 이 문제에 대해 말할 것이 있다.

D 부사적 용법

1 나는 시험에 합격하기 위해 열심히 공부했다.
그녀는 책을 빌리기 위해 도서관에 갔다.
그는 첫 번째 버스를 타기 위해 일찍 일어났다.

2 나는 시험 결과를 들어서 행복하다.
그녀는 고향을 떠나게 되어 슬펐다.

3 그녀는 자라서 시인이 되었다.
그 남자는 100세까지 살았다.

Check-Up p. 141

A 1 부사적 용법 (감정의 원인) 2 부사적 용법 (결과) 3 형용사적 용법
B 1 play with 2 attend 3 to buy 4 to say
C 1 to ask 2 to[in order to] visit 3 to hear 4 to[in order to] stay
D 1 nothing to fear 2 lived to be 3 glad to meet 4 in order to enter

Grammar Practice p. 142

A 1 to take 2 is 3 not to 4 study with 5 to bother
B 1 to get 2 to be 3 to apologize 4 to[in order to] cancel 5 to read
C 1 drive 2 to eat with 3 to meet 4 to stay
D 1 sad to lose 2 time to prepare

문제해설

A 1 동사 want는 목적어로 to부정사를 쓴다.
2 주어로 쓰인 to부정사는 단수 취급한다.
3 「in order to-v」의 부정형은 「in order not to-v」이다.
4 '함께 공부할'의 의미가 되어야 하므로 전치사가 쓰인 study with가 알맞다.
5 감정을 나타내는 형용사 뒤에 to부정사가 쓰여 감정의 원인을 나타낸다.

B 1 보어 역할을 하는 명사적 용법의 to부정사 to get으로 써야 한다.
2 결과를 나타내는 부사적 용법의 to부정사 to be로 써야 한다.
3 앞에 가주어 It이 쓰였으므로 진주어 역할을 하는 명사적 용법의 to부정사 to apologize로 써야 한다.
4 목적을 나타내는 부사적 용법의 to부정사 to cancel로 써야 한다. in order to cancel로 쓸 수도 있다.
5 a newspaper를 수식하는 형용사적 용법의 to부정사 to read로 써야 한다.

C 1 진주어인 to부정사가 와야 하므로 drive로 고쳐야 한다.

2 전치사는 to부정사 뒤에 위치한다.
3 동사 hope는 목적어로 to부정사를 쓴다.
4 '…하기 위해서'는 「(in order) to-v」의 형태로 쓴다.

내신 완성 Grammar Practice p. 143

1 ⑤ 2 ④ 3 ④, ⑤ 4 (1) was surprised to see (2) It is my habit to get up

문제해설

1 첫 번째 빈칸에는 동사 like의 목적어 역할을 하는 명사적 용법의 to부정사 to listen이 와야 한다.
두 번째 빈칸에는 anything을 수식하는 형용사적 용법의 to부정사 to worry가 와야 한다.

2 보기와 ④는 목적을 나타내는 부사적 용법의 to부정사이다. ①은 보어 역할을 하는 명사적 용법, ②는 앞의 명사를 수식하는 형용사적 용법, ③은 목적어 역할을 하는 명사적 용법, ⑤는 진주어 역할을 하는 명사적 용법으로 쓰였다.

3 ④ to부정사의 부정형은 「not to-v」이므로 to not be를 not to be로 고쳐야 한다.
⑤ in order to 뒤에는 동사원형이 와야 하므로 went를 go로 고쳐야 한다.

서술형에 나오는 WRITING p. 144

A 1 His job is to grow rice.
2 We have a lot of clothes to wash.
3 It is not safe to dive here.
B 1 I planned to plant seeds
2 good to waste water
C 1 the kitchen to[in order to] do the dishes
2 shocked to see the price

문제해설

B 1 동사 plan은 목적어로 to부정사를 쓴다.
2 가주어 It이 있는 문장이므로 뒤에는 진주어인 to부정사구가 와야 한다.

READING WITH GRAMMAR pp. 145~146

Reading 1 | 1 ④ 2 ③
Words | [1]과체중의 [2]몹시 싫어하다

해석 | *The Smiths* 제작자 분께
제 이름은 Matt입니다. 저는 당신의 쇼, *The Smiths*의 굉장한 팬입니다. 그것은 정말로 재미있고, 저는 한 편도 절대 놓치지 않습니다. 하지만 저는 어제의 에피소드에 대해 당신께 말씀드릴 것이 있습니다.
그것은 과체중 소년에 관한 것이었습니다. 모든 소녀들이 그 소년을 싫어했고 그에 대해 나쁜 것들을 말했습니다. 그는 이야기할 친구가 없었습니다. 저는 그것을 보니 정말 화가 났습니다. 저도 과체중입니다. 하지만 저는 많은 친구들이 있고, 그들은 모두 저를 좋아합니다. 과체중인 사람들을 놀리는 것은 잘못되었습니다. 저는 이와 같은 에피소드를 더 보지 않기를 바랍니다.

텍사스에서 Matt

구문해설

5행 **It** was about an overweight boy.
▸ It은 앞 문장의 yesterday's episode를 가리키는 지시대명사이다.
5행 **Every** girl *hated* the boy and *said* bad things about him.
▸ every는 '모든'의 뜻이지만, 뒤에 단수명사를 쓴다.
▸ 동사 hated와 said가 접속사 and로 병렬 연결되어 있다.

문제해설

1 ④ 과체중인 소년을 놀리는 내용의 TV쇼를 보고, 이에 대해 제작자에게 불만을 표현하는 글이다.

2 보기와 ③은 감정의 원인을 나타내는 부사적 용법의 to부정사이다. ①과 ②는 형용사적 용법, ④와 ⑤는 명사적 용법의 to부정사이다.

Reading 2 | 1 ⑤ 2 to[in order to] pay
Words | [1]아픈 [2]낫게 하다

해석 | 한 가난한 소년은 먹을 것이 없었다. 그는 가장 가까운 집에서 음식을 달라고 하기로 결심하고 문을 두드렸다. 놀랍게도, 어린 소녀가 나왔고, 소년을 안으로 초대해서, 그에게 햄 샌드위치를 주었다.
20년 후, 그 어린 소녀는 자라서 성인 여성이 되었다. 그러나 그녀는 몹시 아팠다. 그녀의 의사들은 모든 것을 시도했지만, 그녀는 계속해서 더 아팠다. 마침내, 그녀의 가족은 한 유명한 의사에게 그녀를 치료해달라고 부탁했다. 수개월이 걸렸지만, 그는 그녀를 낫게 했다! 여자가 금액을 지불하기 위해 그의 병원에 갔을 때, 그녀는 어떤 것을 알게 되어 충격을 받았다. 모든 것이 공짜였다! 계산서 대신, 간호사가 그녀에게 메모를 주었다. 그것에는 "당신의 요금은 20년 전에 샌드위치로 지불되었습니다."라고 쓰여 있었다.

구문해설

3행 Surprisingly, a young girl **came** out, **invited** the boy in, and **gave** him a ham sandwich.
▸ 동사 came, invited, gave가 접속사 and로 병렬 연결되어 있다.
7행 Her doctors tried everything, but she **kept getting** sicker.
▸ keep v-ing: 계속해서 …하다
10행 **When** the woman went to his hospital to pay her bill, she was shocked to *find* something *out*.
▸ when: …할 때
▸ find out: 알게 되다[알아내다]

문제해설

1 위 글의 제목으로 가장 알맞은 것은?

① 무료 병원 찾기
② 훌륭한 의사들에게 상을 수여하기
③ 가난한 아이들에게 샌드위치 판매하기
④ 최고의 샌드위치를 만드는 사람 찾기
⑤ 무상 치료로 샌드위치값 갚기
▶ ⑤ 한 소년이 지난날 자신에게 샌드위치를 주었던 소녀에게 20년 후 무상 치료로 은혜를 갚은 내용의 글이다.

2 밑줄 친 단어를 바르게 고치시오.
▶ '지불하기 위해'라는 의미로 목적을 나타내는 to부정사가 와야 하므로, pay를 to[in order to] pay로 고쳐야 한다.

내신에 나오는 COMMUNICATION

A 좋아하는 것 묻고 답하기 p. 147

Check-Up | 1 ⑤ 2 ②

문제해설

1 기타 연주하기를 좋아한다고 대답하고 있으므로, 무엇을 하는 것을 좋아하는지 묻는 ⑤가 알맞다.

2 가장 좋아하는 간식이 무엇인지 묻고 있으므로, 감자 칩을 가장 좋아한다는 내용의 ②가 알맞다.

B 상기시켜 주기 p. 148

Check-Up | 1 ④ 2 Remember to wear

문제해설

1 A: 너는 어떤 운동을 제일 좋아해?
B: 나는 야구를 좋아해. 너는 어떠니?
A: 나도 야구를 정말 좋아해! 함께 경기를 하자!
B: 좋아. 네 야구 방망이를 가져오는 것을 잊지 마.
A: 그래, 안 잊을게.

FINAL TEST pp. 149~151

1 ③ 2 ② 3 ⑤ 4 ③ 5 forget to wash 6 ③ 7 ④ 8 ③ 9 ② 10 ③ 11 ③ 12 person to help 13 not to give up 14 in order to succeed 15 ② 16 ② 17 ④ 18 ③ 19 ③ 20 plan is to protect the environment 21 waited a long time to hear the news 22 It isn't possible to finish the work. 23 He will go to the library to return some books. 24 She set her alarm to get up early.

문제해설

1 ③ prize는 '상'이라는 뜻이다.

2 love(사랑하다)와 hate(몹시 싫어하다)는 반의어 관계로, rich(부유한)의 반의어는 ② poor(가난한)이다.

3 밑줄 친 문장은 상대방에게 가장 좋아하는 영화를 묻는 표현이므로, 바꿔 쓸 수 있는 말은 ⑤(너는 어떤 영화를 제일 좋아해?)이다.

4 ① A: 너는 테니스를 좋아하니?
B: 아니. 그건 내게 너무 어려워.
② A: 네가 가장 좋아하는 배우는 누구니?
B: 나는 톰 홀랜드를 정말 좋아해.
④ A: 나는 수영장에 갈 거야.
B: 수영복을 가지고 갈 것을 기억해.
⑤ A: 나는 대구로 여행을 갈 계획이야.
B: 전통 시장을 방문하는 것을 잊지 마.
▶ ③ 집에서 무엇을 하는 것을 좋아하는지 묻는 말에 부엌이 좋다는 대답은 어색하다.

5 「Remember to-v」는 「Don't forget to-v」로 바꿔 쓸 수 있다.

6 ③ 동사 agree는 목적어로 to부정사를 쓴다.

7 chairs를 수식하는 to부정사로 '(위에) 앉을'이라는 의미가 되어야 하므로, 빈칸에는 전치사가 함께 있는 ④가 알맞다.

8 ③ '사기 위해'라는 의미로 목적을 나타내는 부사적 용법의 to부정사 to buy가 와야 한다.

9 ② '(…해서) ~하다'의 의미로 결과를 나타내는 부사적 용법의 to부정사 to be가 와야 한다.

10 ③ '지킬'의 의미인 형용사적 용법의 to부정사 to follow는 수식하는 명사 rules 뒤에 위치한다.

11 ③ '…하는 것은'이라는 의미는 to부정사 주어로 나타낼 수 있다. 이때 주어 자리에 가주어 It을 쓰고, to부정사는 뒤로 보낸다.

13 to부정사의 부정형은 「not to-v」이다.

15 ②는 명사 time을 수식하는 형용사적 용법의 to부정사인 반면, 나머지는 모두 명사적 용법의 to부정사이다.

16 ②는 '그것'이라는 의미의 대명사인 반면, 나머지는 모두 가주어이다.

17 보기와 ①, ②, ③, ⑤의 to부정사는 모두 명사를 수식하는 형용사적 용법이다. ④는 목적을 나타내는 부사적 용법의 to부정사이다.

18 보기와 ③은 감정의 원인을 나타내는 부사적 용법의 to부정사이다. ①과 ⑤는 명사적 용법, ②는 목적을 나타내는 부사적 용법, ④는 형용사적 용법의 to부정사이다.

19 ③ to부정사의 수식을 받는 명사(a house)가 전치사의 목적어인 경우, 전치사를 생략해서는 안 된다. 따라서 to live는 to live in이 되어야 한다.

22 주어로 쓰인 to부정사구 자리에 가주어 It을 쓰고, to부정사구 to finish the work를 뒤로 보낸다.

23, 24 목적을 나타내는 to부정사를 이용해 문장을 연결한다.

CHAPTER 10 동명사

GRAMMAR FOCUS p. 154

A 동명사

1 너와 체스를 하는 것은 재미있다.
그 건물을 찾는 것은 쉽지 않았다.

2 1) 나는 귀여운 동물들의 사진을 모으는 것을 좋아한다.
그들은 악기를 연주하기 시작했다.
2) 그녀는 추리 소설을 쓰는 것을 잘한다.

3 그의 취미는 꽃을 그리는 것이었다.
내 목표는 수학 시험에서 좋은 성적을 받는 것이다.

Check-Up p. 155

A 1 (전치사의) 목적어 2 보어 3 (동사의) 목적어
4 주어
B 1 is 2 Raising 3 using 4 learning
5 doing
C 1 Taking[To take] 2 exercising[to exercise]
3 feeding 4 Not turning
D 1 felt like eating 2 go jogging
3 Not being late 4 instead of going out

GRAMMAR FOCUS p. 156

B 동명사와 to부정사

1 그들은 모바일 게임을 하는 것을 끝냈다.
너는 내일 과학 시험을 보는 것을 피할 수 없다.

2 Amy는 이구아나를 기르고 싶었다.
그는 연설 대회에 참가하기로 결정했다.

3 1) 나는 해변을 따라 걷는 것을 정말 좋아한다.
그 소년은 큰 소리로 울기 시작했다.
2) ① 그녀는 그를 위해 생일 카드를 쓸 것을 기억했다.
네 우산을 가져올 것을 잊지 마.
② 나는 그녀의 목소리를 들은 것을 기억한다.
그들은 창문을 닫은 것을 잊었다.
③ 그는 건강을 유지하려고 노력한다.
Jennifer는 (시험 삼아) 새 프린터를 써 보았다.

Check-Up p. 157

A 1 to ride 2 going 3 turning 4 to set
5 to leave
B 1 running 2 to save 3 cleaning
4 smoking 5 to build
C 1 started burning 2 like to watch
D 1 tries to get 2 forgot to deliver
3 remembered to buy 4 stopped walking

Grammar Practice p. 158

A 1 eating 2 laughing 3 to find 4 taking
5 is
B 1 touching 2 to go 3 Sending[To send]
4 not calling 5 selling
C 1 to take 2 singing 3 to buy
D 1 sending 2 to study

문제해설

A 1 전치사 of의 목적어로 동명사가 와야 한다.
4 '(과거에) …한 것을 기억하다'라는 의미이므로, remember의 목적어로 동명사가 와야 한다.
5 주어로 쓰인 동명사구는 단수 취급한다.

B 1 동사 avoid는 목적어로 동명사를 취한다.
2 동사 decide는 목적어로 to부정사를 취한다.
3 주어 자리에는 동명사나 to부정사가 와야 한다.
5 전치사 about의 목적어 역할을 해야 하므로 sell을 동명사 selling으로 고쳐야 한다.

C 1 forget to-v: (미래에) …할 것을 잊다
2 stop v-ing: …하는 것을 멈추다
3 try to-v: …하려고 노력하다

D 1 문자 메시지를 보냈던 것을 잊었다고 했으므로, forgot 뒤에 과거의 일을 나타내는 동명사를 쓴다.
2 동사 continue는 목적어로 동명사와 to부정사 둘 다 취하는데, 주어진 빈칸이 두 개이므로 to study로 써야 한다.

내신 완성 Grammar Practice p. 159

1 ② 2 ⑤ 3 ⑤ 4 (1) is good at baking
(2) spent lots of money buying

문제해설

1 ② 동사 wish는 to부정사를 목적어로 취한다.

2 동사 mind는 목적어로 동명사를 취하므로 첫 번째 빈칸에는 opening이 와야 한다.
문맥상 경기를 보는 것을 멈췄다는 의미이므로 두 번째 빈칸에는 동명사 watching이 와야 한다.

3 ⑤ '…하러 가다'는 「go v-ing」로 나타낸다.

서술형에 나오는 WRITING

p. 160

A 1 I remembered meeting him on the subway.
2 Running on the escalator is not safe.
B 1 He stopped to take a picture
2 We couldn't help asking for
3 They kept (on) talking
C 1 started eating[to eat] 2 decided to buy
3 forgot to bring

문제해설

B 2 '…하지 않을 수 없다'는 「can't help v-ing」로 나타낸다.
3 '계속 …하다'는 「keep (on) v-ing」로 나타낸다.

C 1 동사 start는 목적어로 동명사와 to부정사 둘 다 취한다.
2 동사 decide는 목적어로 to부정사를 취한다.
3 Lily는 지갑을 가져올 것을 잊었으므로 forgot의 목적어로 to 부정사를 쓴다.

READING WITH GRAMMAR

pp. 161~162

Reading 1 | 1 ②, ③ 2 (A) makes (B) dripping
Words | [1]…이 들어 있다 [2]녹다

해석 | 땅콩버터는 맛있다. 그런데 그것은 유용하기도 하다. 당신은 땅콩버터가 가죽에 좋다는 것을 알고 있었는가? 땅콩버터를 가죽 구두에 문지르는 것은 당신의 구두를 반짝이게 만든다. 이것은 땅콩버터에 천연 기름이 들어 있기 때문이다. 그것은 오래된 스티커도 제거해 줄 수 있다. 스티커에 (땅콩버터를) 약간 문지르고 40분 기다리기만 해라. 스티커가 쉽게 떼어질 것이다.

땅콩버터는 또한 아이스크림콘을 덜 지저분하게 만들어 준다! 당신이 더운 날에 아이스크림콘을 즐기기로 한다고 가정해 보아라. 물론, 아이스크림은 빨리 녹을 것이다. 아이스크림을 얹기 전에, 콘의 맨 아랫부분에 땅콩버터를 조금 넣어라. 그것은 녹은 아이스크림이 흘러내리는 것을 막아 줄 것이다. 그리고 당신이 콘을 먹을 때, 마지막에는 특별한 선물이 있을 것이다!

구문해설

1행 Did you know peanut butter **is good for** leather?
▸ be good for: …에 좋다

3행 **This is because** peanut butter contains natural oils.
▸ This is because: 이것은 …이기 때문이다

4행 The sticker will **come off** easily.
▸ come off: 떼어 낼[제거할] 수 있다

7행 **Suppose** (**that**) you decide to enjoy an ice cream cone on a hot day.
▸ suppose (that)는 '…이라는 것을 가정하다'는 의미로, 뒤에 목적어 역할을 하는 명사절이 온다.

문제해설

1 ② 음식이 상하는 것을 방지해 준다는 내용과 ③ 생선 냄새가 퍼지는 것을 막아 준다는 내용은 언급되지 않았다.

2 (A) 주어로 쓰인 동명사구는 단수 취급하므로, makes로 써야 한다.
(B) '…가 ~하는 것을 막다[방지하다]'를 나타내는 「stop … from v-ing」 구문이 쓰인 것이므로, 동명사인 dripping으로 써야 한다.

Reading 2 | 1 ⑤ 2 (A) to turn (B) making
(C) Adding
Words | [1]쓸모없는

해석 | 사람들은 어디에서나 그들의 휴대 전화를 이용할 수 있다. 그래서 공중전화 부스는 쓸모없어지고 있다. 흥미롭게도, 두 프랑스인 예술가가 이 부스를 특별한 상자로 바꾸기로 결심했다. 그들은 공중전화 부스 수족관을 만들었다!

여기 그것을 만든 그들의 방식이 있다. 문과 틈을 단단히 밀폐하는 것이 첫 번째 단계이다. 이것은 물이 새는 것을 방지한다. 깨끗한 물로 부스를 채우는 것이 두 번째 단계이다. 물고기를 부스에 넣는 것이 마지막 단계이다. 이제, 낡은 공중전화 부스는 하나의 수족관이다. 사람들은 방문해서 아름다운 물고기들을 보는 것을 즐길 수 있다. 그리고 볼 것이 한 가지 더 있다: 낡은 공중전화이다. 예술가들은 재미로 그것을 안에 남겨 두었다!

구문해설

1행 So phone booths are **becoming useless**.
▸ become+형용사: …하게 되다

2행 Interestingly, two French artists decided to **turn** the booth **into** a special box.
▸ turn A into B: A를 B로 바꾸다

5행 **Filling** the booth **with** clean water is the second step.
▸ fill A with B: A를 B로 채우다

9행 People can **visit** and **enjoy** seeing the beautiful fish.
▸ 동사 visit와 enjoy가 접속사 and로 병렬 연결되어 있다.

문제해설

1 위 글의 제목으로 가장 알맞은 것은?
① 최초의 공중전화 부스
② 새로운 유형의 휴대 전화
③ 다양한 물고기가 있는 수족관
④ 세계에서 가장 유명한 수족관
⑤ 아름다운 변화: 공중전화 부스에서 수족관으로
▸ ⑤ 더는 쓸모없어진 공중전화 부스가 수족관으로 탈바꿈한 과정을 설명하는 글이다.

2 (A)~(C)에서 어법상 올바른 단어를 골라 아래에 쓰시오.
▸ (A) 동사 decide는 목적어로 to부정사를 취한다.
(B) 전치사 of의 목적어 역할을 해야 하므로 동명사가 와야 한다.

(C) 문장의 주어 역할을 해야 하므로 동명사가 와야 한다.

내신에 나오는 COMMUNICATION

A 제안하고 답하기 p. 163

Check-Up | 1 ② 2 ⑤

문제해설

1 A: 오늘 밤 여기에서 묵는 게 어때?
B: ____________

▶ ② 오늘밤 여기서 머무르자는 말에 여기에 살지 않는다고 대답하는 것은 적절하지 않다.

2 A: 냉장고에 먹을 것이 없어.
B: ____________

▶ ⑤ 냉장고에 먹을 것이 없다는 말에 음식을 사러 나가자고 제안하는 것이 적절하다.

B 소망 묻고 답하기 p. 164

Check-Up | 1 Do you want to join
2 I would like to feed

문제해설

2 본인이 하고 싶을 것을 말할 때는 「I would like to-v ...」로 표현할 수 있다.

FINAL TEST pp. 165~167

1 ④ 2 am tired of 3 ④ 4 ⑤ 5 ④ 6 ③
7 ④ 8 ③ 9 ④ 10 ⑤ 11 ⑤ 12 O
13 running 14 changing 15 ③ 16 to wear
17 skating 18 ① 19 ③ 20 I couldn't help crying. 21 Solving the math problem is difficult.
22 He kept (on) playing 23 ⑤ Swim → Swimming [To swim] 24 Not leaving the town was a good choice.

문제해설

1 ④ remove는 '없애다, 제거하다'라는 뜻이다.

2 '…에 싫증 나다'는 be tired of로 나타낸다.

4 ⑤ 상자를 열고 싶어 하는지 묻는 말에 유감이라고 대답하는 것은 어색하다.

5 A: 이 빨간 모자를 써 보는 게 어때?
B: 나는 그 색을 좋아하지 않아.
A: 그러면 저 검은 것을 써 보는 게 어때?
B: (잘했어!) 좋아.

6 ③ 전치사 of의 목적어로 동명사가 와야 한다.

8 ③ feel like v-ing: …하고 싶다

9 ④ 동사 enjoy는 목적어로 동명사를 취한다.

10 ⑤ 동사 decide는 목적어로 to부정사를 취한다.

11 ⑤ 동사 avoid는 목적어로 동명사를, 동사 promise는 목적어로 to부정사를 취한다.

12 동사 love는 to부정사와 동명사를 모두 목적어로 취한다.

13 문맥상 '시간을 확인하기 위해 뛰는 것을 멈췄다'가 되어야 하므로, run을 동명사 running으로 고쳐야 한다.

14 동사 mind는 목적어로 동명사를 취하므로, to change를 동명사 changing으로 고쳐야 한다.

15 보기의 informing과 ③의 growing은 보어로 쓰인 동명사이다. ①은 진행형, ②, ④는 동사의 목적어, ⑤는 전치사의 목적어로 쓰인 동명사이다.

16 문맥상 비가 오니 우비를 입을 것을 기억해야 한다는 내용이므로 「remember to-v」 형태로 써야 한다.

17 '…하러 가다'는 「go v-ing」 형태로 쓴다.

18 ① 동사원형은 문장의 주어가 될 수 없으므로 Not be를 동명사의 부정형인 Not being으로 고쳐야 한다.

19 ③ '(과거에) …한 것을 잊다'의 의미일 때는 「forget v-ing」로 쓴다.

23 ⑤ 문장의 주어 역할을 하는 동명사 Swimming 또는 to부정사 To swim이 와야 한다.

24 동명사는 앞에 not을 붙여서 부정형을 만든다.

CHAPTER 11 전치사와 접속사

GRAMMAR FOCUS p. 170

A 전치사

1 1) 나는 너를 공원에서 보았다.
Patrick은 뉴욕에 산다.
누가 회의실 안에 있니?
2) 고양이가 의자 위에 누워 있다.
램프가 침대 위에 걸려 있다.
다리 아래에 벤치가 몇 개 있다.
3) Olivia는 건물 앞에 서 있다.
소년들은 커튼 뒤에 숨어 있었다.
그녀는 항상 내 옆에 앉는다.
4) 내 차는 트럭과 버스 사이에 있다.

2 1) 그는 2017년에 한국을 방문했다.
너는 두 시에 집에 가도 된다.
모든 사람들이 크리스마스에 행복해 보인다.
2) 나는 식사 전에 손을 씻는다.

우리는 방과 후에 발레 연습을 할 것이다.
그는 10분 동안 휴식을 취했다.

| Check-Up | ········· p. 171

A 1 in front of 2 next to 3 over
B 1 in 2 at 3 in
C 1 on 2 at 3 between 4 in
D 1 after lunch 2 for thirty minutes
3 before the show

GRAMMAR FOCUS ········· p. 172

B 접속사

1 Tom과 나는 좋은 친구이다.
이 드레스는 예쁘지만 비싸다.
너는 집에 머무르거나 나가도 된다.
나는 내 가방을 잃어버려서, 분실물 보관소에 갔다.

2 그녀는 일하러 갈 때 항상 지하철을 탄다.
1) 어렸을 때, 나는 채소를 좋아하지 않았다.
Alex는 잠자리에 들기 전에 샤워를 한다.
Sarah는 시험을 본 후에 자유 시간을 즐겼다.
네가 휴식을 취하고 있는 동안 우리는 노래를 연습했다.
나는 나이가 듦에 따라, 잘 잊어버리게 되었다.
2) 추웠기 때문에 나는 두꺼운 코트를 입었다.
3) 그녀가 똑똑하다는 것은 사실이다.
나는 우리가 경기를 이길 수 있다는 것을 믿는다.
그 소식은 Chris가 실종되었다는 것이다.

| Check-Up | ········· p. 173

A 1 or 2 but 3 and 4 so
B 1 ⓒ 2 ⓑ 3 ⓐ 4 ⓓ
C 1 that 2 As 3 or
D 1 when 2 Before 3 and 4 that
5 because

Grammar Practice p. 174

A 1 in 2 on 3 or 4 because
B 1 over 2 that 3 behind 4 so
C 1 in 2 on 3 that 4 finish 5 read
D 1 between, and 2 next to

문제해설

A 1 연도 앞에는 전치사 in을 쓴다.
2 날짜 앞에는 전치사 on을 쓴다.
3 '또는'이라는 의미의 등위 접속사 or가 와야 한다.
4 뒤에 안경을 쓰는 이유가 이어지므로 '… 때문에'라는 의미의 종속 접속사 because가 와야 한다.

B 1 표면에서 떨어진 위를 나타낼 때는 전치사 over를 쓴다.
2 목적어 역할을 하는 명사절을 이끄는 종속 접속사 that이 와야 한다.
3 '구름 뒤로'라는 의미가 되어야 하므로 전치사 behind를 쓴다.
4 앞에서 Tony가 사과한 원인이 제시되었으므로 '그래서'라는 의미의 등위 접속사 so가 와야 한다.

C 1 오전 앞에는 전치사 in을 쓴다.
2 특정한 날 앞에는 전치사 on을 쓴다.
3 보어 역할을 하는 명사절을 이끄는 종속 접속사 that으로 고쳐야 한다.
4 시간을 나타내는 부사절에서는 미래의 일을 현재시제로 나타낸다.
5 등위 접속사 or는 문법적으로 대등한 요소를 연결하므로, 앞에 나온 동사원형 play와 대등한 형태인 read로 고쳐야 한다.

내신 완성 Grammar Practice p. 175

1 ④ 2 ② 3 ① 4 (1) in front of the police station (2) It is impossible that

문제해설

1 첫 번째 빈칸에는 전치사 for(… 동안)이 와야 한다.
두 번째 빈칸에는 종속 접속사 while(… 하는 동안)이 와야 한다.

2 ②에는 시간을 나타내는 종속 접속사 when 등이, 나머지에는 모두 명사절을 이끄는 종속 접속사 that이 와야 한다.

3 (A) '자정'과 같은 하루의 때를 나타내는 말 앞에는 at을 쓴다.
(B) 시간을 나타내는 절에서 미래의 일은 현재시제로 나타낸다.
(C) 문맥상 '그리고'라는 의미의 등위 접속사 and가 적절하다.

서술형에 나오는 WRITING p. 176

A 1 I knew that the rumor was true.
2 As the tiger was sleeping, the vet cured it.
B 1 sat on 2 set up a tent under
C 1 after he reads comic books
2 before he prepares dinner

문제해설

B 1 두 사람은 잔디 위에 앉아 있으므로 sat on을 쓴다.
2 두 사람은 나무 아래에 텐트를 쳤으므로 set up a tent under를 쓴다.

C 1 Tony는 만화책을 읽은 후에 미술 숙제를 할 것이고, after가 이끄는 시간 부사절이므로 미래의 일을 현재시제인 reads로 나타내야 한다.
2 Tony는 저녁을 준비하기 전에 도서관에 갈 것이고, before가 이끄는 시간 부사절이므로 미래의 일을 현재시제인 prepares로 나타내야 한다.

READING WITH GRAMMAR pp. 177~178

Reading 1 | **1** ④ **2** while it grew older
Words | [1] 날카로운 [2] 경험하다

해석 | 어떤 공룡들은 고기를 먹었고, 다른 공룡들은 식물을 먹었다. 그렇지만 당신은 한 육식 공룡이 나이가 들면서 채식주의자로 변했다는 것을 알고 있었는가? 그것은 리무사우루스로, 약 1억 6천만 년 전에 살았던 작은 공룡이었다.

연구에 따르면, 그것은 어렸을 때 날카로운 이빨을 가졌다. 그래서 그것은 아마도 식물과 고기 둘 다를 먹었을 것이다. 하지만 어른이 되면서, 그것은 모든 이빨을 잃었다. 그래서 과학자들은 다 자란 공룡은 식물만 먹을 수 있었을 것이라고 생각한다. "이것은 다 자란 공룡이 어린 공룡들과 먹이로 경쟁하고 싶지 않았기 때문에 일어났습니다"라고 그들 중 한 명이 말했다. 놀랍게도, 리무사우루스는 나이가 드는 동안 신체에 70가지 이상의 다른 변화들도 겪었다.

구문해설

2행 It was the **Limusaurus, a small dinosaur** [***that*** **lived about 160 million years ago**].
- ▸ Limusaurus와 a small dinosaur 이하는 동격이다.
- ▸ that 이하는 a small dinosaur를 수식하는 주격 관계대명사절이다.

8행 Surprisingly, the *Limusaurus* experienced **more than** 70 other changes to its body while it grew older.
- ▸ more than: …보다 많이[… 이상]

문제해설

1 ① 그것의 종을 먹었다
② 그것의 새끼와 싸웠다
③ 훨씬 어려 보였다
④ 채식주의자로 변했다
⑤ 식물과 고기를 싫어했다
▸ 고기와 식물을 먹던 리무사우루스가 자라면서 이빨을 잃어 식물만 먹었을 것으로 추정하는 내용이 뒤에 이어지므로, 빈칸에 알맞은 말은 ④이다.

2 종속절은 「접속사+주어+동사」의 어순으로 쓴다.

Reading 2 | **1** ① **2** ④
Words | [1] 묘사하다

해석 | Sarah와 한 화가가 그의 화실에 앉았다. 그 화가는 커튼 뒤에 앉아 있었기 때문에 그녀를 볼 수 없었다. Sarah는 자신의 얼굴에 대해 이야기했다. 예를 들어, 그녀는 "저는 큰 턱을 가졌다고 생각해요. 그리고 제 볼에 주근깨가 많이 있어요."라고 말했다. 그러고 나서 화가는 그녀를 자신의 화폭 위에 그렸다.

잠시 후, 그는 그녀를 다시 그렸다. 하지만 이번에는, 다른 여성이 Sarah를 묘사했다. 그녀는 "그녀는 아름다운 이마와 깊고 푸른 눈을 가지고 있어요."라고 말했다. 그 화가가 끝마친 후에, Sarah는 두 그림을 비교했다. 그녀는 두 번째 그림에서 더 매력적으로 보였기 때문에 그것을 더 좋아했다. 자, 당신은 자신을 어떻게 생각하는가? 어쩌면 당신은 당신이 생각하는 것보다 더 아름다울지도 모른다!

구문해설

12행 So, **what do you think of** *yourself*?
- ▸ what do you think of ...?: …에 대해 어떻게 생각하니?
- ▸ yourself는 주어와 동일인을 지칭할 때 쓰는 재귀대명사이다.

13행 Maybe you are **more beautiful than you think**!
- ▸ 「비교급+than+주어+동사」 구문처럼 than 뒤에 절이 올 경우, '…하는 것보다 더 ~한[하게]'로 해석한다.

문제해설

1 위 글의 제목으로 가장 알맞은 것은?
① 당신 자신의 아름다움을 보아라
② 그림을 그리면서 시간을 보내라
③ 낯선 사람들의 얼굴을 그려라
④ 당신 자신의 그림들을 비교하라
⑤ 거울을 더 자주 보아라
▸ 스스로를 생각하는 모습보다 다른 사람 눈에 비친 본인의 모습이 더 매력적이라는 내용이므로, ①이 제목으로 알맞다.

2 빈칸 (A)와 (B)에 들어갈 말이 바르게 짝지어진 것은?
(A) 화가가 Sarah를 볼 수 없었던 이유가 뒤에 이어지므로, 빈칸에는 접속사 because(… 때문에)가 와야 한다.
(B) 문맥상 '화가가 끝마친 후에'가 되어야 하므로, 빈칸에는 접속사 After(… 후에)가 와야 한다.

내신에 나오는 COMMUNICATION

A 길 묻고 답하기 p. 179

Check-Up | **1** ③ **2** ④, ⑤

문제해설

1 ③ 서점에 가는 길을 묻고 있으므로, 그것을 서점에서 샀다고 대답하는 것은 적절하지 않다.

2 ① 너는 은행에 가고 있니?
② 너는 어제 어디에 갔니?
③ 네가 가장 좋아하는 건물은 무엇이니?
④ 너는 공원으로 가는 길을 아니?
⑤ 극장을 어디에서 찾을 수 있니?

B 약속 시간·장소 정하기 p. 180

Check-Up | **1** ② **2** Can you make it

문제해설

1 A: 농구 경기를 보러 가자.
B: 그거 좋은 생각이야. 우리 언제 만날까?
A: 오전 11시 어때?
B: 좋아. 어디에서 만나고 싶니?

A: 국립 박물관 앞에서 만나자.

2 A: 언제 만나고 싶니?
B: 저녁 8시 30분까지 올 수 있어?
A: 물론이지.
▶ 동사 make를 이용해 약속 시간을 제안할 때는 「Can you make it by+시간?」으로 표현한다.

FINAL TEST

pp. 181~183

1 ⑤ 2 ① 3 ④ 4 (A)→(B)→(D)→(C) 5 ③
6 ③ 7 ④ 8 ⑤ 9 ② 10 ② 11 ② 12 ⑤
13 next to 14 between, and 15 ② 16 ②, ⑤
17 on the wall 18 for three hours 19 in the morning 20 at lunchtime 21 because I had a toothache 22 after[when] the math teacher came into the classroom 23 begins at 1:30 p.m.
24 bus number 167

문제해설

1 ⑤ compare는 '비교하다'라는 뜻이다.

2 old(나이 든)와 young(어린)은 반의어 관계로, dry(마른, 건조한)의 반의어는 ① wet(젖은)이다.

3 구체적인 시간을 대답하고 있으므로, 빈칸에는 몇 시에 만날지를 묻는 ④가 와야 한다.

4 (A) 우리 어디에서 만날까?
(B) Dream 공원은 어때?
(D) 그래. 그런데 거기에 어떻게 가지?
(C) 너는 지하철을 타야 해.

5 ① A: 우리 언제 만날까?
B: 오후 2시까지 올 수 있니?
② A: 너희 집은 어디에 있니?
B: 미용실 맞은편에 있어.
④ A: 같이 점심 먹자.
B: 좋아. 우리 어디에서 만날까?
⑤ A: Grand 체육관으로 가는 길을 아세요?
B: 네. 세 블록을 곧장 걸어가세요.
▶ ③ 언제 만나고 싶은지 묻는 말에 Star 극장에서 만나자고 대답하는 것은 어색하다.

6 ③ '…할 때'는 접속사 when으로 나타낸다.

7 ④ '… 전에'는 접속사 before로 나타낸다.

8 ⑤ '… 하는 동안'은 접속사 while로 나타낸다.

10 계절 앞에는 전치사 in이 와야 한다.
'… 안에서'라는 의미는 전치사 in으로 나타낸다.

11 첫 번째 빈칸에는 '또는'이라는 의미의 등위 접속사 or가 와야 한다.
두 번째 빈칸에는 시간을 나타내는 부사절에서 미래시제 대신 쓰이는 현재시제인 is가 와야 한다.

15 ②에는 시간을 나타내는 접속사 before 등이, 나머지에는 모두 명사절을 이끄는 접속사 that이 와야 한다.

16 ② 등위 접속사 or로 동사원형 take와 병렬 연결되어야 하므로 walking을 walk로 고쳐야 한다.
⑤ 하루의 때를 나타내는 night 앞에는 전치사 in이 아닌 at을 쓴다.

17 '벽에'의 의미가 되어야 하므로 전치사 on을 쓴다.

18 '세 시간 동안'의 의미가 되어야 하므로 전치사 for를 쓴다.

19 오전을 나타내는 the morning 앞에는 전치사 in을 쓴다.

20 하루의 때를 나타내는 lunchtime 앞에는 전치사 at을 쓴다.

21 이가 아팠기 때문에 치과에 간 것이므로, 접속사 because를 써서 문장을 연결한다.

22 수업이 시작된 것은 선생님이 교실에 들어오셨을 때나 그 이후의 일이므로 접속사 after나 when을 써서 문장을 연결한다.

CHAPTER 12 여러 가지 문장의 종류

GRAMMAR FOCUS

p. 186

A 명령문과 감탄문

1 1) 자신감을 가져라.
저에게 전화해 주세요.
두려워하지 마라.
제한 속도를 넘지 마라.
이 영화를 보자.
우리의 수학 숙제를 하자.
그에 대해서 말하지 말자.
오늘 등산을 하지 말자.

2 1) (너는) 참 귀여운 소녀구나! (← 너는 정말 귀여운 소녀다.)
2) (세상이) 참 좁구나! (← 세상이 정말 좁다.)

Check-Up

p. 187

A 1 How 2 Be 3 What 4 and 5 or
B 1 Let's 2 What 3 Be 4 Don't 5 How
C 1 Wait here 2 Don't play
D 1 What 2 How lucky 3 How funny

GRAMMAR FOCUS

p. 188

B 여러 가지 의문문

1 1) 너는 졸리구나, 그렇지 않니?

그는 경찰이 아니야, 그렇지?
Lisa와 Aaron은 음료를 시키지 않았어, 그렇지?
이것은 네 노트북이야, 그렇지 않니?
바람이 불어, 그렇지 않니?
그는 매운 음식을 못 먹어, 그렇지?
Kate는 미네소타에서 일해, 그렇지 않니?
너는 오늘 아침에 조깅하러 갔어, 그렇지 않니?
지금 점심을 준비해줘, 그럴 거지?
대만을 여행하자, 그럴 거지?
2) A: 너는 서울에 살지 않아, 그렇지?
B: 아니, 살고 있어. / 응, 살지 않아.

2 1) 너는 신이 나지 않니?
그는 디자이너가 아니었니?
그녀는 고기를 먹지 않니?
네가 이 포스터를 만들지 않았니?
Jim은 지금 너를 도울 수 없니?
2) A: 너는 나를 이해하지 못했니?
B: 아니, 이해했어. / 응, 이해하지 못했어.

3 A: 그녀는 선생님이니 아니면 소방관이니?
B: 그녀는 소방관이야.

| Check-Up | .... p. 189

A 1 Isn't 2 don't 3 will 4 didn't 5 or
B 1 I can 2 No 3 Yes
C 1 can't 2 he 3 shall 4 Didn't
D 1 Don't you keep 2 didn't they
3 Will she, today or tomorrow

Grammar Practice p. 190

A 1 be 2 Turn 3 How 4 won't 5 or
B 1 a tiny baby 2 didn't you 3 Let's not go
4 or 5 will you
C 1 No, I won't 2 Yes, he is 3 No, let's not
D 1 Don't touch 2 and you will understand

문제해설

A 1 부정 명령문은 「Don't+동사원형」으로 쓴다.
3 감탄문에서 형용사 exciting 뒤에 바로 주어와 동사가 나왔으므로, How로 시작하는 것이 알맞다.
5 문맥상 '그렇지 않으면'의 뜻이 되어야 하므로, 접속사 or이 와야 한다.

B 1 What으로 시작하는 감탄문의 어순은 「What(+a/an)+형용사+명사(+주어+동사)!」이다.
3 Let's 명령문의 부정형은 「Let's not+동사원형」이다.
5 명령문의 부가 의문문은 will you로 쓴다.

C 1, 2 부정 의문문은 대답하는 내용이 부정이면 No로, 긍정이면 Yes로 대답한다.
3 문맥상 Let's 명령문에 대한 부정 대답이 와야 하므로, No, let's not.을 쓴다.

D 2 '~해라, 그러면 …할 것이다'는 「명령문, and ...」로 표현한다.

내신 완성 Grammar Practice p. 191

1 ⑤ 2 ③ 3 ①, ③ 4 (1) What a cool scarf
(2) Let's not focus on

문제해설

2 ① A: 그들은 노래하고 있지 않아, 그렇지?
B: 응, 안 하고 있어. 그들은 이야기하고 있어.
② A: 잔디 위를 걷지마.
B: 알겠어. 안 그럴게.
④ A: 침대 옆에 알람 시계를 놓자.
B: 아니, 그러지 말자. 그것을 바닥에 놓자.
⑤ A: 너는 초록색 또는 파란색 중 어떤 색을 더 좋아하니?
B: 나는 초록색을 더 좋아해.
▸ ③ 문맥상 Jeremy가 운전 면허증이 없다는 내용이므로, No, he doesn't.로 대답해야 한다.

3 ②는 How beautiful (the bride is[was])!로, ④는 isn't this를 isn't it으로, ⑤는 doesn't를 didn't로 고쳐야 한다.

서술형에 나오는 WRITING p. 192

A 1 Which country is she from, China or Japan?
2 He will visit his hometown, won't he?
3 Tell me the truth, or I will be angry.
B 1 Let's look for something to eat.
2 Didn't they have a Halloween party last night?
3 Don't[Do not] take off your shoes in the hall.
C 1 How bright the lighthouse was!
2 How long these socks are!
3 What a big kitchen she has!

문제해설

B 1 Let's 명령문은 「Let's+동사원형 ...」으로 쓴다.
2 일반동사의 과거형이 쓰인 문장의 부정 의문문은 「Didn't+주어+동사원형 ...?」으로 쓴다.
3 부정 명령문은 「Don't[Do not]+동사원형 ...」으로 쓴다.

C How로 시작하는 감탄문은 「How+형용사/부사+주어+동사!」, What으로 시작하는 감탄문은 「What(+a/an)+형용사+명사+주어+동사!」의 어순으로 쓴다.

READING WITH GRAMMAR pp. 193~194

Reading 1 | 1 ③ 2 How kind they are!
Words | [1] 갑자기 [2] 놀라운

해석 | Josh는 학교에 자주 늦는다. 그는 오늘 아침에도 늦었다. Josh가 그의 선생님을 봤을 때, 그는 "참 운이 나쁜 아침이에요!" 라고 말했다. 그의 선생님은 "이번 네 사연은 무엇이니?"라고 물었다. Josh는 "제가 버스를 기다리고 있었는데요. 갑자기 비가 내리기 시작했어요. 하지만 저는 우산을 가지고 오지 않았어요." "너는 참 운이 나쁘구나!"라고 그의 선생님은 말했다. Josh는 "그래서 저는 다른 사람의 차를 얻어 타려고 시도했어요. 다행히, Nick의 부모님이 저를 보셨고, 그분들이 저를 태워 주셨어요." "그들은 참 친절하시구나!"라고 그의 선생님은 말했다. "그런데 그분들의 차가 고장 났어요. 그래서 저는 학교까지 걸어와야 했어요." 그의 말이 끝나자, 그의 선생님은 "참 놀라운 이야기구나! 그런데 너는 그것을 이미 지난달에 써먹었단다."라고 대답했다.

구문해설

1행 **When** Josh saw his teacher, he said, ...
▸ when은 '…할 때'의 의미로, 시간을 나타내는 종속 접속사이다.

3행 Suddenly it **started raining**.
▸ start v-ing[to-v]: …하기 시작하다

5행 Josh said, "So I **tried hitchhiking**. ..."
▸ try v-ing: …해 보다, …를 시도하다

문제해설

1 ③ 선생님이 학교에 지각한 Josh의 변명을 듣고 그것은 이미 지난달에 쓴 것이라고 대답한 것으로 보아, 선생님은 Josh의 말을 믿지 않는다는 것을 알 수 있다.

2 How로 시작하는 감탄문이므로, 「How+형용사(kind)+주어(they)+동사(are)!」의 어순으로 쓴다.

Reading 2 | **1** ① **2** ⑤
Words | **1** 끔찍한 **2** 증가

해석 | 우리에게 한 달에 단 6분의 햇빛이 있다고 상상해 보아라. 그것은 끔찍할 것이다, 그렇지 않은가? 실제로, 이 일은 최근 러시아 모스크바에서 발생했다. 모스크바는 매년 12월에 보통 약 18시간의 햇빛을 받는다. 그러나 2017년 12월에는, 햇빛을 겨우 6분 받았다! 매일 어둡고 흐렸다. 그때가 모스크바에서 기록상 가장 어두운 달이었다. 이전 기록은 2000년 12월에 세워졌다. 그달에는 단 3시간의 햇빛이 있었다. 우울하게 들리지 않는가? 날씨는 분명히 모스크바 사람들을 우울하게 느끼게 만들었다. 지역 신문에 따르면, 그달에 정신과 의사를 방문한 수가 크게 증가했다!

구문해설

1행 Imagine **that** we had just six minutes of sunshine a month.
▸ that은 Imagine의 목적어 역할을 하는 명사절을 이끄는 종속 접속사이다.

8행 Doesn't it **sound depressing**?
▸ sound+형용사: …하게 들리다

8행 The weather definitely **made the people of Moscow feel** blue.
▸ make+목적어+목적격 보어(동사원형): …가 ~하게 만들다

10행 ..., there was a big **increase in** *the number of visits* to psychiatrists that month!
▸ increase in: …의 증가
▸ the number of+복수명사: …의 수

문제해설

1 다음 문장이 들어가기에 가장 알맞은 곳은?
▸ ① 일반적으로 모스크바가 햇빛을 받는 시간에 대한 주어진 문장 뒤에 역접의 연결어 But으로 시작해서 햇빛을 6분 밖에 받지 못했던 달에 대한 내용으로 이어지는 것이 자연스럽다.

2 빈칸 (A)와 (B)에 들어갈 말이 바르게 짝지어진 것은?
▸ (A) 조동사 would가 쓰인 긍정문의 부가 의문문에서는 wouldn't를 쓴다.
(B) 일반동사 sound가 있으므로 부정 의문문은 Doesn't로 시작한다.

내신에 나오는 COMMUNICATION

A 칭찬하기 p. 195

Check-Up | **1** ② **2** did a great job

문제해설

1 A: 나는 매일 아침에 나무와 식물에 물을 줘.
B: 훌륭하구나!
▸ 상대방을 칭찬하는 말이므로 ②와 바꿔 쓸 수 있다.

B 놀라움 표현하기 p. 196

Check-Up | **1** ③ **2** ①, ④

문제해설

2 A: 이 카메라는 70% 할인을 해.
B: 정말 놀랍다!
▸ 밑줄 친 문장과 ②, ③, ⑤는 놀라움을 표현하는 말이며, ①, ④는 상대방을 칭찬하는 표현이다.

FINAL TEST pp. 197~199

1 ③ **2** happen **3** ⑤ **4** ④ **5** ③, ④ **6** ⑤ **7** ① **8** ② **9** ② **10** ⑤ **11** isn't he **12** can't you **13** ⑤ **14** ⑤ **15** Yes, I do **16** No, we can't **17** ③ **18** ④ **19** How beautifully you sing! **20** Let's take the subway, shall we? **21** Present the coupon, and you'll get a discount. **22** Buy the concert ticket now, or you won't see your favorite singer tomorrow. **23** Turn off your cell phone. **24** Don't[Do not] kick the seat. **25** Don't[Do not] talk during the movie.

문제해설

1 ③ throw out은 '버리다'의 의미이다.

2 happen: 발생하다

3 A: 나는 지하철에서 한 노인을 도와드렸어.
B: ____________________
▶ 문맥상 상대방을 칭찬하는 대답인 ⑤(너 정말 잘했구나!)가 적절하다.

4 A: 믿을 수 없어! 나는 오늘 내 책을 쓰는 것을 마쳤어!
B: 잘했어. (너는 네 책을 읽어 봤니?)
A: 고마워.

6 ① A: 봐! 무지개가 있어!
B: 정말 놀랍다!
② A: 나는 지난 주말에 자원봉사를 했어.
B: 잘했어!
③ A: 나는 과학의 날에 메달을 받았어.
B: 훌륭하다!
④ A: 나는 축구 경기에서 골을 넣었어.
B: 잘했어!
▶ ⑤ 시험에 합격했다는 말에 다시 보게 되어 기쁘다는 대답은 어색하다.

7 ① 선택 의문문에서는 접속사 or를 쓴다.

8 ② 긍정 명령문은 동사원형으로 시작하며, quick과 careful은 형용사이므로 앞에 Be가 와야 한다.

9 ②는 빈칸 뒤에 「형용사+주어+동사」로 이어지므로 빈칸에는 How가 들어가고, 나머지는 모두 What이 들어간다.

10 ⑤는 일반동사 과거형이 쓰인 긍정문의 부가 의문문이므로 빈칸에 didn't가 와야 한다. 나머지는 모두 aren't가 들어가야 한다.

13 ⑤ 평서문에 were가 쓰였으므로, 부가 의문문은 weren't you?가 되어야 한다.

14 ① What → How, ② What lovely → What a lovely, ③ good a player → a good player, ④ has she → she has로 고쳐야 한다.

15 문맥상 부정 의문문에 대한 긍정 대답이 와야 한다.

16 문맥상 부정 의문문에 대한 부정 대답이 와야 한다.

17 ① A: 엘리베이터를 타자.
B: 아니, 그러지 말자.
② A: 하늘을 봐! 맑아.
B: 참 푸르구나!
④ A: 오늘 밤에 눈이 내릴 거야, 그렇지 않니?
B: 응. 눈이 내릴 거야.
⑤ A: 그 빵을 두 조각으로 잘라.
B: 알겠어.
▶ ③ 선택 의문문에는 제시된 대상 중 하나를 선택하여 대답하며 Yes나 No로 대답하지 않는다.

21 문맥상 '쿠폰을 제시해라, 그러면 너는 할인을 받을 것이다.'라고 하는 것이 자연스러우므로, and를 써야 한다.

22 문맥상 '콘서트 티켓을 지금 구입하라, 그렇지 않으면 내일 너는 네가 가장 좋아하는 가수를 못 볼 것이다.'라고 하는 것이 자연스러우므로, or를 써야 한다.

23 명령문은 동사원형으로 시작하므로 Turns를 Turn으로 고쳐야 한다.

24, 25 부정 명령문은 「Don't[Do not]+동사원형」으로 써야 한다.

MEMO

MEMO

MEMO

MEMO

MEMO